"In a time when hope feels scarce, this book offers a grounded and inspiring vision of healing, flourishing, and missional purpose. Rooted in God's redemptive work, it calls the church to embrace and share hope—personally, communally, and beyond its walls. This book will inspire you to look beyond the current struggles and embrace the transformative hope that God provides."

—**Steve Maina**
Bishop, Nelson Anglican Diocese, New Zealand

"One of the great gifts of travel is seeing the world from a broader perspective than one's own limited context and community. This book does that for the church. With all the noise on the 'decline of the church' this book written by practitioners and scholars—who love and serve the church—is a refreshing, helpful perspective. Beneath the hot air of discouragement is a current of new life and hope. Whether you live in New Zealand or New York, this book will stimulate fresh ideas and bear witness to what the Spirit is doing in our churches."

—**MaryKate Morse**
Emerit Professor of Leadership and Spiritual Formation, George Fox University

"For those discouraged by the church's many failures, this book offers fresh hope. The contributors not only point to signs of renewal already emerging; they show how we too can nurture flourishing and health within Christian communities. This is a bold and timely call to believe again in the church as a Spirit-filled body that offers healing, transformation, and hope."

—**Reuben Munn**
Senior Pastor, Shore Community Church, Auckland, New Zealand

"Hope is in rather short supply these days! But hope is to be found in abundance in this excellent book! These perceptive, compelling, and challenging essays speak of hope for individuals, for the church, for healing in the church community, and for the church's mission. While squarely recognizing our brokenness and our need for healing, this book also lifts our gaze to see again the hope we have in God through our Lord Jesus Christ. Read this book—and be prepared to be inspired and to experience new hope!"

—**Paul Trebilco**
Professor of New Testament Studies, University of Otago, Dunedin, New Zealand

"This is a timely and courageous book that engages with the context of Aotearoa New Zealand on behalf of questions that face the global church. With theological depth and pastoral insight, it offers a compelling vision of the church as a community of hope, healing, and transformation. I commend it to all who desire to see the church flourish in faithfulness to Christ and in service to the world."

—**Roshan Allpress**
National Principal, Laidlaw College

Hope

Hope

*Growing Flourishing Church Communities
That Transform and Heal People*

Edited by
GREGORY J. LISTON and SARAH PENWARDEN

WIPF & STOCK · Eugene, Oregon

HOPE

Growing Flourishing Church Communities That Transform and Heal People

Copyright © 2025 Wipf and Stock Publishers. All rights reserved. Except for brief quotations in critical publications or reviews, no part of this book may be reproduced in any manner without prior written permission from the publisher. Write: Permissions, Wipf and Stock Publishers, 199 W. 8th Ave., Suite 3, Eugene, OR 97401.

Wipf & Stock
An Imprint of Wipf and Stock Publishers
199 W. 8th Ave., Suite 3
Eugene, OR 97401

www.wipfandstock.com

PAPERBACK ISBN: 979-8-3852-3599-5
HARDCOVER ISBN: 979-8-3852-3600-8
EBOOK ISBN: 979-8-3852-3601-5

VERSION NUMBER 102325

Scripture quotations marked (NLV) are taken from the *New Life Version*, Copyright © 1969 and 2003. Used by permission of Barbour Publishing, Inc., Uhrichsville, OH 44683. All rights reserved.

Scripture quotations marked (NLT) are taken from the *Holy Bible*, New Living Translation, Copyright © 1996, 2004, 2015 by Tyndale House Foundation. Used by permission of Tyndale House Publishers, Inc., Carol Stream, IL 60188. All rights reserved.

Scripture quotations marked (NRSV) are taken from New Revised Standard Version Bible, copyright © 1989 National Council of the Churches of Christ in the United States of America. Used by permission. All rights reserved worldwide. friendshippress.org.

Scripture quotations marked (WEB) are taken from the World English Bible, public domain. Scripture quotations marked (NMB) are copyright © 2016 by Ruth Magnusson (Davis). Includes emendations to February 2022. All rights reserved.

Scripture quotations marked (WYC) are taken from the Wycliffe Bible copyright © 2001 by Terence P. Noble. Scripture quotations marked (NIV) taken from The Holy Bible, New International Version®, NIV®. Copyright © 1973, 1978, 1984, 2011 by Biblica, Inc. Used with permission of Zondervan. www.zondervan.com.

Scripture quotations designated (NET) are from the NET Bible® copyright © 1996, 2019 by Biblical Studies Press, L.L.C. www.netbible.com. All rights reserved.

Scripture quotations marked (TNIV) are from the Holy Bible, Today's New International Version® TNIV®. Copyright © 2001, 2005 by Biblica®. All rights reserved worldwide.

Copyright material is included from *Common Worship*; copyright © The Archbishops' Council 2000.

Contents

List of Illustration and Tables | ix
Contributors | xi
Acknowledgments | xiii
Abbreviations | xv

Chapter 1
Hope for the Church | 1
—Gregory J. Liston and Sarah Penwarden

SECTION I
Individual Healing: Bodies Flourishing in the Body

Chapter 2
Personal Healing and Flourishing in the Body of Christ | 9
—Mark Keown

Chapter 3
Healthy and Holy Bodies: Reimagining Christian Practice and Discourse to Promote Flourishing in Diversity | 28
—Maja Whitaker

Chapter 4
Discomfort and Diversity as Catalysts for Individual Transformation Within the Church Body | 50
—Jonathan Dove

Chapter 5
Leading from the Center: Body and Place | 70
—MaryKate Morse

SECTION II
Church Healing: Growing Communities That Restore and Transform

Chapter 6
Shepherding Well: Guiding a Theology of Interpersonal Power and Authority | 89
  —Christa L. McKirland

Chapter 7
Compassionate Realism: Reclaiming the Church's Core Identity as a Hope-Filled Community of Healing and Restoration | 102
  —Karen M. Kemp

Chapter 8
The Church Body as a Healing Sacrament | 123
  —Watiri Maina

SECTION III
Church Flourishing: Sustaining the Healing Power of the Church

Chapter 9
At a Loss for Words: How the Spirit Prays When the Children of God Can't (Romans 8:18–27) | 145
  —Geoff New

Chapter 10
A Means of Grace: A Pastor's Listening Within a Church Community as a Way of Sustaining the Body of Christ | 164
  —Sarah Penwarden

Chapter 11
Tūmanako Me Whakahounga: Forms of Hope and Renewal in the Context of Contemporary Aotearoa | 183
  —Lyndon Drake

SECTION IV
Missional Hope: Nourishing the Wider Community

Chapter 12
Different with Distinction: Revitalizing the Church's Mission Through Applying Newbigin's Insights | 205
  —Gregory J. Liston

Chapter 13
Sharing Faith, Imaging God, Nourishing Hope: Faith and Hope That Is Relational, Mysterious, and Transformational | 227
—Lynne Taylor

Chapter 14
Beyond "Them" and "Us": Bumping into God in the Marketplace | 247
—Brian Harris

Chapter 15
Carrying Hope | 260
—Sarah Penwarden and Gregory J. Liston

Author Index | 265
Subject Index | 271

List of Illustrations and Tables

1. The top three most meaningful elements of church life at St. Bede's which contribute to flourishing | 174
2. Luke 1:68–79 in English and Māori | 184
3. Conversion process and affects | 232
4. Proportion of people experiencing loneliness in Aotearoa | 235
5. Carey's framework | 255

Contributors

Rev. Jonathan Dove is the senior pastor of Gracecity Church, a multi-ethnic multi-congregational church located in Auckland, New Zealand. He is also the executive chair of the Auckland Church Network. He holds a master of theology from Dallas Theological Seminary and has served as a pastor for over two decades.

The Venerable Dr. Lyndon Drake was formerly the archdeacon of Tāmaki Makaurau in the Māori Anglican bishopric of Te Tai Tokerau. He has a DPhil in theology and is the author of *Capital Markets for the Common Good: A Christian Perspective* (2017).

Rev. Dr. Brian Harris is the former principal of Vose Seminary (Perth, Australia). He is currently a director at the AVENIR Leadership Institute, which he founded. He is a director of the Australian College of Theology and a distinguished international visiting scholar of Spurgeon's College, London. He has published seven books, the most recent being *Stirrers and Saints: Forming Spiritual Leaders of Skill, Depth, and Character* (2024).

Rev. Dr. Karen Kemp is a senior lecturer in the School of Theology and senior coach in the Laidlaw Centre for Church Leadership. She is an Anglican priest and practical theologian with specialisms in conflict transformation and restorative practice and in leadership and spiritual formation.

Rev. Dr. Mark Keown is the director of evangelistic leadership at Laidlaw College, New Zealand. His recent books include *Galatians* (2024), *Pneumaformity* (2024), and *Jesus as the New Joshua* (2024).

Dr. Gregory J. Liston is a senior lecturer in systematic theology at Laidlaw College, New Zealand. His recent books include *The Anointed Church* (2015), *Kingdom Come* (2022), and *Starting with the Spirit* (2024).

Rev. Watiri Maina is an Anglican priest serving in the Nelson diocese and a lecturer at Bishopdale Theological College. She has a masters degree in counselling psychology and a graduate diploma in theology. She is a spiritual director, retreat facilitator, supervisor, and counsellor in private practice.

Dr. Christa L. McKirland is dean of faculty and lecturer in systematic theology at Carey Baptist College (New Zealand). Her recent books include *God's Provision, Humanity's Need: The Gift of Our Dependence* (2022) and *A Theology of Authority: Rethinking Leadership in the Church* (2025).

Dr. MaryKate Morse is the former executive dean of Portland Seminary at George Fox University and emerit professor of leadership and spiritual formation. She is a church planter and spiritual director. Her recent books include *Making Room for Leadership: Power, Space, and Influence* (2008), *A Guidebook to Prayer* (2013), and *Lifelong Leadership* (2020).

Rev. Dr. Geoff New is the principal of the Knox Centre for Ministry and Leadership (Dunedin). His recent books include *Imaginative Preaching* (2015), *Live, Listen, Tell* (2017), *The Lord's Prayer in the Preacher's Life* (2020), and *Preaching the Parables* (2025).

Rev. Dr. Sarah Penwarden is a practicing counsellor, supervisor, and an Anglican priest. She also teaches in the School of Theology at Laidlaw College on a part-time basis. She has had five book chapters and fourteen articles published.

Dr. Lynne Taylor is the Jack Somerville Senior Lecturer in pastoral theology at the University of Otago, New Zealand, and Theology and Psychology Fellow, University of Birmingham. She has a PhD in theology and has written over a dozen articles and book chapters.

Rev. Dr. Maja Whitaker is the Academic Dean and a lecturer in practical theology at Laidlaw College, New Zealand. She is the author *of Perfect in Weakness: Disability and Human Flourishing in the New Creation* (2023) and editor of *Pursuing Perfection: Faith and the Female Body* (2025).

Acknowledgments

With a multiauthored, edited book, many people are involved in its creation. I would like to thank Greg Liston for his vision, dedication, and persistence in believing in the message of the book and in bringing it to life. I'd also like to thank Laidlaw College, and the School of Theology in particular for their support of the book, and to all the contributors. On a personal note, I'd like to thank my husband David for his ongoing calmness and support in all my endeavors. The vision of this book might speak to those who have experienced toxic elements in church life *and also* know the hope of a church community where people can grow spiritually and relationally. Thus, I'd like to acknowledge the many people who struggle with, and also hope in, the church. I'd also like to acknowledge my own church community in Titirangi for being a real, human, funny, and often joyful place.

—Sarah Penwarden

My sincere thanks to the many contributors to this book. I have appreciated both your willingness to contribute and your astute thoughtfulness in what you have contributed. I am also grateful to Laidlaw College and its leadership for giving us an opportunity to explore this important topic with its many significant ramifications and implications. In terms of direct contribution, Sarah Penwarden has been an extremely competent and engaging colleague and collaborator. Thanks so much for taking on this project! The final vote of thanks goes to my family—my caring mother, Frances, my loving wife, Diane, and my beloved children, Emily (now joined with Alex) and James. My prayer for us as a family, and particularly for my children, is that you will continue to abide in hope (1 Cor 13:13).

—Greg Liston
Soli Deo Gloria

Abbreviations

BECNT	Baker Exegetical Commentary on the New Testament
EEC	Evangelical Exegetical Commentary
ICC	International Critical Commentary
LBD	*The Lexham Bible Dictionary*. Edited by John D. Barry, et al. Bellingham, WA: Lexham, 2016. Digital Logos Edition.
LCC	Lexham Context Commentary. Digital Logos Edition.
LRC	Lexham Research Commentaries. Digital Logos Edition.
NICNT	New International Commentary on the New Testament.
PG	*Patrologia Graeca*
PDTT	*Pocket Dictionary of Theological Terms*. Edited by Stanley Grenz, et al. Downers Grove, IL: InterVarsity Press, 1999.
ZECNT	Zondervan Exegetical Commentary on the New Testament

Chapter 1

Hope for the Church

Gregory J. Liston and Sarah Penwarden

Many people are writing about how the Western church is failing. One author even ironically comments that the only thing currently growing in the Western church is literature on its decline.[1] These works often explore at great length what the church is doing wrong and describe in detail how it is not living up to its calling. It is, of course, entirely appropriate to acknowledge the many challenges facing the contemporary church, and to fully own the (sometimes grievous) mistakes that have been made. But this tale of decline and despair is not the whole truth. There is another side to the story. For the church is God's church, so there is always hope for us. This volume, emerging primarily from writers located within the South Pacific context of Aotearoa New Zealand, seeks to highlight this hope.

Without denying the Western church's challenges and failures, the motivation underlying this volume is to speak hope into our current situation and to identify the (sometimes unexpected) places where hope is already present. Each of the four sections that follow examine a core facet of the church and discusses in what ways hope can and sometimes does exist in each of these areas. The four sections are: (1) hope for individual healing; (2) hope for healing in the church community; (3) hope for sustained flourishing within the church; and (4) missional hope—hope that extends beyond our church borders. Inspired by our hope in God, each section explores how

---

1. Jinkins, *Church Faces Death*, 12.

he is working through the challenges we are currently facing, and how this work of God can inspire us.

So this volume is intentionally and unapologetically full of hope. But it is also intentionally and unapologetically cross-disciplinary. Each topic is commented on from perspectives across the theological landscape. So every section of this volume has at least one practitioner,[2] one systematic theologian or biblical scholar, and one interdisciplinary or applied scholar examining the same overarching subject. By bringing together these various perspectives, we aim to demonstrate that a broad range of people with a variety of viewpoints and voices can have a rich and mutually beneficial discussion about the church—a discussion that genuinely brings hope.

The first section, entitled "Individual Healing: Bodies Flourishing in the Body," explores how we can have hope for the individuals who make up the church body. As is appropriate, Mark Keown's introductory chapter explores the flourishing of individuals within the body of Christ from a biblical perspective. It surveys how the apostle Paul uses the image of the church as Christ's body, and through this provides insight into the expectations and hopes we can have for the individuals located within this church body. In the next chapter, Maja Whitaker brings her combined experience in anatomical science and theology together to explore the church's attitude to our physical bodies. Recognizing the immense challenges that arise from overemphasizing health and particular notions of beauty, she explores how some attitudes within the church have adopted these unhelpful Western perspectives on our bodies. The chapter goes on to draw on the richness of the Christian tradition, both in terms of theological reflection and embodied practice, to offer a challenge to contemporary Christian communities to support the holistic flourishing of their members, particularly in their treatment of and attitude to their physical bodies. The third chapter comes from Jonathan Dove, senior pastor of Gracecity Church, a multi-campus, multicongregation church based in suburban Auckland. Written from a practitioner's perspective, this chapter explores seven stories of actual transformation experienced by individuals. Focusing on these stories, Dove helpfully reflects on how discomfort and diversity interacts with the divine to foster healing and missional engagement for individuals within church communities. MaryKate Morse, the writer of the final chapter in this section, is unique among the authors of this volume in that she is a visitor to Aotearoa New Zealand. As an international guest contributor, she insightfully develops a theological understanding of how bodies and places

---

2. By "practitioner," we refer to someone deeply immersed in pastoral ministry, such as a priest or pastor.

intersect and explores how this recognition can positively affect our Christian leadership.

The second section, entitled "Church Healing: Growing Communities That Restore and Transform," explores flourishing and healing, not just for individuals but within entire local church communities. Exploring this question from a biblical perspective, Christa McKirland reaches for a metaphor to describe the workings of the church, in this case the image of shepherding. Tracing this image from the beginning to the end of Scripture, from God shepherding Jacob as an individual and Israel as a nation, through Jesus's self-identification as the good shepherd, and ultimately to his crowning as the lamb on the throne. McKirland urges a restrained understanding of spiritual authority that in hopefulness under God's guiding hand can lead towards healing and flourishing for the entirety of God's flock. In the next chapter, Karen Kemp draws on her applied insights in both pastoral leadership and spiritual formation to suggest that the posture and practice of compassionate realism is an appropriate communal response to the significant abuses that have been inflicted by and suffered within the church. In this intense but very necessary chapter, Kemp explores how in thought and action the church might grow its capacity to be a hope-filled, transforming community that increasingly reflects God's reconciling intent. The final chapter in this section, from Watiri Maina, intentionally explores, from a practitioner's perspective, how the church is a healing sacrament. Her theological reflections on how the church can embody the reality of Christ among us are given clear expression through the examples she outlines of her own church experience.

Moving beyond the question of how the church *is* a healing community, the third section, entitled "Church Flourishing: Sustaining the Healing Power of the Church," asks the question of how the church can *continue* to be a flourishing community. What practices and understandings are necessary for the church to constantly renew and remember her calling? Once again, the chapters within this section include a biblical exploration, an interdisciplinary approach, and a practitioner's perspective. Geoff New begins with a biblical exploration of groaning. Examining Rom 8 leads to a thoughtful reflection of how the Spirit participates in our groaning. New suggests that the appropriate response to such groaning is patience, as we learn to wait and trust in who God is and what he has done, is doing, and will do for us. Sarah Penwarden brings her multi-faceted experience as a counsellor and ordained priest to the next chapter, arguing that the sustaining of a church's healing power comes from being intrinsically participatory, and that this participation is best facilitated through listening. Penwarden provides a helpful example of listening within her own church and provides some beautiful glimpses of hope in the reaction of church attenders to her Appreciative Inquiry. In the final chapter in this section, Lyndon Drake, having recently moved on from his position as the archdeacon of the Māori Anglican church in Tāmaki Makaurau (Auckland) to take up a research position at Oxford University, leverages his experience both with the contemporary church and his awareness of Māori history. In this chapter, he not only insightfully names the false hope the church in Aotearoa is placing on implausible strategies but also explores how true hope can come from noticing afresh God's "pattern" for Aotearoa New Zealand, using as examples the need for acknowledging the historical injustices of Māori land confiscations and for supporting Māori leadership and evangelists.

The final substantive section of this volume looks beyond the church itself and towards its impact on the world around it. Entitled "Missional Hope: Nourishing the Wider Community," this section explores the hope the church can bring to the surrounding society. In the first chapter, Greg Liston argues that the Western church is best served by leaning into the differences it has with the culture around it. Sound theology, an analysis of historical trends, and recent cases studies all lead to the conclusion that in contrast to the common approach of pursuing contextual relevance, the New Zealand church can be truest to its calling and have the most impact on society by intentionally being different with distinction. Lynne Taylor draws on her practical theological experience, and particularly her qualitative research over the last several years, to explore what Christians are offering to the world around them that is both faithful to the gospel and meaningful for those beyond the church. Through several encouraging and hope-filled stories of people who have recently become Christians, Taylor shows the value of communicating a faith that is relational, mysterious, and transformational. Brian Harris's final chapter provides a wonderful case study of precisely the kind of missional contribution that reaches beyond the walls of the church. Utilizing his position as a founder of the Avenir Leadership Institute and his experience consulting to both Christian and non-Christian organizations, Harris argues that it is possible to engage with the implicit "theological architecture" present in secular organizations and seek to grow this. In this sense, effective missional engagement with the wider community requires orthodoxy (right belief), orthopraxy (right actions), and orthopathy (right feeling). While all three are important, Harris suggests that in our current climate it might be the last of these that is the most telling.

Hope is a virtue. Christians do not hope simply when there is some earthly circumstance to be hopeful about. We hope because of God. The writer of Lamentations provides a stirring example. Chapter 3 begins in a dark place. The writer has known afflictions, darkness, disease, anguish, distress, homelessness and worse, and all this at the hands of the Lord (Lam 3:1–20). But then comes a significant change in attitude:

> Yet I still dare to hope when I remember this: The faithful love of the Lord never ends! His mercies never cease. Great is his faithfulness; his mercies begin afresh each morning. I say to myself, "The Lord is my inheritance; therefore, I will hope in him!" (Lam 3:21–22 NLV)

A hope that is centered on God is a hope that can remain and grow even in the darkest of times. A hope that is centered on God is a hope that can heal individuals and communities; it is a hope that can lead to flourishing churches; it is a hope that drives churches to missionally engage with the society around them. This is a hope that does not disappoint us (Rom 5:5), for it is a hope that rests on God and his graciousness—not on our human flaws and frailties—a graciousness fully revealed in the incarnation, life, death, and resurrection of Jesus Christ our Lord.

The authors who have contributed to this volume believe in the church and are genuinely hopeful for its future. Even with all the church's failings, and despite all our current challenges, we genuinely think the church is something worth believing in. And we're not alone. The early church fathers almost exactly seventeen hundred years ago explicitly included the phrase "We believe in. . . [the] church" in the Nicene Creed.[3] This clause, in probably the most profound and significant statement of faith ever written, is even more remarkable when you realize that the only other things the creed encourages us to believe in are the Father, the Son, and the Holy Spirit. But neither the early church fathers nor the authors of this volume believe in the church because of our proud story, our inspiring leaders, our world-shaping impact, or our transforming potential. Neither do we stop believing when we recall our flawed history, our ministers who have fallen, our failure to stand for justice, or our too-easily-abandoned communal calling. Rather, we believe in the church simply because it is God's church. We walk by faith and not by sight. God's presence means that we can have a genuine and certain hope, not just in the church's future but also in its present.

The theologian Stanley Hauerwas says the primary missional task of the church in the world is simply to be the church.[4] The (increasingly and incredibly pragmatic) Western church might benefit from a reminder of that reality. Perhaps our current challenges can help us to remember that

---

3. Pelikan and Hotchkiss, *Creeds and Confessions*, 169.
4. Hauerwas, *Peaceable Kingdom*, 99.

our significance has never come from having an influential position in society but rather from our humble participation in God's inner life. Being church means that we get to join in with the life of the Trinity, and that our present just as much as our future lies securely in God's hands.

BIBLIOGRAPHY

Hauerwas, Stanley. *The Peaceable Kingdom*. Notre Dame: SCM, 1983.

Jinkins, Michael. *The Church Faces Death: Ecclesiology in a Post-Modern Context*. New York: Oxford University Press, 1999.

Pelikan, Jaroslov, and Valerie Hotchkiss, eds. *Creeds and Confessions of Faith in the Christian Tradition: Early, Eastern, and Medieval*. New Haven: Yale University Press, 2003.

Section I

Individual Healing
Bodies Flourishing in the Body

Chapter 2

Personal Healing and Flourishing in the Body of Christ

MARK KEOWN

INTRODUCTION

What does it mean to flourish and experience healing? How can humans experience it in their bodies in a world blighted by sin, pain, and death? Understanding healing in terms of wholeness and freedom from corruption and sickness, this chapter will explore Paul's "body of Christ" references to consider how individuals can find wholeness in relation to the body of Christ. Paul is well-known for describing the church as the body of Christ. He is unique in this, although some ideas among other New Testament writers approximate it.[1] As a result, scholars debate the origin of the notion, raising a few possibilities but nothing concrete, leading to the strong possibility that Paul innovated with the idea.[2]

In using this "body of Christ" analogy, Paul likens the church of God to the human body. He does so in two main ways. First, in Romans and 1 Corinthians, he speaks of the local church as an individual body of Christ. Also relevant to this discussion is Christ's body in Phil 3:21. Second, in

---

1. Especially John's writings; see e.g., John 6:56; 14:20; 15:27; 16:33; 17:21; 1 John 2:28.

2. For a simple explanation of the body of Christ in Paul see Lee, "Body of Christ."

Ephesians and Colossians, Paul extends the metaphor so that all believers form the cosmic body of Christ.

In this chapter, I will argue that individual healing, wholeness, and flourishing flow from God through the actual body of Christ—crucified for us and raised. At times, God intervenes with healing and release from suffering. These moments of direct intervention are wonderful and experienced in and through the body of Christ. However, this chapter focuses on how, even as we suffer, we experience inward wholeness through connection with the body of Jesus. Ideally, that experience of flourishing and inner healing and God's spasmodic direct intervention is deepened within the church, the body of Christ. True individual healing comes through Christ's body—actual and spiritual (the church).

This chapter will first consider Paul's use of the idea of the body of Christ concerning the local church and its implications for individual flourishing and health. Next, it will discuss his view of the whole world church as the cosmic body of Christ and its consequences in the same space.

CHRIST AND THE LOCAL CHURCH AS THE BODY OF CHRIST

In Romans and 1 Corinthians, each local church is the body of Christ. As such, the body of Christ in these two letters will be briefly discussed. In addition, I will consider Paul's mention of Christ's body in Phil 3:21, as it has important implications for living in the present.

The Body of Christ in Romans

There are two sections where Paul mentions the body of Christ, which are now considered.

Romans 7:4

In Romans, the first mention of "the body of Christ" is in Rom 7:4. Here, Paul addresses those "who know the law" (v. 1) and so speaks primarily to Jewish believers. Still, when gentiles become familiar with Jewish law and are challenged to yield to it by law-observant preachers,[3] his words extend

---

3. The early church faced the dilemma of whether new gentile converts should be circumcised (if male) and be submissive to the Torah with its many regulations and rituals. Paul advocated passionately that such submission was not required. Others

to them.[4] Paul tells his readers that just as a woman is free from the law of marriage when her husband dies, so also the Roman Jewish believers died concerning the law through the body of Christ. Thus, they are freed from the Torah as a system, as a means by which they are declared right by God, as the basis for how they live and the condemnation it brings. Instead, as he will expound, they are justified by faith, and the power of the Spirit shapes their lives. This death to the law is through "the body of Christ."

Here, this body is Jesus's actual body. Moo says, "Paul has laid no groundwork in Romans for this application; he must be referring to the physical body of Christ, put to death on the cross for us."[5] The actual body of Christ lies at the heart of Paul's understanding. This body was destroyed by crucifixion for our sins and their consequences and raised to life. Believers participate in his redemptive death and resurrection. On the face of it, this passage says nothing about individual flourishing and health in the body of Christ. However, on deeper inspection, it lays a foundation for what Paul goes on to say about the body of Christ in Rom 12. In speaking of Christ's body here, Paul is referring to Christ's human body, spent through sustained service, mangled through crucifixion, and yet now raised from the dead, healed and fully alive in the Spirit. The answer to our question—How can a human person flourish and experience healing?—is not found in the law but via the body of Jesus. In him is our healing (Isa 53:5; 1 Pet 2:24).

Thus far in Romans, Paul has made the charge that Jews and gentiles alike are under sin, captive to its power (Rom 3:9). Our sin and idolatry have fractured our relationship with God, with the creation, with one another, and our personal mental and physical health. We are incapable of resolving these problems ourselves through human effort. Rather than bringing healing and flourishing, the external code of the law illuminates our incapacity to find wholeness (Rom 3:20; 7:7–9). Seeking health through bloody-minded determination to live God's law deepens our entrapment to sin and leads to despair. It also fails, for ultimately, our bodies fail us, and we die.

However, the human quest for *shalom* is found in the crucified and raised body of Jesus. His death fulfils the hopes of the Day of Atonement and the mercy seat of God. When a person believes in Jesus, they are declared right before God by faith. What the law was impotent to do, Jesus has done for us (3:21–26). Declared righteous by his blood through faith, we have access to God and are formed into the character of Jesus, the image of God

---

continued to preach a gospel requiring people to Judaize. The church sided with Paul at the Jerusalem Council (Acts 15); still, advocates for the law continued to afflict churches like the Philippians (Phil 3:2–11) up to the fall of Jerusalem in AD 70.

4. Moo, *Romans*, 443.

5. Moo, *Romans*, 443.

through suffering, by the power of the love poured into our inner beings by the Spirit (5:1–9). We are reconciled to God through his death (5:10). Despite the inevitability of death due to our sin, we are given a new identity in Christ and live for God through the work of the new Adam (5:12–21). We are freed from sin, alive to God, and destined for eternal life. We can and must now serve righteousness by the power of the Spirit. What the law could not do, the body of Christ has done, and all that is required is faith—trust, allegiance, submission, yielding, assent, and love of God, Father, Son, and Spirit.

Romans 12:4–5

The second mention of the body of Christ is in Rom 12:4–5. As we all experience, we humans have only one body. That body comprises multiple parts; however, they do not all have the same function. Within the one body of Christ, we are joined together as one to the extent that we are members of one another through our shared relationship with Christ.[6] Paul explains that each member has different gifts of grace from the Lord. They must be encouraged to express their various gifts liberally and joyfully for the good of others in the church (Rom 12:6–8).

As with 1 Cor 12, these verses tell us that the path to healing and flourishing is not found in the rugged individualism that characterizes New Zealanders. Nor is it merely found in our personal relationship with God, as some forms of evangelicalism stress. Indeed, Christians must be people determined to please God in themselves. They must also be people living in a personal relationship with God, governed by Christ, and led by the Spirit. However, on their own, these are not enough. The true and deep wholeness we seek is found in and through our relationship with others in the body of Christ, the church. These verses stress our mutual indwelling and need for one another. They also indicate that wholeness comes through service with our God-given gifts. As the church encourages each member to express their gifts, wholeness is experienced through the body. As we minister to one another, we hear from God, serve one another and are served, teach and learn, encourage and are encouraged, lead and follow zealously, and experience mercy as we give to one another. As we do this, we are nurtured in life; even in the dark times of suffering, we grow in maturity (see Rom 5:2–5).

---

6. Theilman, *Romans*, 575.

The Body of Christ in 1 Corinthians

In this letter, Paul provides more detail concerning his view of the body of Christ. He mentions it in his discussion of idolatry in 1 Cor 10:15, where he relates it to the Lord's Supper. He refers to it again in his critique of the Corinthian abuse of the Supper in 1 Cor 11:17–34. In 1 Cor 12:12–31, the body of Christ provides the framework for his discussion of the use of spiritual gifts in the church.

1 Corinthians 10:15

The first mention is in 1 Cor 10:15 when Paul discusses participation in feasts at pagan temples. In the previous verses, Paul strongly urges the Corinthians to "flee from idolatry." It seems that some of the Corinthian Christians have continued to attend pagan festivals and participate in feasts devoted to their deities.[7] Paul is adamant that this must end because attendance at these feasts violates the exclusive relationship a Christian has with Christ. This exclusive and intimate relationship is remembered at the celebration of the Lord's Supper. As we drink of the cup and eat of the bread we break, we participate in "the body of Christ." We must not violate this deep sacramental connection by participating in feasts celebrating other deities. If Christians do this, as they sever their intimate relationship with Jesus the vine (see John 15:1) and create divisions in the body, they become vulnerable to sickness and even death (1 Cor 10:6–10; 11:30).[8]

Whereas in Rom 7:4, the law is a danger to our health, here it is idolatry that violates our exclusive relationship with Christ. In a Western context like New Zealand, there are a myriad of idols that call us away from Jesus and poison our souls. Behind these are demonic forces that feed us what we long for through our consumeristic, materialistic, hedonistic, and self-centered society. If we allow ourselves to dine out on the wrong things, our loves become disordered, we fall prey unwittingly to the patterns of this age, and we fall away from the radical discipleship Jesus calls us to. We must ensure that Jesus is the center of our existence and not the gods of this age. Western nations are full of spiritually-ill Christians infected by the idolatries

---

7. As Fee says of 1 Cor 10:14–22, "With this paragraph Paul finally brings to a conclusion the long argument with the Corinthians that began with his forbidding them to go to the temples to join in the idolatrous feasts (8:1)." Fee, *First Epistle*, 511.

8. "Probably the rash of illnesses and deaths that have recently overtaken them is here being viewed as an expression of divine judgment on the whole community." Fee, *First Epistle*, 625.

of the age. As we gather and unmask the idols, repent, and serve God with the exclusive allegiance he deserves, we will be well again.

1 Corinthians 11:17–34

Paul turns more explicitly and directly to the Lord's Supper in 1 Cor 11:17–34. Paul is deeply disturbed that the Corinthians are broken into factions as they come to share the meal (vv. 17–20). They do not share food, and they do not eat and drink together. Some are even left hungry at the meal, and others get intoxicated—the poor are being oppressed at the shared church meal.[9] Paul has no praise for the Corinthians. He then recalls Jesus's last meal, where Jesus declares the bread broken as "my body which is for you" (v. 24). They are to partake of such consecrated bread and drink from the communion cup in remembrance of him and as a proclamation of his death (vv. 25–26). When they come together, divided into factions, and fail to share the meal so that some are left hungry and others get drunk, they eat and drink in an unworthy manner. Moreover, they are then guilty of the body and blood of the Lord. As Garland puts it, "They are charged with his death" (v. 27).[10] As such, each person should examine themselves as they come to the Supper to rid themselves of such attitudes that violate Jesus and what he stood and died for. They must "recognize the body" in the sense of "reflect on his death, as they eat" (v. 29).[11] In other words, they must reflect on Jesus's death and repent of all things that are inconsistent with his call for intimate *koinōnia*. If they fail to, they eat and drink judgment on themselves (v. 30).

The communion meal is utterly central to our health and flourishing. While ideas like transubstantiation and consubstantiation go too far for some Christians,[12] the gathering is not merely a remembrance of Jesus. It is a place where we ingest God's health through Christ's body *by the Spirit* as we humbly and genuinely receive the elements that signify the blood and body of Jesus.[13] We lay all idolatries aside as we gather, and our loves are

---

9. "The problem is simply this: when they eat the Lord's Supper, they divide along socioeconomic lines." Garland, *1 Corinthians*, 533.

10. Garland, *1 Corinthians*, 550.

11. Fee, *First Epistle*, 622.

12. Transubstantiation means "essential change," holding that at the Catholic Mass "the bread and wine change substance into the actual substance of Jesus' body and blood, even though they seem to retain their natural characteristics." Luther developed the idea of consubstantiation whereby "the body and blood of the Lord is present 'in, with and under' the actual bread and wine." See Grenz et al., *PDTT*, 29, 115.

13. See Calvin, *Institutes*, 4.17.7–10.

reordered. Knowing that we need each other profoundly and must love one another despite our differences and disagreements, the body of Christ is made more whole and so are we as individuals. God fills us afresh as we enact our oneness and binds the body closer together. Individually, we experience God's grace and are empowered to impart that grace to other believers and into the world through our witness. The meal is not magic, as if we no longer are subject to weakness of the flesh, sin, decay, and death. Indeed, in his following letter, Paul mentions his mysterious "thorn in the flesh" as a means of God's grace (2 Cor 12:7–10).[14] But, as we *together* "ingest" Christ, we are healed even as we die. Our oneness is deepened, hope is rekindled, we are reminded of our identity in Christ, and we are impelled to love one another.

1 Corinthians 12:12–31

The most detailed development of the idea of the body of Christ comes in 1 Cor 12:12–31. As in Romans, the body of Christ, the people of God, is one entity with multiple members (vv. 12, 14). All believers of all ethnicities are baptized into this one body by the one Spirit of whom they have drunk (v. 13). In vv. 15–17, referring to the unique and different parts of the body (foot, hand, ear, eye), Paul stresses that all are equal, necessary, and unique parts of the body. Each contributes something different, which is good, as the body needs all parts to fully function. God has arranged the various members of the one body just as he wants them (vv. 18–20). In verses 21–24, Paul restresses the necessity of all members of the body without exception. Even the seemingly weaker and shameful parts of the body are vital and part of God's composition of the body. Those who make up the body must be deeply concerned for each other, suffering and rejoicing together in good times and bad.

In vv. 27–30, he directly addresses the Corinthian believers. As is every church, they are a body of Christ made up of individual parts. Each has a role to play through the diverse spiritual gifts God has given them. These gifts include those listed earlier in vv. 8–11 and in vv. 27–30. The many members are differently gifted, and the church needs all its members to express their gifts in unity for the good of the body and the common good (v. 7).

---

14. With Witherington, I consider this most likely a physical ailment and perhaps his eyesight. Witherington, *Conflict and Community*, 461–63.

Notable among these gifts are healing and miracles. Paul believed in miracles and performed many of them in his ministry.[15] We should also believe in them, laying hands on the needy with absolute faith in God. When we cry out, God acts in accordance with his cosmic purposes, and we will see his power bring healing and respite as he wills. However, Paul's theology of healing and wholeness runs deeper than temporary relief—we can experience wholeness even as humankind's last enemy—death—stings and swallows us up (see 1 Cor 15:54–55).

This passage adds to Rom 12, stressing our unity as God's people as one unit. We are a team, bound together in Christ by the Spirit. The passage also reemphasizes the importance of people expressing their individuality and diversity for the community's common good. The community flourishes as gifts are used. Sometimes, this flourishing is seen through direct healing and deliverance. Yet, whatever the outcome of our prayers, the Spirit flows and is experienced inwardly and in the community.

As individuals, we grow as we are given the confidence to use our gifts and talents in the community. The passage also touches on times of celebration where we rejoice together when there is cause for festivity. We also emphasize deeply in times of trouble. The gifts are to be used with love and for love's sake. They are to be used with the intent of edification, encouragement, and consolation. Healing flows not merely through us using our gifts and God's intervention in healing and miracles but by humbling ourselves by expressing our needs and accepting the service of others.

The Body of Christ Philippians 3:21

Although Phil 3:21 technically falls outside the "body of Christ" and local church references, Paul's mention of the body of Christ is essential for this discussion. The verse culminates in Paul's warnings to the Philippians concerning false teachers who syncretize the gospel in the direction of Jewish law (3:2) and Greco-Roman licentiousness (3:18–19).[16] After warning them not to emulate the enemies of the cross who violate the gospel with gentile debauchery and factionalism (3:18–19), he reminds the Philippians of their hope. Jesus, their Savior, will return from heaven. The Savior Christ will transform their bodies trapped in mortality and perishability due to their sin, into bodies like that of the risen Lord Jesus.

---

15. See in his letters Rom 15:19; 2 Cor 12:12; Gal 3:4. See also Acts 14:3, 8–18; 15:12; 16:16–18; 19:11.

16. On this view of 3:2 and 3:18–19, see Keown, "Paul's Answer," 28–45.

Paul here describes Jesus's body as a "body of glory," or a "glorious body."[17] This reframes the spiritual body of 1 Cor 15:44, which contrasts with the Adamic body of dust. Christ's raised body remains that of a human but is now transformed, utterly alive by the Spirit, freed from death, immortal, imperishable, and truly glorious. This same kind of body awaits the Philippians at Christ's return when they meet him alive or after being raised from the dust (1 Thess 4:17).

Here, then, Paul pictures our complete healing when Jesus returns. We will be no longer subject like Epaphroditus to sicknesses that can bring death (2:25–30). We will no longer age but be ageless. We will be healed. This outcome is assured because of the undeniable power of Christ to subject all things to himself, seen as the gospel floods the world and hearers bend the knee and confess he is Lord (see 2:10). In the meantime, the Philippians are to emulate Paul and renounce all claims to greatness and devote all they have and are to knowing Christ, gaining him, and being found in him (3:6–9). They are to embrace Christoformity with all their hearts, even to suffering and death (3:10), for in him is healing. They are to press on to take hold of this prize that awaits them (3:12–16). They must renounce all claims to honor that violate unity and take on the mindset and virtues of Christ (2:5). By their love, all will know they are Christ's disciples (John 13:34–35). They will shine as lights of the world, holding out the word that brings life and health to the world (2:15–16a).

We are to walk in the same path as Christ, Paul, his coworkers Timothy and Epaphroditus (2:19–30), and the Philippians themselves (1:5). We are to renounce all worldly glories and empty ourselves for the world, pour ourselves out like a drink offering on the sacrifice of others (2:17). Whole in Christ, we spend ourselves for the world. We do so with the knowledge that we are renewed inwardly by the Spirit and strengthened for the task (2 Cor 4:16). We are also confident we will watch health flow into a sick world, bringing the transformation we need as the gospel is preached. We also know we will face opposition because evil lurks, seeking to devour us (see 1 Pet 5:8). Yet, we know the path of faith is the path to glory, and God will strengthen us and carry us through to *shalom*.

Conclusion to Romans, 1 Corinthians, and Philippians

How does Paul utilize the body of Christ motif to urge us on to life in all its fullness (see John 10:10) in these letters? First, the idea of the body of Christ

---

17. "The gen[itive] is attributive or a gen[itive] of quality, 'body of glory,' meaning 'glorious body.'" Keown, *Philippians*, 2:280.

is premised on the physical body of Jesus, particularly his redemptive death. In the death of his body, Jesus dealt with the law and its power to enslave people in sin and its consequences. Believers are, thus, dead to the law, freed from bondage to law, sin, and death. We experience spiritual healing at the moment we believe and receive the Spirit. However, we remain bound in bodies of flesh that will decay and die. We will be vulnerable to sin and never be fully healed on this side of eternity. Still, if we stay the course, living in grace, with faith, hope, and love, while we age and face trials, we will grow in wholeness, and through us, God will do the same for others.

Secondly, and related to the physical body of Christ, is the sacrament of communion, as we remember his sacrifice, we are inwardly renewed and experience Christ's death by the Spirit. We must renounce all other worship and false behaviors, sexual and otherwise, that violate the exclusive "marriage" we have with Christ. We must partake of the Supper with careful self-examination, ensuring our attitudes to other Christians, our affections, worship, and lifestyle commitments are aligned with Christ. Failure to do so, especially during the meal itself, as at Corinth, and to address relational brokenness and economic oppression as we gather may lead to God's discipline. Communion is a time of inward personal healing as we renew our relationship with God and are refreshed in the Spirit. We experience this renewal in community, and our challenge each time is to arise and again serve others and allow ourselves to be served. In this way, we all grow in the experience of *shalom*.

Thirdly, Paul's *charismata* include healing and miracles, indicating that he believed in miracles. We are to lay hands on each other and allow the healing power of God to flow. We will see people released from suffering, pain, illness, and hostile forces. As we pray, God acts as he wills. Whatever the outcome, God will pour his love into us afresh, renew us inwardly, and strengthen us for the future.

Fourthly, a local church is one body of Christ with multiple, spiritually-connected, and interdependent members. Within this body, there is no room for racial and status inequality—we have all undergone the same baptism and drink of the same Spirit. Each member is variously gifted, yet all have equal value and are to be cherished. Indeed, the less gifted and seemingly ignoble, often the unhealed, are to be honored even more than those who seem more gifted. All members are also necessary and should express their gifts for the common good. Healing comes as we give of ourselves to God and others. Healing is received as others minister to us.

Finally, we are reminded that Jesus will return, and our lowly bodies will be transformed to be like his glorious body. We will be immortal and imperishable, free forever from all shades of illness and weakness. We will be whole. In the meantime, sustaining ourselves by Christ and together as his people, we press on to form communities of faith that change villages, towns, suburbs, nations, and the world.

THE BODY OF CHRIST IN EPHESIANS AND COLOSSIANS

In Ephesians and Colossians, Paul uses the same metaphor but extends it to the whole church. While the body is a collective cosmic notion in Ephesians, it applies to all body members in each local context. We begin with the body of Christ in Ephesians and then consider Colossians.

The Body of Christ in Ephesians

The body of Christ is, in various ways, referred to eight times in six passages (Eph 1:23; 2:16; 3:6; 4:4, 12–16; 5:23, 30). I will consider each briefly.

Ephesians 1:23

The first mention of Christ's body is toward the end of Paul's prayer in Eph 1:15–23. Paul prays for God to deepen their understanding and insight in Christ, their hope and inheritance, and the greatness of power exerted for them (vv. 15–19). This power raised Jesus, exalted him above all creation, and placed everything under his feet. God's power also exalted Christ to be the head of all things, including his people, the church. This church is "his body." This body, the church, is "the fullness of the one [Christ] filling all things [in creation] in every way."[18] Here,

> the church is filled with power and grace from its exalted Lord, who, in turn, extends his reign throughout heaven and earth through the church. The church accomplishes this through dependence on the one who fills her and by proclaiming the gospel and manifesting the kingdom of God to all in an extensive way.[19]

Notably, it is through prayer that Paul envisages readers of Ephesians experiencing a deeper knowledge of God's wisdom and revelation in their hearts. Paul realizes that prayer leads to a deeper knowledge of God and an unleashing of God's power. As our minds are renewed, we perceive God

---

18. On this interpretation, see Arnold, *Ephesians*, 116–20.
19. Arnold, *Ephesians*, 120.

meeting us in whatever we are facing physically and relationally. Healing comes through prayer and a more profound mind-and-heart experience of God.

Ephesians 2:16

Here, the "one body" in view is the Christ mentioned in 1:23. Whereas Ephesians 2:1–10 focuses on individual salvation, this passage focuses on the equally critical collective aspects of being in Christ. Through the passage, Paul carefully distinguishes between gentiles and Jews, who were formerly separate people before God. In Christ, gentiles and Jews are reconciled in "one body" to God through the cross.[20] God has brought together all who believe in this body, the church, forming them into one people without prejudice or favoritism. This body is held together in Christ and is growing (v. 21).

A cause of great personal pain is marginalization from others based on being perceived differently. This difference may be due to a person's race, ethnicity, culture, age, idiosyncrasies, status, capacities, abilities, health, sex, gender, or sexuality. Such perspectives lead to marginalization, loneliness, isolation, and pain. The church is to be a place of grace in which not only is the gospel upheld, but it is done so in a way that allows space for difference, struggle, and weakness. Paul did, at times, admonish and even instruct his readers to break fellowship with others. He did so for three reasons: (1) extreme unrepentant ethical violations (1 Cor 5); (2) violation of the essence of the gospel (Galatians; 2 Cor 11; Phil 3); and (3) extreme divisiveness (Titus 3). However, in the racist, sexist, and elitist world of the Romans, he summoned believers to embrace one another with a deep *koinōnia* of love and acceptance. People flourish when they know they are welcomed, loved, and given the freedom to express their differentness in the people of God.

Ephesians 3:6

Ephesians 3:1–13 focuses on Paul's mission of proclaiming the mystery of the gospel in which Jew and gentile (and all races) are one in Christ's church and body. In the present age, God has revealed the mystery of Christ—that Jews and gentiles are fellow heirs of God's promises and eternal life. They are now fellow members of the body [the church] and fellow sharers of the

---

20. Lincoln rightly states that "one" indicates that this is the church, not the body of Christ. See Lincoln, *Ephesians*, 145–46.

promise in Christ Jesus through the gospel. His mission is to serve God by his grace and, through his power, preach this to the world.

The mission of Paul was not just preaching a gospel that others are saved. His gospel heals the world as people radically different from one another come together to form one people bound by love. The vision of Eph 2:11–21 comes to pass as the gospel is preached, a diversity of people believe in Jesus, and together, they live out the call of the gospel to unity. Our gospel may be technically correct but is deficient if it does not challenge the various isms that separate us. It is in a saved people that healing comes.

Ephesians 4:4

In Eph 4, having laid a brilliant theological foundation for life in the body of Christ in Eph 1–3, Paul turns to what that looks like. He exhorts the Ephesians to live lives worthy of the call of Jesus, marked by humility, gentleness, patience, and forbearance in love (4:1–2). With all these attributes binding them together, they are to be zealous to maintain the unity produced by the Spirit in the bond of peace. Paul then poetically speaks of seven "ones" that point to the call to oneness the readers are to live out. The first is "one body," referring to the church.[21] For Paul, although there were multiple church expressions across the Roman world, and today there are a plethora of denominations and streams of the church, there is only one body of Christ—one catholic apostolic church. This oneness is as axiomatic as there is one Spirit, one hope, one Lord, one faith, one baptism, and one God.

Paul's "one body" theology is expounded magnificently here. Paul packs into the passage the keys to healing the world and its people. As we are exhorted by Paul every time we meet to live out our calling and allow the Spirit to shape in us the virtues of God listed in v. 2 and rely on the one Spirit, body, Lord, faith, baptism, and God, the one body is able to grow. That body comprises people like you and me, and we flourish as we experience such *agapē*. We experience gentleness, patience, love, and spiritual reconciliation, even when we err.

Ephesians 4:12–16

Within this one church (v. 4), each member has received gifts of grace (vv. 7–10). Paramount among these are the leadership charisms (v. 11). Those so

---

21. Best writes, "There can be no doubt that [the author of Ephesians] understands it to refer to the church and not to the eucharistic or physical body of Christ." Best, *Ephesians*, 366.

gifted are to equip the saints for the work of ministry and the building up of the body of Christ—the church. As the leaders and church members do their various work, the church grows in the unity of faith, knowledge of the Son of God, and the maturity of the fullness of Christ. It is then safeguarded from false teaching that sweeps and blows away the immature. Through "truthing in love," the people of God, the body of Christ, grow up into Christ, the head of the church and body. From him, the whole body, beautifully formed by God with various parts and held together by sinew and ligament, grows in love. The church is a unified and growing organism in which spiritual gifts are used to grow the body internally and numerically.

Notably, healing here is both collective and individual. The church grows in health as leaders equip and congregants serve. In ministering to others and truthing in love,[22] both ministers and recipients experience renewal, leading to a flourishing community of faith.

Ephesians 5:21–33

The context of this passage is family relationships in the households of the Ephesians. As Paul gives his vision of life in the family, as mentioned in Eph 4:15, in v. 23, he refers to Jesus's relationship to his church, the body. Jesus is both the head and Savior of the church (see Eph 1:22–23). The church should, therefore, be subject to Christ in everything. In vv. 29–30, as a healthy person nourishes and cherishes their own body, Christ nourishes and cherishes his body, the church. He does so, because we are members of his body, indicating that Christ's cherishing of the church is because it is made up of his people whom he loves.

This passage imagines the family as a place of flourishing. Both spouses experience wholeness through mutual submission (5:21) and Christ-emulating service.[23] Children grow up healthy and resilient as they are cherished by their parents and grow in obedience. Nothing can replace the home as a place of healthy human development. Paul's vision is of the family as a community of shalom, love, and service, in which all members of the *oikos* flourish.

---

22. The Greek here is the verb *alētheuō*, literally meaning "truthing." It speaks of expressing love toward others.

23. For my take on this passage see Keown, "Paul's Vision," 47–60.

The Body of Christ in Colossians

In Colossians, the body of Christ is mentioned five times, which this essay will now consider. Paul's ideas resonate with those in Ephesians, and several additional elements extend our understanding.

Colossians 1:18, 22

As in Eph 1:22–3; 5:23, and 30, Christ is the head of the body, the church. His position of preeminence is based on his being the beginning, the firstborn from the dead, and the first and preeminent in everything. In Christ, God's fullness dwells, and in turn, Christ's fullness dwells in the church (Col 1:19; Eph 1:23). He does not merely reconcile believers of different ethnicities in his body, but all things by making peace through his blood on the cross (Col 1:20). Despite the Colossians being alienated from one another ethnically and in other ways, now they have been reconciled by the body of his flesh—his redemptive death. The purpose of this is that he may present believers holy, blameless, and above reproach before God (Col 1:22). This outcome is conditional on believers remaining established and steadfast in the faith, without shifting from the hope of the gospel proclaimed throughout the creation, which they heard from Epaphras (Col 1:7, 23).

This passage recalls the discussion of Rom 7:4, in which the actual body of Christ is the basis of good health and human flourishing. Here, Christ's blood reconciles all things, including humankind, who find personal well-being and reconciliation with God, one another, and the creation in Christ. Where believers grow rooted and established in Christ, they experience the fullness of the deity in them via Christ by the Spirit and grow in holiness, blamelessness, and freedom from reproach. Such a heart state can flourish despite the struggles of suffering, which Paul was aware of and experienced daily on behalf of the readers (1:24–2:1; 1 Cor 15:31). The body is wasting away, but the faithful are renewed day by day through Christ by the Spirit (2 Cor 4:16).

Colossians 1:24

Paul here shifts to his ministry of proclamation, calling to mind Eph 3:6, but with the added nuance of suffering. Paul rejoices in his sufferings on behalf of the Colossians. In these afflictions, he fills up in his flesh what is lacking in those of the risen Christ. Paul sees his ministry as an extension of Christ, so his sufferings add to what Jesus suffered to save humankind. His suffering, like that of Jesus, is for the sake of Christ's body, the church. Paul's sufferings do not save the church, but Christ brings people to salvation and adds them to the church through them. Unbelievers are brought into the orb of Christ's salvation through his suffering gospel preachers. Christ, then, absorbs the sufferings of his servants to himself through the Spirit and grows his body.

Ultimate healing comes at the eschaton. In the meantime, like Paul, all believers suffer in multiple ways, filling up Christ's sufferings. Yet, Paul can press on ministering to others so that they may be mature in Christ. Paul here speaks of a heart state where humans face the withering array of pain, especially in a preindustrial world with a life expectancy of around forty,[24] and yet live in wholeness. As in Christ are hidden "all the treasures of wisdom and knowledge," he remains steadfast (2:3, 5). We can live in the same way. God intervenes as he wills when we pray for miracles, yet more profound is the health of Christ flowing through our inner beings, sustaining us and enabling us to continue to serve even when it hurts.

Colossians 2:19

Colossians 2 suggests many of the Colossians had fallen prey to a syncretistic blend of Christianity, combining angel worship, asceticism, philosophy, and Jewish tradition. Recalling Rom 7:4, Paul urges them to reject this special *gnōsis* forsaking their reliance on doing for Christ. They are to hold fast to their head, Jesus, who holds together his body. This body comprises them—they are its ligaments and sinews, and as they hold firm individually and are bound together in Christ, they and the church grow in divine health and renewal. They have died with Christ and must not allow themselves to be subject to the *stoicheia*,[25] the elemental spirits and philosophies that corrupt believers and God's church. The answer to good health is not human, Jewish, or church law that seeks to conform behavior to God through command and obedience (2:20–23). Both we and the law are impotent in generating the life of God in us and the church. Rather, we must set our minds on the things of Christ, which he embodies in the right hand of God (3:1–5). As such, we renounce earthly works and find wholeness in the virtues of God clothed in love (3:5–17). These virtues are worked out in the community so that we grow in maturity and wholeness despite our frail humanness.

---

24. Mangum, *Acts and Paul's Letters*, Titus 2:1–5 .

25. On the *stoicheia*, see Mangum and Brown, *Galatians*, Galatians 3:1—4:7, "Stoicheia, 'Elemental Spirits.'"

Colossians 3:15

Central to Paul's vision for a healthy life in Christ (whatever our psychological, physical, political, or social situation), Col 3 is allowing the "peace of Christ" to rule in our hearts. The genitive *eirē nētou Christou* is one of production whereby Christ generates in us individually the *shalom* of God. Peace here is, first, reconciliation with God; however, this individual experience of peace spills over to the church, where believers are called to share peace and experience it as a body. From this experience flows gratitude.

True peace is found where believers renounce the works of the flesh that inhabit our fallen bodies and live by the virtues of the eschaton in the present. Health and wholeness flow to the body with its cultural and ethnic diversity (3:11) and to the family as the following passage expounds (3:18–4:1). True health flows from God, is experienced in community, fills our hearts, and flows to the world as we root ourselves in the head of the body, Jesus Christ our Lord.

Conclusion to Ephesians and Colossians

Paul's use of "the body of Christ" in these letters informs our understanding of the world church. First, the church made up of all the saints, past, present, and future forms a cosmic body of Christ that experiences his full power and presence and extends his kingdom to the world by proclaiming the gospel. Secondly, the emphasis on cultural unity in the local church is extended to the world. In Christ, the enmity of Jew and gentile is washed away in his redemptive death. All believers from all races and ethnicities are reconciled together in the one body of Christ.

Thirdly, while the proclamation of the gospel includes an appeal for the heart, the gospel is a proclamation of the reconciliation of all peoples (2 Cor 5:18). In Christ, all are *fellow* partakers in the promises of the gospel. Fourthly, we are to form one body by embodying the virtues of Christ in our fellowships. By the one Spirit, the one body then is healthy and whole, and people find the fullness of God's healing.

Fifthly, the whole church generates good health as spiritually gifted leaders share their charisms with the whole church. Unthreatened by others intruding in their ministry space, these leaders treat others with integrity and seek to develop them to excel in acts of service that grow the church. The church grows as people find integrity, value, and esteem as they serve. Equally, as they give honor to others as they are served, others share the limelight of cruciform service. The church not only grows in knowledge and maturity, but new converts are made as people seek this quality of life in a world that so often crushes them and their hopes. Sixth and finally, this quality of life flows into the family where husbands, wives, and children, love and serve one another, dissolving hierarchies in the balm of love.

OVERALL CONCLUSION

The Spirit of God brings healing and wholeness. Sometimes, it is direct intervention to alleviate sickness, demon possession, and need. Still, Christians will never attain complete bodily wholeness, for decay and death still hold us in a vicelike grip. However, through it all, they can be renewed and grow in wisdom and maturity. This flourishing comes as healing is received through and in the body of Christ. This renewal begins in the heart as a person believes in Jesus. It comes through Christ's shattered and restored body, as the Spirit of Jesus fills the faithful who exist in him and relive his experience of death and resurrection. Healing is also experienced in the church community as we serve one another in love, even as we traverse the struggles of being human. Ultimately, through Jesus, we will be fully healed with bodies as glorious as his spiritual body. We will be forever free and whole, as will the cosmos itself. The key to the human quest for wholeness is Jesus. He died and rose for us. We believe and receive him. We are welcomed into his people, and as we serve and are served in the church, we and others flourish. As we negotiate this increasingly perplexing world, what is needed more than ever are redemptive communities of grace in which healing is experienced. May we join with Jesus to build them.

BIBLIOGRAPHY

Arnold, Clinton E. *Ephesians*. ZECNT. Grand Rapids: Zondervan, 2010.
Best, Ernest. *A Critical and Exegetical Commentary on Ephesians*. ICC. Edinburgh: T&T Clark, 1998.
Calvin, John. *Institutes of the Christian Religion*. Bellingham, WA: Logos Bible Software, 1997.
Fee, Gordon D. *The First Epistle to the Corinthians*. Rev. ed. NICNT. Grand Rapids: Eerdmans, 2014.
Garland, David E. *1 Corinthians*. BECNT. Grand Rapids: Baker Academic, 2003.
Keown, Mark J. "Paul's Answer to the Threats of Jerusalem and Rome." In *The Gospel in the Land of Promise: Christian Approaches to the Land of Promise*. Edited by Philip Church et al., 28–45. Eugene, OR: Pickwick, 2011.
———. "Paul's Vision of a New Masculinity." *Colloquium* 41 (2016) 47–60.
———. *Philippians*. 2 vols. EEC. Bellingham, WA: Lexham, 2017.
Lee, Yongbom. "Body of Christ." In *LBD*.

Lincoln, Andrew. *Ephesians*. Word Biblical Commentary 42. Dallas: Word, 1990.
Mangum, Douglas, ed. *Acts and Paul's Letters*. Vol. 2 of *Lexham Context Commentary: New Testament*. LCC. Bellingham, WA: Lexham, 2020. Digital Logos Edition.
Mangum, Douglas, and Derek R. Brown. *Galatians*. LRC. Bellingham, WA: Lexham, 2012. Digital Logos Edition.
Moo, Douglas J. *The Letter to the Romans*. NICNT. Grand Rapids: Eerdmans, 2018.
Theilman, Frank. *Romans*. ZECNT. Grand Rapids: Zondervan, 2018.
Witherington, Ben, III. *Conflict and Community in Corinth: A Socio-Rhetorical Commentary on 1 and 2 Corinthians*. Grand Rapids: Eerdmans, 1995

Chapter 3

Healthy and Holy Bodies
Reimagining Christian Practice and Discourse to Promote Flourishing in Diversity

Maja Whitaker

INTRODUCTION

It was a lovely summer day, and our family had headed to the beach. I was playing in the sand with my youngest daughter, and around us were the chatter and laughs of people both young and old. An older man was walking along the waterline, and as he came closer we made eye contact, and after I smiled he initiated conversation. It started as a lovely interaction, but this is what he opened with: "Good to see you're not as large as *her*," indicating a woman out in the waves. I did not know how to respond, and mistaking my silence as agreement, he followed up with, "I don't think I've ever seen anyone so *large*." I found my voice enough to comment on what I noticed of the woman he was referring to. She looked like she was having a good time—she was stylishly dressed in a glorious red bathing suit and a wide sun hat, obviously enjoying the waves and the water on her body. Having realized that I was not going to be a partner in his body-shaming commentary, the man moved on quickly, leaving me to unpack the interaction with my daughter. At seven years of age she is wholly unselfconscious of her body. Yet I know that the years of body insecurity and body shame will soon be upon her. Hard as I try to help her interpret and filter the world, she is bombarded, as her older sisters have been, by the messaging that only some bodies are good bodies, and so she had better work hard at how her own body looks.

A second vignette comes from some feedback I received after a women's event I spoke at, at a church in Napier last year. The organizer told me that some months afterwards, when they announced a baptism service, a woman had come forward for baptism. This woman explained how she had been wanting to get baptized for some time, but that she couldn't bear the thought of being seen coming up out of those waters in a clinging T-shirt and shorts, her larger body exposed and, she assumed, shameful. It was hearing the message that I shared, that all bodies are good bodies, and wrestling with that for herself, which had given her the felt sense of freedom to take the step of baptism. I was deeply encouraged, but also heartbroken for this woman, whose experience is, I fear, not uncommon. People are withholding themselves from baptism for the fear of how their body will be seen and perceived by their church community.

This feels deeply incongruent, because there is no place for fatphobia within a biblical worldview and Christian communities should be places of full inclusion for all people, regardless of their body's size, appearance, ability, or disability. An understanding of the human body that is shaped by Scripture is good news for all people. It rewrites the scripts of shame and stigma that characterize contemporary society, particularly for people whose bodies do not meet the aesthetic standards that are demanded. However, in order for us to share this good news with the world, we must first examine ourselves. The log in our own eyes is pretty big on this one. The reasons for this are two-fold, I think. Firstly, we are dealing with some biases that are deeply entrenched in human cultures and even in human brains. Secondly, we need to deal with the fact that historically the Christian tradition has, frequently, been more harmful than helpful here. Historically, we have not allowed a biblical anthropology to shape our practice and have succumbed to other cultural forces and powers. A recovery of Scripture's good news about the body, particularly its definition of what it means to be healthy and holy, opens the door to an experience of genuine hope in and for the body—one that offers flourishing within the full diversity of humanity to people both inside and outside the church.

In this chapter I will trace some aspects of the history of the body in the Western philosophical and Christian tradition, and explore how the fallenness of human ways of thinking and relating have distorted us away from a biblical understanding of the goodness of the body. This will entail some challenging critique, but the intention here is to highlight how deeply we need the Spirit to transform our thinking away from the patterns of this world by the renewing of our minds (Rom 12:2). In response, a recovery of a biblical anthropology, one that defines health holistically and beauty rightly, points us towards the rich resources that the church holds both for her members and for the world. The *telos* of the body is not conforming to an ideal of health or beauty, but loving God and loving neighbor, and within this there is space for the generous hosting of diverse bodies. Finally, I will explore how the discourse and practices in Christian communities might be reimagined and refined to support the holistic flourishing of all people.

THE BODY IN WESTERN CHRISTIANITY

Historically the Christian tradition has struggled with the nature of human persons as embodied beings, often dismissing the body or viewing it as primarily something to be disciplined. Bryan Turner offers this summary:

> At least in the West (during the classical and Christian eras) the body has been seen to be a threatening and dangerous phenomenon, if not adequately controlled and regulated by cultural processes. The body has been regarded as the vehicle or vessel of unruly, ungovernable, and irrational passions, desires, and emotions. The necessity to control the body (its locations, its excretions, and its reproduction) is an enduring theme within Western philosophy, religion, and art.[1]

Much of the blame for this can be laid at the feet of the disproportionate influence of Greek philosophies on early Christian thinking. In broad terms, these tended to denigrate the body and elevate the rational soul as the true essence of the human person.[2] Bodies were generally viewed as dangerous and as an anxious burden which one longed to escape, because materiality itself is viewed as contemptible or evil. In addition, fluidity or change is fundamentally problematic, and biological organisms, which are characterized by change whether in development or decay, exemplify this fluidity. It is for this reason that critics such as Celsus, a second century anti-Christian polemicist, struggled to conceive of how bodily resurrection could be in any way desirable to Christians, let alone an ultimate hope. In the prevailing worldview of the cultural milieu, the immortal soul would not seek to inhabit a lifeless body, and so resurrection is only a hope "which might be cherished by worms."[3] Nevertheless the early church fathers strove

---

1. Turner, "Body in Western Society," 20.
2. See Ware, "'My Helper,'" 90–110.
3. We can read his objections as recorded by Origen in his apologia *Contra Celsum*,

to make the idea both palatable and reasonable to intellectuals both inside and outside the church. Despite this hard-fought commitment to the doctrine of the resurrection of the body, the esteem of the rational soul and the aversion to changeable bodies continued. Bodies of course must be tolerated for biological survival, but they should be under the control of the rational soul.

I have often wondered how the Christian tradition might have developed differently if the voices and experiences of women had been given more room in theological conversation. Generally speaking, the rational intellect was equated with the masculine, and the physical body with the feminine, so much so that Caroline Walker Bynum claims that the Western religious tradition "had long told women that physicality was particularly their problem."[4] Male bodies are, generally speaking, more static and amenable to control, at least between the end of puberty and the onset of old age. Female bodies, in contrast, are naturally more fluid: the regular monthly rhythm of ovulation and menstruation; the changes wrought by pregnancy, birthing, breastfeeding, post-pregnancy, and ultimately menopause. Change is a given when it comes to the female body. In addition, our relations with others are more closely embodied, particularly with our children: with a newborn in your arms the boundaries of your bodily self are dissolved. In medieval times the enfleshment and porosity of women was celebrated as an access point to a kind of transcendent spirituality. The female mystics bled and lactated, their bodily fluids and fluidity considered sacred sites of power.[5] This medieval understanding of spirituality as largely sensuous and the body as unproblematically porous, intercorporeal, and volatile, gave way to the rise of rationalism in the period of the Enlightenment.

Once again, the rational soul was elevated above the body. The soul was located in, or at least connected with the body in some way, but it was subordinate in both meaning and value.[6] The body came to be conceived of as a machine, even a container or "earthsuit,"[7] which is filled, activated and controlled by the soul—the interior life of which is "the real me." This fundamental dualism still pervades much of our theological worldview, spiritual

---

5.14.

4. Bynum, *Fragmentation and Redemption*, 146.

5. Bynum, *Holy Feast*; Louth, "Body in Western Catholic," 111–30; Bynum, "Fast, Feast, and Flesh," 1–25; Bynum, *Fragmentation and Redemption*.

6. Descartes suggested that perhaps it was the pineal gland that formed the tethering point, though his assumption was likely based on the mere fact this is the only anatomical feature of the brain that does not appear, on dissection, in a paired duality. See Descartes, "Letter to Meysonnier, 29 January 1640," 103.

7. A term used in Copeland, "4 Keys to Understanding."

practice, and general being in the world. The biblical hope of the resurrection of the body to come has faded from popular view, in both wider culture and in the minds of many Christians. As Sarah Coakley writes,

> Devoid now of religious meaning or of the capacity for any fluidity into the divine, shorn of any expectation of new life beyond the grave, [the body] has shrunk to the limits of individual fleshliness; hence our only hope seems to reside in keeping it alive, youthful, consuming, sexually active, and jogging on (literally), for as long as possible.[8]

The Christian worldview has moved away from the center of broader Western society, and, in response, Christians have attempted to stall the shift and regain cultural power and influence. However, in doing so in relation to matters of the body, Christian discourse has often focused on a narrow range of particular concerns, rather than addressing broader currents in society. Ethical reflection has been characterized by a preoccupation with sexuality and reproduction, but has largely neglected to speak into issues such as food insecurity, body shame, or sexual abuse. This is not to say that the former issues are not important, but the attention to the control of bodies—women's bodies in particular—is painful to trace. One of my core claims here is that, as the church, we should be focussing our attention regarding the body, not on a narrow range of ethical concerns or hot-button issues but on those deeper cultural currents that underlie the shame and stigma placed on diverse bodies—shame and stigma that are so common that strangers can assume them as common currency when they want to strike up conversation with you on the beach.

Health, Beauty, and the Body as a Project

Of the broader currents in modern Western culture, it is the foundational notion of the body as a reflexive project of the self that I find particularly troubling.[9] Here the body is conceived of as something to be shaped in order to not only express one's individual self but also as an active way to reflexively shape the self. That is, I "work on" my body in order that it will reflect who I really am in an interior sense, but also in order to actively shape my interior sense of self. This worldview is so pervasive that it is hard to distinguish. It shows up when we exercise in order to attain a bodily form appropriate to the kind of person we want to be, when we dress in ways that

---

8. Coakley, *Powers and Submissions*, 155.
9. See Whitaker, "Shaping Our Bodies," 182–90.

reflect the sub-groups with which we wish to identify, when we consciously or unconsciously adopt a different manner of speaking in order to project a certain persona. These everyday examples are not particularly concerning. Yet underneath them is the same current that leads to practices such as disordered eating, compulsive exercise, body dysmorphia, cosmetic surgery, and extreme body modification. This intensification of the discontented relationship with the body as a project is alarming, and it reveals the pressure brought to bear on the body in the pursuit of health or beauty.

Health and beauty are, of course, goods in themselves—when rightly conceived, that is. However, both health and beauty can become totalizing ideals that subsume other goods, and we end up with healthism and beautyism, which are deeply problematic not least because of their stealthy pervasion of Western culture. Nicole Morgan defines healthism as

> the prioritization of health to an extreme degree, where persons living with disease or disabilities find themselves to be second-class citizens. In this way of thinking, health becomes a moral obligation, and those who fail to pursue health become outcasts.[10]

Thus, healthism leaves no space for true belonging for people who are ill, disabled, or with bodies that are deemed categorically "unhealthy." Health has been used to justify the stigmatization or shaming of fat people into weight-loss behavior "for your own good." In response, the Health at Every Size (HAES) movement takes aim at "the cultural unintelligibility of the healthy fat person."[11] It uses a weight-neutral approach to health and fitness, and recognizes that fatness is not necessarily associated with ill health but that all people can work towards better health.[12] There is much merit in this approach, yet it is still incomplete in dethroning healthism. The "fat and fit" discourse can become normative, setting up a "good-fat-person" vs. "bad-fat-person" dichotomy, stigmatizing those who do not or cannot pursue health as a moral obligation.[13] As in many of these supposedly liberatory movements, the chronically ill are overlooked and marginalized.

Anthony Synnott describes beautyism as follows:

> Beautyism, and its attendant, facism, the prejudice and discrimination in favour of the beautiful and attractive (however defined) and against the ugly and less attractive, are virtually

---

10. Morgan, *Fat and Faithful*, 104.
11. Boero and Mickulas, *Killer Fat Media*, 131.
12. Bacon, *Health at Every Size*.
13. Morgan, *Fat and Faithful*, 99–128.

institutionalized in our society, and they are the last major bastion of inequity.[14]

This "aesthetic stratification"[15] is founded in physiognomic assumptions that link appearance with moral character. This is a foundational piece to every form of eugenics, yet it is thoroughly normalized. Heather Widdows's academic work has extended to the #everydaylookism campaign,[16] in which snippets of stigma and shaming are shared by anonymous participants. What makes the reading even more heart-rending is how *normal* it feels. Participants share comments from strangers, family, and lovers on how they are too fat, too skinny, not conventionally pretty, too hairy, too dark-skinned, too light-skinned, or not paying enough attention to styling their hair, clothes, or make-up as they supposedly should. The comments are confronting when isolated, but in everyday life they often go unexamined and unquestioned. The structural injustice of beautyism is embedded in social systems and norms of relating.[17] "Pretty privilege" is a social dynamic that my teenaged daughters can name that they are consciously navigating; it is simply a social reality.[18]

The Powers Underneath This Painful Trajectory

We can discharge some of our frustration and anger at where we have ended up by offering a harsh retrospective of Western culture, body theology, and the Christian tradition in general. Yet this is insufficient if it is deep and long-lasting change that we hope for—and it is to this that we must orientate ourselves. That is, rather than merely asking "Where did we go so wrong?" in terms of history and culture, a more helpful question is "How did we get here so easily?" That is, how have we so easily adopted and absorbed harmful and prejudicial worldviews, particularly when, as I will go on to argue, they run counter to the good news that a biblical worldview is for the body?

14. Synnott, *Body Social*, 100.
15. Synnott, *Body Social*, 100.
16. See everydaylookism.com.
17. Widdows, "Structural Injustice," 251–69.
18. "Pretty privilege" plays out in vocational contexts. For example, one report finds that blonde women are paid more for equal work. Johnston, "Physical Appearance and Wages," 10–12. In an Italian study, women deemed attractive are more likely to be given interviews when applying for a job with a call-back rate of 54 percent for "attractive" women versus 7 percent for "unattractive" women. For men, the rates are also lower but not as starkly so, with a call-back rate of 47 percent for "attractive" men versus 26 percent for "unattractive" men. Busetta et al., "Searching for a Job."

These prejudicial assumptions are encoded in our neural makeup, deeply enfleshed, and they color the cultural waters that we swim in. One of the starkest examples in the literature of this embedded and enculturated stigma is provided by the neurocognitive response to viewing anomalous bodies and the consistent conflation of that anomaly with evil of some kind.[19] Testing with functional MRI reveals that viewing faces with anomalous characteristics tends to elicit neural activity indicating a disgust response. In addition, people with facial anomalies have their character evaluated more negatively and receive less prosocial behavior. That is, when we view a face that deviates from the biological norm in a significant way (whether by trauma or genetic difference), a sense of disgust is unconsciously provoked, and we tend to assume that this person is morally worse in some way and act in a less friendly manner towards them. The neurocognitive explanation for this lies in the way that the neural networks for visceral and moral disgust are arranged, and the fact that at one point this arrangement served us well. Evolutionary psychology suggests that a disgust response can promote protective responses such as avoiding pathogens (visceral disgust), avoiding sexual contact with partners who would likely jeopardize the fitness of any offspring (sexual disgust), and avoiding behaviors that transgress social taboos and cultural norms in order to protect social relationships within the in-group (moral disgust).[20] These various kinds of disgust all activate the same neural systems, and so the intuitive experience of the person is not dissimilar.[21] In the case of facial anomalies, the lack of symmetry could be an indicator of an unstable genome or disease that might produce limited function and an evolutionary disadvantage. Yet this does not make them rationally justifiable, particularly in a modern context in which attention to biological fitness and evolutionary advantage has been mitigated by medical, technological, and social progress.

The research of Workman, Humphries, Hartung, Aguirre, Kable, and Chatterjee takes this deeper into even more discomforting territory: the increased neural activity indicating disgust and lower prosociality is correlated with a stronger just-world belief and a higher socioeconomic status.[22] That is, if a person believes that people generally get what they deserve in life, then the disgust response is more intense, and people who are better off socioeconomically tend to be less friendly towards people with anomalous

19. Workman et al., "Morality Is in the Eye of the Beholder," 3–17.

20. Tybur et al., "Disgust," 65–84.

21. See, for example, Sanfey et al., "Neural Basis of Economic Decision-Making," 1755–58.

22. Workman et al., "Morality Is in the Eye of the Beholder," 3–17.

faces. It is not difficult to understand how these biases might fit together in ways that appeal to our sinful nature. If we are generally doing well at life, we would like to believe that this isn't mere accident but something that we somehow deserve, and so by parallel people who are in unfortunate situations have probably done something to deserve that somehow, and so they are less deserving of our kindness.

I would like to think that most of us would blush if we had to articulate a reasoning like that, for it is no longer socially acceptable to say out loud. We might regularly enact stigma, but when forced to reflect on it consciously we would (hopefully) struggle to justify it.[23] However, we do not need to go far back into the Christian tradition to find the generally agreed belief that people with any kind of disability are afflicted as such because of some kind of sin—despite the fact that Jesus explicitly denied this kind of causal connection in John 9:3—and I have heard far too many people with disabilities report that it remains.[24] When it comes to fatness, it is often assumed that the overweight body is due to a lack of personal responsibility or laziness; the assumption is that if someone just tried harder to eat better and exercise more, then of course they will lose weight. However, the weight range of any individual body is largely genetically determined, the heritability of Body Mass Index is very close to that of height.[25] Certainly no one would suggest that short people are morally lazy and should take responsibility for increasing their height.[26] While the connection between moral character and diverse bodies has been loosened (except in the case of fatness), the connection between aesthetics and diverse bodies largely remains.

Yes, there are hopeful signs in the slow rise of more inclusive beauty campaigns, in which "diverse" models are featured. However this is a "naïve integration"[27] that reinforces the ideology of normate bodies, for the diverse models only ever diverge on one aspect of the beauty ideal that Widdows

---

23. Similarly, it is unlikely that the stigma against facial anomalies would be explicitly articulated in the broader culture (that is, "the world"), but it is implicitly reinforced. R. J. Palacio's wildly popular book *Wonder*, and the accompanying movie, portrayed the experience of Auggie Pullman whose anomalous face made him subject to relentless isolation and bullying. His inclusion was celebrated but it was a surprising reversal of the way things normally go.

24. Eiesland, *Disabled God*, 70.

25. Body Mass Index (BMI) appears to have a heritability of 0.7, which suggests that 70 percent of the variation of BMI in the population is due to genetic inheritance. By comparison, height has a similar heritability of 0.79. Manne, *Unshrinking*, 84.

26. Note, however, the association between shortness and smallness of character that persisted in the ancient world and is exemplified in the account of Zaccheus in Luke 19:1–10. Parsons, *Body and Character*, 705.

27. Heiss, "Locating the Bodies."

has articulated—for example, if they are plus-size they are still firm, youthful, and smooth.[28] It is worth noting that Widdows's beauty ideal ("thin, firm, smooth, and youthful") makes no mention of disability. It almost does not need to; "without markers of physical or intellectual disability," goes without saying. Similarly, if disabled models are used in inclusive beauty campaigns, they tend to be thin, firm, smooth, and youthful. That is, while attempts are made to push against the norms of advertising (likely in an attempt to garner a broader market), the fundamental ideology of beautyism remains untouched.

We must acknowledge the brokenness of our human nature and human systems that makes us so susceptible to adopting the kinds of ideologies and practices that promulgate prejudice and harm. In these efforts I find it helpful to employ the framework of "the flesh, the world, and the devil." This was first outlined most clearly by Evagrius of Pontus (345–399).[29] In his 2021 book *Live No Lies*, John Mark Comer has articulated this ancient framework for contemporary audiences: "Deceptive ideas (the DEVIL) . . . that play to disordered desires (the FLESH) . . . that are normalized in a sinful society (the WORLD)."[30] This entails a more realistic view of ourselves as human persons, what David Zahl terms a "low anthropology," one that recognizes our inherent limitation, doubleness, and self-centeredness.[31] It is this kind of approach that allows us to humbly admit our own complicity in harm, to seek deep transformation, and to protect against future harms.

I suggest that the shame and stigma attached to diverse bodies are one of the "patterns of this world" that Paul calls us to be transformed away from by the renewing of our minds (Rom 12:2). That is, while prejudice against diversity might come naturally to us, for it is deeply embedded in "the flesh," we must work and participate in the Spirit's work to root it out. In doing this we are also participating in spiritual warfare. These lies that appeal to the flesh and have become normalized (and repeated/spread) in the world have their source in the father of lies (John 8:44), that "old deluder,"[32] and the enemy of us all. I suspect that the healthism and beautyism that underlie dynamics such as disgust at diversity and what Michelle Lelwica calls "the

---

28. Widdows, *Perfect Me*, 118–19, 220.

29. Particularly in the prologue to his *Praktikos*. See Foster and Beebe, *Longing for God*.

30. Comer, *Live No Lies*, xxiii.

31. Zahl, *Low Anthropology*.

32. This name for the devil is enshrined in the Massachusetts School Laws of 1647.

religion of thinness"[33] fall into the category of the "powers of this age" that Eph 6:12 warns us that we are at war with.

THE CHURCH AS (HOPEFULLY) A PLACE OF HOPE FOR THE BODY

The church could be a place of hope here, and she should be. The marginalization of particular groups of people is antithetical to the gospel, and there are clear mandates to not focus on outward appearance (e.g. 1 Sam. 16:7; John 7:24; Jas 2:1–5). However, Christian culture has often absorbed uncritically many of the values of our cultural milieu. As with the early Christian thinkers who failed to filter out problematic elements of Greek philosophy, modern Christians have uncritically adopted the paradigm of the body as a project and the tenets of both healthism and beautyism.[34] These have been theologically reframed, repackaged with Christianese, and touted from celebrity Christian platforms and the common pulpit.

In the case of healthism and fatphobia, a lush landscape of Christian programs, books, and diet devotionals have arisen, particularly in North America where the connection between thin white women, social power, and racism is particularly potent.[35] Where fat was once a marker of social privilege, the parameters of an ideal body shifted under the weight of colonial constructs and the larger body was identified with the black body. As Michelle Lelwica explains, "In the context of colonialism, robust appetites belonged to 'savages,' while slenderness came to represent self-control, intelligence, spiritual virtue and high social rank, all of which economically privileged White Christians claimed for themselves."[36] Thus weight loss and maintenance became a central concern for affluent white women, one which was frequently held within religious constructs and communities.

Marie Griffith has traced the disturbingly prolific history of Christian weight-loss programs and literature in North America, revealing their grounding in Anglo-Protestant culture married with the secular conception of the body as a perfectible project.[37] She claims that the latter is "deeply indebted to currents that have perceived the body as essential for pushing

---

33. Lelwica, *Religion of Thinness*.

34. Whitaker, *Pursuing Perfection*.

35. Shamblin, *Weigh Down Diet*; Shedd, *Pray Your Weight Away*; TerKeurst, *I'll Start Again Monday*; Warren et al., *Daniel Plan*.

36. Lelwica, "Shameful Perfection," 158–9. See Strings, *Fearing the Black Body*.

37. Griffith, *Born Again Bodies*.

the soul along the path to redemption."[38] This connection between fatness and spiritual weakness or sin is exemplified by the writing of Charlie Shedd who claimed that fatness is outside of God's good plans for each person, that failed attempts at weight loss evidence a lack of personal faith, and that fatness is in itself sinful; he wrote, "We fatties are the only people on earth who can weigh our sin."[39] While the weight-loss behaviors and programs promoted by Christian advocates and celebrities vary, unifying them is the assumption that there is, as Griffith writes, a "basic religious obligation to cultivate correct bodily practice and create a proper looking body."[40]

Christian culture has been more subtle in its advocacy of beautyism. The apparently obvious connection between health and slimness does not parallel with the same power in questions of beauty, and there is a clear injunction in Scripture that physical beauty is not to be pursued above personal holiness or more internal qualities (1 Pet 3:3–4; Prov 31:30; 1 Tim. 2.9). Yet physical beauty is still unduly celebrated in many Christian communities, particularly in American evangelicalism and the many church communities here in New Zealand that are influenced by them, and as almost always, the implications are particularly felt by women. There is plenty of anecdotal evidence of the implicit and explicit pressure placed on women to conform to a certain aesthetic standard whether they are on the stage, behind the pulpit, or in the pews. This could be in the direction of the "modest is hottest" approach,[41] or in a more sexually explicit way. At one point in time this dynamic reached a peculiar height, particularly in American megachurch and aspiring-megachurch contexts, where a male speaker would wax lyrical about his "smoking hot" wife.[42] Whatever the approach or the intention, the outcome is still the objectification and control of bodies, women's bodies in particular.[43]

The woman who does not attend to personal grooming—whether by controlling weight, applying makeup, tanning or lightening skin, or

38. Griffith, *Born Again Bodies*, 240.
39. Shedd, *Pray Your Weight Away*, 11.
40. Griffith, *Born Again Bodies*, 239.
41. See Miller, "How 'Modest Is Hottest.'"
42. Demuth, "I'm Sick of Hearing."

43. Naomi Wolf traces "the sense that [women's] bodies are second-rate, an afterthought" to the order of creation in Gen 2: "Eve's body is twice removed from the Maker's hand, imperfect matter born of matter." She goes on to identify the hierarchical interactions between Adam and Eve as the foundation for why, as she writes, women "often need to offer their bodies to any male gaze that will legitimize them. . . . Many women don't believe that they are beautiful until they win the official seal of approval that men's bodies possess in our culture." Wolf, *Beauty Myth*, 93.

straightening curly or Afro hair—is deemed to be "not taking care of herself" or "letting herself go," or even worse failing to "tend her temple."[44] Body maintenance is here conceived of as an act of personal responsibility and discipline that is an outworking of the faith-filled life. The appearance of a healthy body (read: thin and conventionally attractive) has become a defining mark of a holy body. Note of course that a thin and conventionally attractive body is not necessarily a healthy body; the behaviors employed to achieve a thin and conventionally attractive body may be directly harmful to one's health. As we shall see, our definitions of health, beauty, and holiness are skewed in this worldview. Thankfully, a biblical approach to the body offers not only a hope-filled corrective to this, but also an invitation to a freer and more flourishing embodied life than many women can imagine for themselves.

The Rich Resources of a Biblical Anthropology

From start to finish, the grand narrative of Scripture affirms the place of the body in God's good purposes for his created order. The first words spoken over the human body are that it is very good (Gen 1:31), and the hope of human existence in the new creation is for fullness of eternal life in the resurrection body. In between we see embodiment incorporated into expressions of worship in the Hebrew Bible—yes, the impurity of the body is something to be managed, but there are ways to do that; that is, the pathway to embodied holiness is prescribed, it is not blocked by the mere fact of embodiment.[45] The act that signals the greatest affirmation of human embodiment is surely the incarnation. Let us not forget that Christ has not shed his body post-crucifixion, he rises in a resurrection body, which, while both continuous and discontinuous with our earthly bodies, is still a body, and with this he ascends to heaven. All this runs so very counter to the themes of the Greek philosophers who generally despised the body with its materiality and fluidity. It also runs counter to the more modern assumption that it doesn't really matter what one does with one's body, a foundational presupposition for the so-called sexual revolution. Where the prevailing perception of the Christian tradition, rightly or wrongly, has been that it has a low view of the body, Nancy Pearcey has shown how this is, in fact, characteristic of the anthropology that undergirds many of Western modernity's

---

44. Here 1 Cor 6:19–20 is usually in mind.

45. For example, as Mary Douglas's influential work in *Purity and Danger* reveals, "By rules of avoidance holiness was given a physical expression." Douglas, *Purity and Danger*, 57.

response to body issues from gender and sexuality, to abortion and euthanasia.[46] Christianity in fact has a high view of the body. Thus, Paul writes to the church in Corinth that what they do with their body *does* matter, in an attempt to correct the dualist anthropology that both denigrated the material order and gave licence to sexual immorality (1 Cor 6:12:20). Along similar lines, a biblical anthropology does not lead us to rubbish the desire for health or beauty, instead it redeems these from healthism and beautyism and the perceived achievement of their superficial goals, offering back to us a worldview that leads to holistic flourishing.

Where the Western model is overly reductionist, relying primarily on medical categories and measures, a biblical approach to health is more consonant with indigenous frameworks, such as *Te Whare Tapa Whā*.[47] Here health is conceived of holistically, incorporating the emotional, spiritual, and social facets of the human person, in addition to the physical, in good alignment with a biblical anthropology. John Wilkinson has articulated how in the Old Testament health is characterized by wellbeing, righteousness, obedience, strength, fertility, and longevity, all of which come under the umbrella of *shalom*.[48] Health is about far more than biological functioning, and it cannot be described by medical measures alone. The focus is instead on right relationship, and the person must be considered as embedded in 360 degrees of relationship: with God, with herself, with other persons, and with the environment. Thus, it is possible to conceive of a chronically-ill person who is healthier than even an athlete at the prime of life. The pursuit of a healthy body, thus, is one that supports this kind of being, rather than taking a toll on emotional, mental, spiritual, or social wellbeing.

A redeemed understanding of beauty requires a similarly deepened and more holistic approach. Where the common conception of beauty focuses on an attractive outward appearance, a biblically-informed conception goes beneath the surface and also interrogates the nature of attractiveness. Jessica Schroeder offers this definition: "Beauty, in the most basic sense, is that which, being perceived, rightly pleases or ought to please with respect to what it is."[49] It is possible, then, that something may be attractive, but in being so does not please as it ought, and thus is by definition ugly. The character of "oughtness" here is crucial, and Schroeder defines this by reference to image of Christ and the transcendentals of goodness and truth that sit alongside that of beauty. Thus, a thing or a person may be of minimal or

---

46. Pearcey, *Love Thy Body*.
47. Rochford, "Whare Tapa Wha," 41–57.
48. Wilkinson, *Bible and Healing*.
49. Schroeder, "Mirrors, Pedestals," 31.

faded beauty, perhaps not even outwardly attractive in conventional terms, but be truly beautiful. The fundamental difference here is one of perception, and it is our perceptions that must be redeemed and renewed away from the patterns of this word. This is the work of formation, which will only be complete at our final transformation of resurrection. Brian Brock writes of his expectation of the resurrection that "bodies and minds that today some find repulsive will be gloriously visible to all in the beauty that God's eyes behold in them."[50]

This renewal of perception is an example of the level at which Christian thought and practice can work on the problem at hand. We have much to say about the issues at the surface, guidelines for action and response in the case of particular ethical issues. Yet we also have more than this; we have the tools to deal with what is going on underneath—not least the fundamental lies that thread through the action of the flesh, the world, and the devil. For example, let us return to the functional MRI studies of Workman and colleagues.[51] Alongside the neurally embedded pathways that prompt a disgust response to the viewing of anomalous faces was the just-world belief that people tend to get what they deserve. This just-world belief can be amended by a more accurate view of providence, an appropriately realized eschatology, and a critique of the causality of suffering and disability. Instead of the assumption that the person with an anomalous face has done something to deserve their disfigurement, either in a past life or this one, we can assert the brokenness of creation and our great hope for its renewal, alongside calling all bodies, even the most diverse, good.

Discipling the Body

In the case of facial anomalies is relatively easy to dispute the correlation between sin and diverse bodies. We can take the words of Jesus regarding the man born blind and declare over those born with anomalous faces, "It was not because of his sins or his parents' sins" (John 9:3, NLT). Similarly, for those with faces disfigured by accident or disease, we are less likely to attribute their suffering to their sin. But what about the issue of fatness? Obese bodies prompt similar responses of disgust and dread.[52] As earlier described, the assumption is that a person can and should do whatever is required to maintain a body size within a range that is deemed healthy and attractive. The inability to do so is often put down to a lack of discipline, or

---

50. Brock, *Disability*, 132.
51. Workman et al., "Morality Is in the Eye of the Beholder," 3–17.
52. Fahs, "Imagining Ugliness," 237–58.

indulgence in the obvious sin of gluttony. But is gluttony actually about the overconsumption of calories? No, it may include this, but the source of the sin is in the harm it causes to others. Nicole Morgan writes,

> Gluttony is not feasting. Gluttony is not fatness. We can just as easily be a thin glutton as we can be a fat person who is not prone to gluttony. Gluttony is the consumption of food at the expense of others. If racism is prejudice plus power, gluttony is overconsumption plus power.[53]

In addition to excessive eating that harms our neighbor, there are other forms of gluttony, such as being overly fastidious or unthinking as regards our food choices.[54] All things being equal, the demanding guest who asserts her unsubstantiated food intolerances upon her host is more open to the accusation of gluttony than the fat person. Behind this claim is the questioning of whether saying "yes" to the body's desires is inevitably sinful, and saying "no" to the body is always the path to holiness.

In 1 Cor 9:24–27 Paul writes of his aspiration for the sake of the gospel and of the need to exercise self-control and discipline in order that he might, as an athlete would, achieve the "prize." He writes of the necessity to "punish" his body (NRSV), variously translated as "beat" (WEB), "discipline" (NLT), "tame" (NMB), or "chastise" (WYC). Paul's language here is strong and could be read to bolster a body-hatred in which asceticism or even self-flagellation is required—particularly if we read this portion of Scripture forgetting everything else that it says about the goodness of the body. However, instead of the physical body per se, it is more likely that Paul has in mind "day-to-day life as a whole in the public domain"; it is the whole person that needs to be restrained in its attitudes and practices in the world.[55] That is, Paul is not here advocating harsh treatment of the physical body, as if it was the opponent against which we fight. The metaphor of the athlete is more successful here: a wise athlete trains in such a way as to avoid injury and carefully nourishes her body. Yes, the training is often uncomfortable and self-discipline is required, but this does not equate to the kind of punitive disciplining that takes the body out of the "stretch

---

53. Morgan, *Fat and Faithful*, 63.

54. DeYoung, *Glittering Vices*, 139–58.

55. Thiselton, *First Epistle*, 716. Fee attributes the potential confusion to Paul's mixed metaphors and writes, "He hardly intends them to understand his physical body as such as the 'opponent' that he must subdue in order to gain the prize. He uses 'body' because of the metaphor; what he almost certainly intends by it is 'myself,' as before (v. 19) which would include the body, but only as it is the vehicle of his present earthly life. His point, after all, is the need for self-restraint, not asceticism (which he thoroughly rejects) or self-flagellation." Fee, *First Epistle*, 484–85.

zone" and into the zone of harm. I suggest that we will avoid the dangers of harmful asceticism and body-hatred if we talk more about "discipling" the body rather than "disciplining" it, if we must talk about our bodies as third-person objects in this way, rather than our very being.

Discipleship entails denial, and I am not arguing here for indulgence of every bodily whim. However, this target must be distinguished from the kinds of "bodily imperatives" that moral philosopher Kate Manne describes: "They tell us, for example to go to sleep or quench our thirst. They tell us to pull our hand away from a flame, or gasp for air when we are starved of oxygen."[56] She goes on to argue that these constitute "our most important *moral* imperatives" towards both ourselves and other creatures. Whims and impulses do not carry the profundity or urgency of imperatives, yet in training ourselves to rightly ignore our bodily "whims" and impulses we have often also learned and taught others to ignore their bodily imperatives. And so some women simply quit eating for days on end in a desperate effort to lose weight, doing violence to themselves.[57]

Practical Suggestions for Church Communities

There is hope here for the body, and it is hope that many both inside and outside the church are deeply aching for. But how might we share it and enact it? I will finish with a few practical suggestions.

Firstly, let us interrogate our assumptions and identify the impact of these problematic cultural discourses in our contexts—you could consider it a body-shame audit. This will vary according to the shape of our church communities, particularly the life stage of those who make them up. Consider how various people or groups might experience your communal thinking and practice—ask them if you are not confident in your imagination. How might their particular vulnerabilities need particular care—youth and young people, young mothers, those with naturally heavier bodies, those with naturally skinnier bodies, aging bodies, people with disabilities? Be curious about how they might be experiencing your community, and invite candid feedback.

Consider your preaching and messaging; watch your language! Be careful not to conflate sin and disability, or equate fatness with a lack of discipline or gluttony. Speak carefully about the body and about health. Consciously rebuke healthism in favor of a holistic framing, and draw on

---

56. Manne, *Unshrinking*, 173.
57. As Manne describes of her own and others' experience. Manne, *Unshrinking*.

Te Whare Tapa Whā.[58] This is particularly important in those seasons of the calendar and church year when we focus on fresh starts or on denial, such as Lent. When speaking about fasting, be particularly careful and consider those with disordered eating. Tread carefully to avoid a "self-help" approach to well-being. Self-care for women is often framed as attention to personal grooming, and women's ministries can fall into this trap, not realizing that it reinforces beautyism.

Pay attention to the practices and behaviors that reinforce culture. Be particularly careful about how you might celebrate a person's experience of weight loss. Do not tell people who appear on the stage or behind the pulpit, either implicitly or explicitly, that their bodies need to be different to fulfil this role. Do not offer weight-loss tips or beauty advice to the vocalists on the worship team—this should not need saying out loud, but in too many contexts it does. We can move beyond merely correcting thinking to the practices that form us. Spiritual practices that are deeply embodied, such as Eucharist and baptism, offer a way to affirm our shared identity alongside affirming our bodies and even the very act of eating.[59]

Note that we must be careful to take aim at the powers of this age, at cultural discourses, and social dynamics, rather than at individual bodies. We cannot move from the claim that fat bodies should be embraced and beauty ideals need not be pursued, to the claim that individual persons should not attempt to lose weight for health reasons.[60] Similarly, we cannot argue that individual persons should not spend their time and money on making themselves look beautiful. That would merely be shifting the shame around and would continue the oppression, particularly of women, and the segregation of power to a privileged few. Heather Widdows writes,

> I have rejected the approach of telling women what to do and not do. Such an approach is women-blaming and divisive, and it does not address the beauty ideal. Only collectively can change happen, and if we seek to mitigate the harms and costs of the emerging inhuman and punishing beauty ideal, we should focus collectively.[61]

---

58. Mental Health Foundation, "Te Whare Tapa Whā."

59. Kent, "Consuming the Body."

60. This problematic dynamic is outworked in the public shaming of those in the fat acceptance movement who have pursued interventions to lose weight. See Bacon, "Unspeakable Fat," 91–92.

61. Widdows, *Perfect Me*, 257–58.

HOPE FOR THE BODY

We must take a compassionately-realist dive beneath the surface if we are to properly address the embedded and enculturated stigma that we so easily tend to attach to bodies that diverge from the idolized ideal of health and beauty. It is to this effort that the Christian tradition can and should add its weight. We have the resources, both theoretical and practical, to ground, focus, and energize this collective aim. The gospel is good news for the body.

It is within church communities that diverse bodies can be offered a full inclusion and where scripts of stigma and shame can be rewritten in light of the belonging offered by the redeemed community and the good news that all bodies are good. The *telos* of the body is not conforming to an ideal of health or beauty, but loving God and loving neighbor, and within this there is space for the generous hosting of diverse bodies.[62] From this flows the call for Christians, and Christian leaders in particular, to carefully examine our ways of thinking: Do they align with Scripture and scriptural values? This is basic work, but often overlooked, particularly outside of the hot-button issues that preoccupy conversations about faith, culture, and practice. What also follows is the possibility of discovering promising avenues towards freedom and flourishing—avenues that we ourselves may walk down and that we also may share with other journeyers.

The simmering discontentment with the body that characterizes modern Western culture, where we are both body-denying and body-obsessed, has created a state of tension in which many are desperate for relief. To those aching for freedom, burdened by shame, and hurting from harm, we can speak words that echo those spoken over the first human body: "It is very good" (Gen 1:31). We can enact those words and offer healing and reconciliation between bodies and within bodies, however diverse they might be. This is hope for us, as embodied beings, and hope for the world.

BIBLIOGRAPHY

Bacon, Hannah. "Unspeakable Fat, Unspeakable Beauty: Fatness, Apophasis and the Overflowing of Excess." In *Pursuing Perfection: Faith and the Female Body*, edited by Maja I. Whitaker, 77–98. London: SCM, 2025.

Bacon, Linda. *Health at Every Size: The Surprising Truth About Your Weight*. Dallas: BenBella, 2010.

Beck, Amanda Martinez. "Christian Hope Through an Embodied Telos." In *Pursuing Perfection: Faith and the Female Body*, edited by Maja I. Whitaker, 7–23. London: SCM, 2025.

---

62. Beck, "Christian Hope."

Boero, Natalie, and Peter Mickulas. *Killer Fat: Media, Medicine, and Morals in the American "Obesity Epidemic."* New Brunswick: Rutgers University Press, 2012.

Brock, Brian. *Disability: Living into the Diversity of Christ's Body*. Grand Rapids: Baker Academic, 2021.

Busetta, Giovanni, et al. "Searching for a Job Is a Beauty Contest." *Economia Politica* 38 (2021) 171–201. https://mpra.ub.uni-muenchen.de/49825/10/MPRA_paper_49825.pdf.

Bynum, Caroline Walker. "Fast, Feast, and Flesh: The Religious Significance of Food to Medieval Women." *Representations* 11 (1985) 1–25.

———. *Fragmentation and Redemption: Essays on Gender and the Human Body in Medieval Religion*. New York: Zone, 1992.

———. *Holy Feast and Holy Fast: The Religious Significance of Food to Medieval Women*. Berkeley: University of California Press, 1987.

Coakley, Sarah. *Powers and Submissions: Spirituality, Philosophy, and Gender* Oxford: Blackwell, 2002.

Comer, John Mark. *Live No Lies: Recognize and Resist the Three Enemies That Steal Your Peace*. New York: WaterBrook, 2021.

Copeland, Gloria. "4 Keys to Understanding the Spirit, Soul and Body." Kenneth Copeland Ministries, Jan. 14, 2015. https://blog.kcm.org/4-keys-to-understanding-the-spirit-soul-body/?gad_source=1&gad_campaignid=944301260&gbraid=0AAAAADGr4oJZuXc-piGuS9rbdrfK4Ih95&gclid=CjoKCQjwzOvEBhDVARIsADHfJJRKxM7dGiucUcF-go8aIyf4bGf3ks-xjqyQdQl_3qULLHFz8gIR-6oEaAuOdEALw_wcB.

Demuth, Mary. "I'm Sick of Hearing About Your Smoking Hot Wife." *Christianity Today*, Apr. 19, 2013. https://www.christianitytoday.com/ct/2013/april-web-only/im-sick-of-hearing-about-your-smoking-hot-wife.html.

Descartes, René. "Letter to Meysonnier, 29 January 1640." Pages 103–4 in "Selected Correspondence of Descartes." Edited by Jonathan Bennett. "Some Texts from Early Modern Philosophy," 2017. https://www.earlymoderntexts.com/assets/pdfs/descartes1619.pdf.

DeYoung, Rebecca Konyndyk. *Glittering Vices: A New Look at the Seven Deadly Sins and Their Remedies*. Grand Rapids: Brazos, 2009.

Douglas, Mary. *Purity and Danger: An Analysis of Concepts of Pollution and Taboo*. London: Routledge, 1966.

Eiesland, Nancy. *The Disabled God: Toward a Liberatory Theology of Disability*. Nashville: Abingdon, 1994.

Fahs, Breanne. "Imagining Ugliness: Failed Femininities, Shame, and Disgust Written onto the 'Other' Body." In *On the Politics of Ugliness*, edited by Sara Rodrigues and Ela Przybylo, 237–58. London: Palgrave Macmillan, 2018.

Fee, Gordon D. *The First Epistle to the Corinthians*. Rev ed. Grand Rapids: Eerdmans, 2014.

Foster, Richard J., and Gayle D. Beebe. *Longing for God: Seven Paths of Christian Devotion*. Westmont, IL: InterVarsity, 2009.

Griffith, R. Marie. *Born Again Bodies: Flesh and Spirit in American Christianity*. Berkeley: University of California Press, 2004.

Heiss, Sarah. "Locating the Bodies of Women and Disability in Definitions of Beauty: An Analysis of Dove's Campaign for Real Beauty." *Disability Studies Quarterly* 31 (2011). https://dsq-sds.org/index.php/dsq/article/view/1367.

Johnston, David W. "Physical Appearance and Wages: Do Blondes Have More Fun?" *Economics Letters* 108 (2010) 10–12.

Kent, Elizabeth. "Consuming the Body: The Church and Eating Disorders." PhD thesis, Durham University, 2013. http://etheses.dur.ac.uk/6905/.

Lelwica, Michelle. *The Religion of Thinness: Satisfying the Spiritual Hungers Behind Women's Obsession with Food and Weight*. Carlsbad, CA: Gürze, 2010.

———. "A Shameful Perfection: Racism and the Religion of Thinness." In *Pursuing Perfection: Faith and the Female Body*, edited by Maja I. Whitaker, 153–72. London: SCM, 2025.

Louth, Andrew. "The Body in Western Catholic Christianity." In *Religion and the Body*, edited by Sarah Coakley, 111–30. Cambridge: Cambridge University Press, 1997.

Manne, Kate. *Unshrinking: How to Face Fatphobia*. New York: Crown, 2024.

Mental Health Foundation. "Te Whare Tapa Whā." https://mentalhealth.org.nz/te-whare-tapa-wha.

Miller, Sharon Hodde. "How 'Modest Is Hottest' Is Hurting Christian Women." *Christianity Today*, Dec. 15, 2011. https://www.christianitytoday.com/2011/12/how-modest-is-hottest-is-hurting-christian-women/.

Morgan, J. Nicole. *Fat and Faithful: Learning to Love Our Bodies, Our Neighbors, and Ourselves*. Minneapolis: Fortress, 2018.

Origen. *Contra Celsum*. https://www.newadvent.org/fathers/0416.htm.

Palacio, R. J. *Wonder*. New York: Black Swan, 2013.

Parsons, Mikeal C. *Body and Character in Luke and Acts: The Subversion of Physiognomy in Early Christianity*. Grand Rapids: Baker Academic, 2006.

Pearcey, Nancy R. *Love Thy Body: Answering Hard Questions About Life and Sexuality*. Grand Rapids: Baker, 2018.

Rochford, Tim. "Whare Tapa Wha: A Māori Model of a Unified Theory of Health." *Journal of Primary Prevention* 25 (2004) 41–57.

Sanfey, Alan G., et al. "The Neural Basis of Economic Decision-Making in the Ultimatum Game." *Science* 300 (2003) 1755–58.

Schroeder, Jessica J. "Mirrors, Pedestals, and a Cross: The Cult of Perfection and the Beauty of Self-Sacrifice." In *Pursuing Perfection: Faith and the Female Body*, edited by Maja I. Whitaker, 24–42. London: SCM, 2025.

Shamblin, Gwen. *The Weigh Down Diet*. New York: Doubleday, 1997.

Shedd, Charlie. *Pray Your Weight Away*. Philadelphia, PA: J. B. Lippincott, 1957.

Strings, Sabrina. *Fearing the Black Body: The Racial Origins of Fat Phobia*. New York: New York University Press, 2019.

Synnott, Anthony. *The Body Social: Symbolism, Self, and Society*. London: Routledge, 1993.

TerKeurst, Lysa. *I'll Start Again Monday: Break the Cycle of Unhealthy Eating Habits with Lasting Spiritual Satisfaction*. Nashville: Thomas Nelson, 2022.

Thiselton, Anthony C. *The First Epistle to the Corinthians*. Grand Rapids: Paternoster, 2000.

Turner, Bryan S. "The Body in Western Society: Social Theory and Its Perspectives." In *Religion and the Body*, edited by Sarah Coakley, 15–41. Cambridge: Cambridge University Press, 1997.

Tybur, Joshua M., et al. "Disgust: Evolved Function and Structure." *Psychological Review* 120 (2013) 65–84.

Ware, Kallistos. "'My Helper and My Enemy': The Body in Greek Christianity." In *Religion and the Body*, edited by Sarah Coakley, 90–110. Cambridge: Cambridge University Press, 1997.

Warren, Rick, et al. *The Daniel Plan: 40 Days to a Healthier Life*. Grand Rapids: Zondervan, 2013.

Whitaker, Maja I., ed. *Pursuing Perfection: Faith and the Female Body*. London: SCM, 2025.

———. "Shaping Our Bodies to Our Shape Our Selves: A Theological Remedy to the Discontented Pursuit of the Body I Want to Be." *Dialog* 63 (2024) 182–90. https://doi.org/https://doi.org/10.1111/dial.12862.

Widdows, Heather. *Perfect Me: Beauty as an Ethical Ideal*. Princeton: Princeton University Press, 2018.

———. "Structural Injustice and the Requirements of Beauty." *Journal of Social Philosophy* 52 (2021) 251–69.

Wilkinson, John. *The Bible and Healing: A Medical and Theological Commentary*. Edinburgh: Handsel, 1998.

Wolf, Naomi. *The Beauty Myth: How Images of Beauty Are Used against Women*. 1st ed. New York: W. Morrow, 1991.

Workman, Clifford I., et al. "Morality Is in the Eye of the Beholder: The Neurocognitive Basis of the 'Anomalous-Is-Bad' Stereotype." *Annals of the New York Academy of Sciences* 1494 (2021) 3–17.

Zahl, David. *Low Anthropology: The Unlikely Key to a Gracious View of Others (and Yourself)*. Grand Rapids: Brazos, 2022.

Chapter 4

Discomfort and Diversity as Catalysts for Individual Transformation Within the Church Body

JONATHAN DOVE

INTRODUCTION

CONTEMPORARY DISCOURSE ABOUT THE church is often dominated by narratives of decline and dysfunction.[1] This is evidenced by a proliferation of titles expressing disillusionment with institutional Christianity such as *Life After Church*, *Dear Church*, *Quitting Church*, *UnChristian*, and *They Like Jesus But Not the Church*.[2] Each story becomes another reason to potentially give up on or rethink the biblical concept of the church. Yet, despite these critiques, the local church remains a vital instrument for spiritual and social transformation, serving as the primary means through which divine grace enables the renewal of people and places.

This chapter emerges from my perspective as a pastor and practitioner—someone immersed daily in the rhythms and realities of church life, including a local church that has its own share of disappointments and

---

1. For example Dan Kimball's *They Like Jesus but Not the Church*; David Kinnaman's and Gabe Lyons's *UnChristian*; and Alan Jamieson's *A Churchless Faith*.

2. Additional examples include Lyz Lenz's *God Land*; Jake Meador's *In Search of the Common Good*; and Wayne Jacobsen's and Dave Coleman's *So You Don't Want to Go to Church Anymore*.

pain. Gracecity Church in Auckland represents a significant case study in congregational adaptation and transformation. Originally established as Greenlane Christian Fellowship, later known as Greenlane Christian Centre and GCC, the church adopted its current name in early 2021. This rebranding reflected both the centrality of grace in its messy history and its expanded vision for church planting beyond its original geographical base. Throughout its history, the church has maintained a significant presence in Auckland's Christian landscape, particularly through its Alpha courses and extensive mission work. The congregation's current identity is marked by remarkable diversity, comprising members from fifty-five countries and spanning multiple generations, socioeconomic backgrounds, political affiliations, and religious histories. The church now has locations across three Auckland locations—Greenlane, Howick, and Flat Bush. I was called to serve as senior pastor in October 2014.

Like many religious institutions, our church has weathered significant challenges over the years. These difficulties have included leadership transitions, financial complexities, staff turnover, and questions about governance and accountability. It's fair to say that our journey has been tumultuous. Yet amid these challenges, this chapter presents seven narratives of individual transformation within our church community.[3] These stories suggest that even churches facing significant challenges can foster genuine spiritual and social transformation. As these narratives unfold, particular attention should be paid to the recurring themes of discomfort and disruption—elements that prove central to understanding these transformative journeys.

Story One: Rose—An Enigma

Rose is an enigma. She is an attractive, well-presented beauty consultant who enjoys spending any spare time in her flower garden. She is a gentle soft-spoken Pākehā woman now in her seventies. But for over a decade she has led a team of more than forty volunteers to run church services in three

---

3. These interviews were conducted following approval from the Laidlaw College Research Ethics Committee. Participants were selected based on their previously shared experiences of transformation within the church community. Each participant gave informed consent, was interviewed in a private setting at the church premises, and their stories have been anonymized to protect confidentiality. The interviews followed a semi-structured format using prepared questions while allowing for open-ended responses. Digital recordings were made and securely stored, and participants were given the opportunity to review and verify their contributions to the research. The pseudonyms were chosen by the author.

Auckland prisons each Sunday. She defies conventional expectations. It's hard to reconcile these things.

I mention this enigma to Rose. "How did this happen?" I ask inquisitively. More surprises were to come. Rose's life took an unexpected turn when she became an unmarried mother at sixteen years old. During this challenging period, she received support from the Salvation Army but also experienced the pain of losing her son to adoption, which she described as feeling like "a dagger entered my heart." Years later, changes in New Zealand's adoption laws allowed her to reunite with her birth son. This reunion was pivotal. After an awkward meeting, he sent her a Bible with these inscribed words: "To dear Rose. In appreciation for everything you have done for me, Lots of Love Eddie xxx."[4] She phoned to thank him and ask how he could say such kind things. He spoke about how she had given him life and he knew someone who wanted to give her new life—Jesus.

This encounter catalyzed Rose's spiritual transformation. Encouraged by a colleague, she joined Gracecity, was baptized, and experienced a profound divine love. She says her broken heart was healed. Inspired by her newfound faith, Rose embarked on mission trips to developing countries, leading annual teams over eleven years. These experiences were transformative, enhancing her faith through witnessing divine provision and community renewal. Hearing her stories builds my faith in what God can do. Sadly, this chapter of global mission didn't end well: Rose explains how her leadership role in the mission was closed down. She looks up and says, "For whatever reason—I never found out." While she did eventually receive an apology, the process was appalling; but she chooses not to dwell on this. Instead, I notice the way she reworks the conversation to highlight the way God continued to work even amid the dysfunction.

She was invited to consider prison ministry, a prospect she initially resisted due to preconceived notions about prison environments. She recalls the mental image of the place filled with gangs and tattooed people. As a beauty consultant who works with skin, this was a massive barrier. However, her heart softened, allowing her to embrace this new calling. She recognized the commonalities between incarcerated individuals and church members, fostering empathy and understanding: "Those incarcerated come from all walks of life, just like our church." This ministry has now grown with a team of forty-five volunteers providing weekly church services across three prisons.

Rose's story is one of overcoming personal struggles and societal challenges through faith and service. Her journey from a beauty consultant to

---

4. "Eddie" (along with "Rose") is a pseudonym to protect confidentiality.

a leader in prison ministry exemplifies how life's disruptions can lead to profound personal growth and fulfillment. She summarizes all her experiences with four simple words: "I feel very blessed."

Story Two: Eve—"I Belong to Him"

"I belong to him." It was a recurring line in her story. For Eve, this wasn't a statement of subjugation, but a powerful revelation of divine love and purpose discovered through her Christian journey. Eve's roots lie in mainland China, where she was raised as a devout Buddhist for over two decades. Her life was marked by waiting for a partner who promised marriage but remained in an additional relationship to another. This stagnation, coupled with her struggle with English, left her feeling trapped. The revelation of her son's sexuality further disrupted her world, culminating in a period of deep unhappiness in early 2019.

Hearing the word "unhappiness" was a surprise to me. After all, Eve is the most joyful person I have met in my life. She is constantly encouraging me—always with an energizing smile on her face. "What happened?" I asked. Her transformative journey began when she attended free English classes at Gracecity and was introduced to Alpha and Sunday services. In June 2019, she says she experienced a profound sense of divine love that led her to remove Buddhist idols from her home. By December 2019, she was baptized, began studying the Bible, and in 2022, began attending a Bible college.

Eve reflects on how realizing she is loved changed her fundamentally. She describes herself as having been selfish and controlling before knowing Jesus. Now, she embraces patience and forgiveness—concepts previously foreign to her upbringing—and this has softened her relationship with her son and provided empathy with people so different to her. She speaks of the value of diversity within our church community, which helps her to see the way God accepts everyone even though they are so different from each other. In her words, "Being part of a diverse church has helped me appreciate differences." "Usually when there is conflict," she says, "there is often misunderstanding. Understanding our differences and abilities can create unity and harmony. . . . Diversity helps us to learn from one another." Her transformation extended beyond personal relationships. Recently, she has expanded her home in order to welcome more people into her life.

For Eve, all this derived from a profound awareness of being loved and accepted by Jesus and being surrounded by such diversity in people. "Where else have you seen change?" I inquired. She spoke of the way her newfound faith reshaped her relationship with money. Once a source of security that never satisfied, she now trusts in divine provision even when financially strained. "I was never satisfied," she said. "I held onto it for safety." But now "even with (just) $2 in my account, I know that God will provide." The change occurred from hearing the divine words from Scripture—"I am with you" (Isa 41:10 NRSV). She believed it. It broke a stronghold in her life, enabling her to sacrifice and find contentment.

Hearing someone speak about transformation so definitively brought some skepticism to these pastoral ears. But, Eve's transformation is evident not only in herself but also in those around her. Her partner, once distant in faith, was baptized in October 2023 and married Eve. He is now actively serving the homeless—something that would have been an anathema to him five years prior. Eve's parents-in-law also embraced faith, and she enjoys a restored relationship with her son. This journey came at a cost; some family members rejected her new beliefs, including a younger brother who ceased communication. Yet, Eve finds solace in belonging to Jesus, experiencing a joy that is genuine and unmanufactured. Reflecting on the past five years, Eve likens her growth to "a mustard seed growing bit by bit," illustrating the profound and steady transformation that has reshaped every aspect of her life.

Story Three: Mac—A Surprising Journey to Faith and Awareness

Mac, a successful CFO from a comfortable middle-class background in New Zealand, has been an integral part of our church community since 2010. He arrives at our interview in his sports car, exuding confidence and success. When asked about his journey to faith, he intriguingly credits "the Moonies, the unification church."[5] I begin to wonder if this particular interview was a good idea.

Mac recounts the manipulation he faced within the Moonie commune, where he spent four challenging months while traveling in the USA during his overseas experience. Breaking free from the commune propelled him into a personal pilgrimage of prayer and Bible study, reactivating a faith return to orthodox belief and understanding beyond the confines of the commune. Returning to New Zealand, he came to Gracecity with his first

5. The Unification Church, founded by Sun Myung Moon in 1954, is a controversial religious movement that blends Christian themes with Moon's teachings that he and his wife were humanity's "True Parents." Known colloquially as "the Moonies," the group gained notoriety in the 1970s and 1980s for its mass weddings and aggressive recruitment practices that often involved isolating converts from their families. See Chryssides, *Advent of Sun Myung Moon*; and Melton, *Encyclopedia of American Religions*.

observation being the diversity of what he saw. His spiritual journey took a pivotal turn when a church member invited him to lead a group focused on helping people find employment. This opportunity exposed him to individuals from diverse backgrounds, particularly immigrants who had borrowed money to reach New Zealand. Something began to change within him. This exposure to ethnic diversity and social needs profoundly transformed Mac.

Mac highlights that his change has been a gradual process. Comparing himself to other successful business leaders, he observes the way his experiences have developed in him a desire to be with people who are different along with a deep empathy for those facing challenges he has never personally encountered. Mac eagerly shares an email he received the week prior from a Muslim lady interested in Christianity because of what he was doing: "I am interested in becoming a Christian and would love to learn more about the faith. Could you assist me in taking the next steps?" This individual goes on to describe being touched by the warmth and kindness experienced at the church's community ministries, finding comfort and belonging in a new country.

"What are some of the factors that affected this?" I ask. Mac highlights three areas: "I spent five plus years volunteering at the Auckland City Mission serving the rough sleepers. It was very challenging but also a privilege to serve them. Most days when I arrived I was reminded of Jesus's words in Matthew 25:40–45—'Whatever you did for one of the least . . . you did for me.'" He continues, "Another big factor in my life has been the four years of part time study at Bible college—this has changed my life for the better, as both a Christian and a human being." He finishes with mentioning the church community—being surrounded by people who were "serious about what they believe," has reshaped his perspectives on life, death, and sacrifice.

Through these experiences, Mac has witnessed how Christian love attracts people and fosters a sense of community. His negative experiences with the Moonies paradoxically disrupted his life to find an authentic relationship with Jesus. His journey reflects the power of faith to transform lives through exposure to diversity and need.

Story Four: Grace—"Giving Up Is Not an Option"

Grace's journey is a testament to her resilience, largely shaped by her diverse cultural experiences and her deep commitment to her faith community. Born in West Africa, she spent her early years in Saudi Arabia before moving to New Zealand as a teenager in 2002. Describing herself as deeply introverted, Grace preferred quiet nights at home with a tim-tam biscuit and a movie, yet she found herself deeply involved in her church community, Gracecity, which she says "always felt like a second home."

Grace is well aware of the internal and external challenges our church has faced over the years. Early in our conversation, she candidly shares stories of how these challenges affected her personally. She is not a person in denial about the sad failings. It's been heart-breaking for her; deeply disappointing. Despite witnessing many of her peers leave the church due to its failings, Grace chose to stay. "Why?" I asked. "Why are you still so positive about our church?" She speaks about how her immigrant journey—from her home country through Saudi Arabia to New Zealand—instilled in her the conviction that "giving up is not an option." For her, it has motivated her to add kindness to a world full of challenges. She goes on to speak about the way difficulty deepened her reliance on divine grace. Once again, she acknowledges the dysfunction and heartbreak but emphasizes her decision to remain and contribute positively. Her experiences of being in the "not-so-cool group" at school taught her the importance of inclusivity and compassion. She reflects, "I found it difficult to make new friends . . . there were cliques growing up," but this pushed her to develop resilience and empathy.

As the only black person in many settings, Grace appreciates the ethnic diversity within Gracecity, which includes members from over fifty-five countries. This diversity fosters understanding and grace among its members. With a background in law, Grace values political diversity and church initiatives that have encouraged dialogue across different viewpoints within the church community. She recalls an evening where people sat at round tables with people from different political affiliations in an effort to understand the variety of perspectives people had through a lens of faith. Video interviews with leaders from each mainstream party were shown. This was followed by discussion questions that helped people identify potential connection points to the teachings of Jesus and explore why such views were important to them personally. Experiences like this remind her that we are all different—and to grow in grace towards each other. She seeks to speak well of people. "After all," she says, "I have learned to love God more here and to love and understand people more."

Story Five: Andy—"The Biggest Change I Have Gone Through"

Andy, a self-confessed, privileged, middle-class white man, has transitioned from working behind the scenes to actively engaging with the complex issues faced by rough sleepers and ex-convicts. His journey began during the COVID-19 pandemic when his wife volunteered him to help cook meals for the homeless. Known for his willingness to work hard away from the public eye, Andy didn't anticipate how this would change his life.

Reflecting on the concept of "middle-class charity," Andy discusses how it's often easy to donate food or money without truly engaging with social issues. However, his experience was different. He now finds himself preaching to small groups on the street, praying for those in need, and welcoming Māori and Chinese communities, including ex-prisoners, into his life and home. Although this has pushed him out of his comfort zone, it's evident that he thrives in this environment. "This is the biggest change I have gone through," Andy states, surprising those familiar with his past challenges, including the death of a spouse, family conflicts, and health issues. Despite these hardships, he insists that his involvement with rough sleepers has been the most transformative experience for him.

Initially aware of social needs but viewing them as others' responsibilities, Andy's direct involvement opened his heart in new ways. It wasn't just about serving; it was about understanding shared pain and connecting with disadvantaged individuals on a deeper level. A poignant moment came when a Māori friend expressed surprise at being welcomed into Andy's home: "I never thought I would be in a house like this with an old white couple sitting here having some real yum food." This interaction allowed Andy and his wife to share their own histories of abuse and pain, highlighting how pain is a universal equalizer and God's love extends equally to all.

It wasn't long ago that Andy challenged the use of te reo Māori and kept rough sleepers at a distance. Now, he finds his life being shaped by serving the very communities he once overlooked, as he embraces the transformative power of empathy and inclusion.

Story Six: Alan and Miriam

Alan's story is a captivating journey of unexpected transformation. Born in Asia, Alan immigrated to New Zealand in 2004 to work as a chef and ran a small local dairy. His introduction to Gracecity came through Sharon,[6] a regular customer known for her daily *New Zealand Herald* reading habit. One day, Alan forgot to reserve her paper, prompting Sharon to complain. Despite her grumpiness, she felt compelled to invite Alan to an Alpha dinner at Gracecity. Surprisingly, Alan accepted the invitation, driven by a mix of fatigue and hopelessness from a shoplifting incident the day before and guilt over Sharon's complaint.

---

6. "Sharon" (along with "Alan" and "Miriam") is a pseudonym to protect confidentiality.

Alan attended the dinner with his Chinese girlfriend Miriam, and both were struck by the hospitality and diversity they encountered. Although Alan had been in New Zealand for five years, this was his first meaningful interaction with non-Chinese individuals. Both emphasize how culturally isolated they had been, never having had a conversation with a non-Chinese person that lasted more than ten minutes. Yet at Gracecity, they recall how friendly and interested people were in them.

Miriam was already searching for a church, inspired by readings at the public library, and began attending Alpha regularly while Alan joined occasionally. Jesus's story of the Prodigal Son[7] deeply resonated with Miriam, marking a turning point in her spiritual journey. As they settled into their new community, Miriam embraced faith and invited their church connect group to their home. During one gathering, Alan heard about Nick Vujicic, an Australian preacher born without limbs who spoke of "abundant life in Jesus."[8] This testimony inspired Alan to take Jesus seriously; he was baptized in 2013 and later married Miriam.

Alan's insatiable desire to learn led him to serve wherever possible. The concept of grace was foreign to him and Miriam initially, but they found patience and understanding within their church community as they navigated various life challenges. The ethnic diversity at Gracecity broadened Alan's compassion for the wider world. Before his conversion, he focused solely on business success and lacked empathy for certain social groups.

Reflecting on his journey, Alan believes that joining a single-ethnicity Chinese church would have limited his growth. Engaging with people from diverse backgrounds helped him understand cycles of poverty and develop compassion for marginalized groups. This shift replaced his ambition for business success with a desire to study at a local Bible college. Today, Alan and Miriam are planting churches in Asia, modeling the diversity they experienced at Gracecity.

Story Seven: My Story

As I reflect on these stories of Rose, Eve, Mac, Grace, Andy, Alan, and Miriam I am struck by a profound realization: transformation rarely occurs in comfortable, predictable spaces. It emerges from the very disruptions we often seek to avoid. My own journey mirrors these narratives.

---

7. Luke 15:11–32.

8. A similar documentary about Nick Vujicic is 60 Minutes Australia, "Inspiring Man."

In October 2014, I stepped into my role as senior pastor with ambition, vision, and a desire to bring change. Little did I know that the most profound transformations would take place within my own heart. Initially, my faith journey had been primarily shared with people of similar backgrounds. As I looked out at the diverse faces in my congregation, I quickly realized the variety of experiences represented before me. Deep down, I harbored an unconscious desire for a community that mirrored my own identity—one filled with individuals who shared my ethnicity and passion for learning and creativity. I admired other churches that embodied this vision, silently wishing for a similar environment—one that was funky, edgy, and artistic.

However, alongside this personal preference was a deeper theological conviction that resonated within me: the dream of Jesus for unity amid diversity. This realization prompted me to take action and lean into this space of difference. I began inviting people from various ethnicities within Gracecity to share meals and stories, creating an open environment where we could connect on a deeper level. Through these interactions, I listened to diverse experiences and witnessed how God engaged uniquely with each individual. This openness brought about significant changes in my own life.

As I embraced the church's diversity, I discovered a deeper understanding of God and life itself. My capacity to love expanded in ways I had never anticipated. During this time, I also faced significant disappointments from leaders and members who breached written and unwritten codes of conduct. I heard the pain stemming from our past experiences as a community. The unexpected disruptions caused by COVID-19 added another layer of complexity to our journey. Amid these challenges, I came to realize that personal transformation often occurs not in spite of disruptions but because of them. This seems to be the way God works—using challenges to deepen our understanding and expand our hearts. Ten years in, I can honestly say I am a better person and leader because of the disruptions and discomfort I have experienced.

THEMES AND LEARNINGS

Gracecity has a complex history—investigations, public splits, staff turnover, and lingering questions of integrity. Many would have walked away. Indeed, some did. But something deeper was happening. Each story I've shared reveals a common thread: disruption is not the enemy of faith, but potentially its most powerful catalyst. Rose found healing through an unexpected reunion. Eve discovered love after years of waiting. Mac's manipulation became a pathway to discovering genuine faith. Grace chose resilience over rejection. Andy transformed his privileged perspective through service.

Stories like these can provide hope. They suggest that when we embrace discomfort, when we remain committed despite dysfunction, genuine transformation can emerge. Our church—with its fifty-five nationalities, complicated history, and ongoing journey—became a living laboratory of grace. Not a perfect place, but a transforming one. As I've listened to these stories and watched these lives change, I've become convinced: hope is not found in avoiding pain or mess, but in walking through it together. The local church, with all its imperfections, remains God's primary vehicle of renewal. Transformation happens, not in spite of disruption but because of it. Four key themes stand out to me. You may see others.

Loving the Church as She Is

One of the key themes is learning to love the church in its imperfect form. Despite facing significant challenges, such as family rejection or church setbacks, each person found transformation through the messiness of church life. This journey taught us to love our community rather than leave our community. While there is no excuse for poor behavior or toxic culture, we must acknowledge that every church is far from ideal. It is too easy to impose a hope and vision for the local church, even a biblical one, and ignore the reality that each church is and will be far from this beautiful ideal.

The early church provides a compelling framework for this perspective. The apostle Paul's letters to the Corinthians reveal a community plagued by toxic culture, rifts, and dysfunction: sexual immorality (1 Cor 5:1–5), lawsuits between believers (1 Cor 6:1–8), divisions over leadership (1 Cor 1:10–17), social and economic disparities where the wealthy ate separately from the poor at the Lord's Supper (1 Cor 11:17–22), and chaos in worship (1 Cor 14). Yet, remarkably, Paul neither minimizes these issues nor abandons hope. He still addresses them as "the church of God that is in Corinth" and as those "sanctified in Christ Jesus, called to be saints" (1 Cor 1:2 NRSV). Similarly, the book of Acts, while showcasing the dynamic spread of the gospel, doesn't gloss over institutional challenges: the deceit of Ananias and Sapphira (Acts 5:1–11), cultural tensions over the distribution of food to widows (Acts 6:1–7), sharp disagreements between Paul and Barnabas over John Mark (Acts 15:36–41), and heated debates over the inclusion of Gentiles (Acts 15:1–35). These biblical accounts suggest that imperfection and transformation can coexist within the same community.

However, this recognition of church imperfection must be carefully balanced. As Scot McKnight and Laura Barringer argue in *A Church Called Tov*, there's a danger in using this reality to enable toxic positivity or defend unhealthy environments. There are indeed legitimate reasons for leaving a church, particularly when it becomes unsafe or deviates from orthodox historical theology.[9] The challenge lies in discerning the difference between normal community dysfunction and truly toxic environments.

Dietrich Bonhoeffer wisely observed, "Those who love their dreams of a Christian community more than they love the Christian community itself become destroyers of that Christian community even though their personal intentions may be ever so honest, earnest, and sacrificial." He continues, "God hates this wishful dreaming because it makes the dreamer proud and pretentious. Those who dream of this idealized community demand that it be fulfilled by God, by others, and by themselves. They enter the community of Christians with their demands, set up their own law, and judge one another and even God accordingly."[10] This serves as a reminder that it's naive to expect a community without dysfunction or problems, as each church comprises diverse peoples with their own challenges, biases, and difficulties. Indeed, the Christian gospel itself reminds us that God works and saves, not despite our problems but because of them—our very need for grace is what draws us to Christ, and this need never diminishes for any of us.

Grace's story of choosing to stay despite disappointments challenges our contemporary impulse to leave when things become difficult. Her experience raises an important question: What transformative opportunities do we miss when we give up too quickly? This doesn't minimize legitimate reasons for leaving but suggests that working through difficulties can itself be a path to growth.

The question of unity presents particular challenges. Too often, leaders have wielded biblical texts about unity as weapons, casting those who disagree as opponents of God's purposes. A more nuanced approach recognizes that many church conflicts aren't simple matters of right versus wrong. Instead, as Grace's story demonstrates, transformation often emerges when we choose to work through issues with humility and grace, acknowledging that different perspectives can coexist within the same community. This approach doesn't demand uniform agreement but rather a commitment to journey together despite our differences.

We can love the church, not because we turn a blind eye to the problems but because we believe in the reality of sin and the hope of the gospel.

9. McKnight and Barringer. *Church Called Tov*.
10. Bonhoeffer, *Life Together*, 36.

Through these stories and biblical examples, we see how God continues to work, not despite the problems but even amid them. This is the paradox and promise of church community.

Disruption Can Be Transformational

Disruption has proven to be a powerful catalyst for personal growth. Each individual's journey was marked by significant life disruptions that led to profound personal growth. Rose's unexpected motherhood and reunion with her son, Eve's struggle with English and family issues, Mac's escape from the Moonies, Grace's cultural transitions, and Andy's engagement with social issues all showcase how disruptions can catalyze an awakening and transformation. These moments of upheaval allowed for openness to new learning and unlearning what wasn't working. Disruptions break down old patterns, making way for new insights and growth. We are challenged to pay closer attention to what God is doing in these moments of disruption.

The biblical narrative itself is filled with transformative disruptions. Abraham's call required leaving his homeland,[11] Moses encountered God in exile,[12] Joseph's betrayal by his brothers led to Egypt's salvation,[13] and the early church's persecution led to the gospel's spread beyond Jerusalem.[14] In each case, disruption served, not as an obstacle to God's purposes but as a vehicle for them. Joseph's declaration to his brothers—"You intended to harm me, but God intended it for good to accomplish what is now being done, the saving of many lives"[15]—offers a powerful lens through which to view our own experiences of disruption.

This pattern echoes through our contemporary stories. Just as Joseph's imprisonment became the unlikely path to leadership, Rose's painful adoption experience became the very means of her encounter with faith through her son's witness. Like Moses finding his calling in exile, Mac's manipulation by the Moonies created a hunger for authentic faith that eventually led him to serve others. Eve's cultural isolation and family challenges, much like Abraham's journey from the familiar, opened her heart to a new understanding of divine love. These experiences suggest that transformation often occurs, not in spite of disruption but because of it.

---

11. Gen 12:1–3.
12. Exod 3:1–12.
13. Gen 37–50.
14. Acts 8:1–4.
15. Gen 50:20 NIV.

However, mere disruption alone doesn't guarantee growth. What distinguishes these stories is how each individual responded to their disruptions within the context of community. They didn't face their challenges in isolation but found in their church community both the support and the theological framework to interpret their experiences. This suggests that while disruption may be the catalyst, transformation requires both a receptive heart and a supportive community.

This understanding has significant implications for church leadership and community life. Instead of reflexively minimizing disruption, we can learn to discern God's transformative work within it. The question shifts from "How do we fix this problem?" to "What might God be developing through this season?" Such reframing doesn't diminish the real pain of disruption but invites us to remain open to its transformative potential. For leaders, this means cultivating environments where disruption can be engaged thoughtfully rather than avoided entirely. The goal isn't to celebrate difficulty for its own sake, but to recognize that God often works most powerfully in these challenging moments.

Embracing Diversity

The diverse environment of Gracecity played a crucial role in the spiritual journeys in each of these stories. Recent research in church communities suggests that diversity fosters not only understanding and empathy but also deeper spiritual formation and community transformation.[16] Michelle Sanchez argues that "when we step into diverse church communities, we enter spaces where God intentionally stretches our capacity for understanding and compassion. These encounters with difference become catalysts for both personal and communal transformation."[17] Similarly, Soong-Chan Rah observes that such diversity challenges our cultural assumptions and creates opportunities for genuine spiritual growth that monocultural environments simply cannot provide.[18]

We experience this reality when travelling to a new country. The language, the food, the chaos, the new environment can be unsettling. But these disorienting experiences often become our most powerful memories, fundamentally altering how we perceive and engage with the world around us. Through discomfort in new contexts, we begin to see things that were always present but previously invisible to us—our cultural blinkers removed

---

16. Sanchez, *Color-Conscious Discipleship*, 45–47.
17. Sanchez, *Color-Conscious Discipleship*, 52.
18. Rah, *Many Colors*, 32–33.

through exposure to difference. Like travellers in a foreign land, our stories illustrate this pattern of transformation through encounter: Alan and Miriam's first meaningful conversations with non-Chinese people, Andy's transformation through engaging with Māori communities, Mac's growing awareness of immigrant struggles, and Grace's navigation of being the only black person in many settings. Each experience created what David Anderson calls "gracious space"—environments where difference becomes a catalyst for growth rather than division.[19]

Before these encounters, each person was comfortable in their familiar space and place. But through discomfort in new contexts, they began to see things they hadn't noticed earlier. As Eve reflects, "Being part of a diverse church has helped me appreciate differences." This isn't merely about tolerance or superficial inclusion. Rather, it speaks to a deeper theological truth about the nature of the church itself—what Miroslav Volf describes as "the practice of embrace," where we learn to make space for those who are different from us.[20]

These stories demonstrate how this embrace of diversity operates on multiple levels. Cultural diversity among fifty-five nationalities created natural opportunities for cross-cultural learning and understanding. Socioeconomic diversity through Andy's engagement with rough sleepers challenged middle-class assumptions deeply ingrained in his worldview. Political dialogue events described by Grace fostered understanding across different viewpoints within a framework of shared faith. Rose's prison ministry brought together people from vastly different backgrounds and life circumstances, creating bridges between worlds that rarely intersect.

The transformation that occurs through these encounters isn't automatic. This is evident in how Mac's exposure to immigrant struggles fundamentally altered his worldview, or how Andy's engagement with marginalized communities transformed his perspective on privilege. Through these various expressions of diversity, our church community has become not just a meeting place of differences, but a transformative space where those differences shape us into people who better reflect God's heart for all humanity.

Creating Opportunities That Stretch

Service to others emerged as a powerful catalyst for transformation in each narrative. As Christine Pohl observes, when we extend ourselves in service,

19. Anderson, *Multicultural Ministry*.
20. Volf, *Exclusion and Embrace*.

particularly through hospitality to strangers, we often find ourselves transformed in unexpected ways.[21] The very act of making room for others creates space for our own growth.

Significantly, these transformative acts of service often began with resistance or hesitation. Rose, the beauty consultant, initially recoiled from prison ministry. Andy, secure in his middle-class world, resisted engagement with rough sleepers. Eve expanded her home specifically to welcome more people into her life, overcoming earlier cultural isolation. Yet in each case, this very resistance marked the beginning of profound change.

The transformative power of service in these stories operated through multiple dimensions. Rose crossed significant social boundaries by entering prisons and engaging with incarcerated individuals. Andy welcomed ex-convicts into his home, challenging his previous social comfort zones. Mac bridged economic divides by engaging with struggling immigrants who had borrowed money to reach New Zealand. Grace demonstrated sustained commitment by building inclusive community despite repeated disappointments and obstacles.

Creating these opportunities requires intentional leadership and community support. Robert Lupton's research demonstrates that lasting change emerges, not through isolated acts of kindness but through sustained, relationship-based engagement.[22] Our stories demonstrate the importance of creating opportunities that push people beyond their comfort zones while providing the support needed for genuine growth. This approach to service differs significantly from traditional volunteer programs or ministry assignments. Rather than matching people solely based on their existing skills or preferences, there's value in encouraging people to serve in ways that stretch them. As Samuel Wells suggests, this kind of service becomes, not just about what we do for others but about what God does in us through the encounter.[23]

Boundaries and Balance: When Themes Become Unhealthy

While these four themes emerge powerfully in our stories, it's important to recognize their limitations and potential pitfalls. Each theme requires careful balance and discernment. The selection of these seven stories naturally raises questions of methodology and representation. These narratives, while powerful, represent a specific subset of experiences within our church

21. Pohl, *Making Room*, 56–71.
22. Lupton, *Toxic Charity*, 31–33.
23. Wells, *Learning to Dream Again*, 89–90.

community. Many others encountered similar disruptions but reached different conclusions—some found the challenges overwhelming, others left for different congregations, and some sadly abandoned faith entirely. Their experiences, while beyond the scope of this chapter, remind us that transformation through disruption is neither automatic nor universal. Understanding why some find growth through challenge while others experience damage is crucial for pastoral leadership.

Loving the church as she is should not mean accepting dysfunction blindly. While Grace's story demonstrates faithful commitment through disappointment, this differs significantly from enabling abuse or overlooking serious ethical breaches. When churches deviate from orthodox teaching or engage in abusive practices, loving the church might actually require speaking up, seeking reform, or, in some cases, leaving. The biblical pattern shows prophets and apostles both loving and confronting God's people.

Diversity, too, needs thoughtful boundaries. While our fifty-five nationalities create rich opportunities for growth, this only works because we maintain unity in essential beliefs and values. Alan and Miriam's story shows how diversity within a framework of shared faith creates transformation, but diversity without common ground can lead to fragmentation. Our political dialogue events succeed precisely because they operate within agreed parameters of mutual respect and shared Christian conviction.

Creating stretching opportunities must be balanced with pastoral wisdom. Andy's story demonstrates transformation through challenge, but pushing people too far too fast can be harmful. Some in our community needed longer periods of healing before engaging in challenging ministry. Leadership requires discernment about when to stretch and when to support.

Practices for Nurturing Transformation

These stories of transformation amid diversity and disruption have profoundly shaped my approach to pastoral leadership. Four key practices have emerged from my decade of leading Gracecity:

First, I've discovered the essential role of intentional solitude and supervision in processing transformation. Henri Nouwen's insight resonated deeply with my experience: "Solitude is where community begins. If we do not know we are the beloved sons and daughters of God, we're going to expect someone in the community to make us feel that way. They cannot."[24] Through monthly external supervision, I've found structured space to

---

24. Nouwen, *Spiritual Direction*, 92.

reflect on community dynamics and recognize God's grace amid challenges. Similarly, adopting Peter Scazzero's practice of the Daily Office[25] has given me rhythms of silence that reinforce my identity as a beloved yet imperfect leader.

Second, our emphasis on hospitality has created tangible opportunities for transformative encounters. I've found the most profound connections happen through sharing meals with people from diverse backgrounds. As Christine Pohl observes, "Hospitality is not about a perfect meal or a perfect home; it is about opening our lives to others."[26] I've watched countless relationships form across cultural boundaries as people gather around our tables, mirroring the transformative encounters in our seven stories.

Third, leading through several challenging seasons has taught me to understand the systemic nature of both dysfunction and transformation. While discussions often focus on toxic leadership, the biblical narrative suggests a more complex reality. The golden calf incident (Exod 32) illustrates how entire communities can participate in toxic patterns—the people pressured Aaron, and he acquiesced. At Gracecity, this perspective has helped us move beyond simplistic solutions focused solely on leadership changes, recognizing instead how our entire community participates in both challenges and healing.

Fourth, I've learned the value of transparent communication during seasons of change and uncertainty. Rather than presenting decisions as uniquely spiritual imperatives, I now acknowledge complexity and alternative viewpoints. Taking Nieuwhof's advice, I often tell our congregation, "Our team has prayerfully considered the options. We believe this is the best move we can make at this time for these reasons . . . ."[27] Upfront and honest admission has built trust and enabled our community to navigate change together. These practices don't guarantee transformation but create conditions where stories like those of Rose, Eve, Mac, Grace, Andy, Alan, and Miriam become more common, allowing our community to experience genuine renewal and growth together.

CONCLUSION

These seven stories—Rose, Eve, Mac, Grace, Andy, Alan, and Miriam— reveal how transformation often emerges from unexpected places: a prison ministry, cultural isolation, a manipulative cult experience, repeated

25. Scazzero, *Daily Office*.
26. Pohl, *Making Room*, 73.
27. Nieuwhof, "What Not to Say."

disappointments, cooking for the homeless, or a forgotten newspaper. Each narrative demonstrates that meaningful change rarely occurs in comfortable, predictable spaces. Instead, transformation emerges through disruption, diversity, and opportunities that stretch us beyond our familiar boundaries.

Michelangelo is often credited with the insight that his sculpture of David already existed within the marble block—his task was simply to remove everything that wasn't David.[28] This metaphor illuminates how God works through local churches. Like a master sculptor, God uses various tools—the chisel of disruption, the hammer of diversity, the rasp of stretching experiences—to reveal what we are meant to become. Sometimes the process requires forceful strikes, as when Rose faced the pain of adoption or when Mac escaped the Moonies. Other times it needs gentle, persistent smoothing, as with Grace's patient commitment to community or Eve's gradual opening to hospitality. The four themes we've explored—loving the church as she is, recognizing disruption as transformational, embracing diversity, and creating opportunities that stretch us—are like the sculptor's tools, each playing its part in revealing the beauty hidden within.

When supported by practices like intentional solitude, genuine hospitality, systemic understanding, and transparent communication, communities can create environments where such transformation becomes more likely. Our stories demonstrate that hope isn't found in avoiding pain or maintaining comfort, but in walking through difficulties together. The local church, despite its imperfections, remains God's primary vehicle for renewal—not because it is perfect, but because it provides a context where grace, diversity, and disruption can intersect to shape us into people who better reflect God's heart for humanity.

BIBLIOGRAPHY

60 Minutes Australia. "Inspiring Man Born Without Arms or Legs—Nick Vujicic." www.youtube.com/watch?v=tJnJ_fTYofQ.

Anderson, David A. *Multicultural Ministry: Finding Your Church's Unique Rhythm*. Grand Rapids: Zondervan, 2004.

Bonhoeffer, Dietrich. *Life Together and Prayerbook of the Bible*. Translated by Daniel W. Bloesch and James Burtness. Edited by Geffrey B. Kelly. Dietrich Bonhoeffer Works 5. Minneapolis: Fortress, 2005.

Chryssides, George D. *The Advent of Sun Myung Moon: The Origins, Beliefs, and Practices of the Unification Church*. London: Macmillan, 1991.

---

28. Wallace, *Michelangelo*, 89.

Lupton, Robert D. *Toxic Charity: How Churches and Charities Hurt Those They Help (And How to Reverse It)*. New York: HarperOne, 2011.

McKnight, Scot, and Laura Barringer. *A Church Called Tov: Forming a Goodness Culture That Resists Abuses of Power and Promotes Healing*. Carol Stream, IL: Tyndale Momentum, 2020.

Melton, J. Gordon. *Encyclopedia of American Religions*. Detroit: Gale Research, 2003.

Nieuwhof, Carey. "Exactly What Not to Say When You're Leading People Through Change." Careynieuwof.com. https://careynieuwhof.com/exactly-what-not-to-say-when-youre-leading-people-through-change/

Nouwen, Henri J. M. *Spiritual Direction: Wisdom for the Long Walk of Faith*. Edited by Michael J. Christensen and Rebecca J. Laird. New York: HarperOne, 2006.

Pohl, Christine D. *Making Room: Recovering Hospitality as a Christian Tradition*. Grand Rapids: Eerdmans, 1999.

Rah, Soong-Chan. *Many Colors: Cultural Intelligence for a Changing Church*. Chicago: Moody, 2010.

Sanchez, Michelle T. *Color-Conscious Discipleship: Healing the Divide in Our Churches*. Grand Rapids: Baker, 2023.

Scazzero, Peter. *Daily Office: Remembering God's Presence Throughout the Day*. Grand Rapids: Zondervan, 2008.

Volf, Miroslav. *Exclusion and Embrace: A Theological Exploration of Identity, Otherness, and Reconciliation*. Nashville: Abingdon, 1996.

Wallace, William E. *Michelangelo: The Artist, the Man, and His Times*. Cambridge: Cambridge University Press, 2010.

Wells, Samuel. *Learning to Dream Again: Rediscovering the Heart of God*. Grand Rapids: Eerdmans, 2013.

Chapter 5

Leading from the Center[1]
Body and Place

MaryKate Morse

I've learned that people will forget what you said; people will forget what you did; but people will never forget how you made them feel.
—Maya Angelou

No matter how much knowledge you have, there is still a limitation to what you can do around "this table."
—Doretha O'Quinn

INTRODUCTION

Recently I traveled from Charlotte, North Carolina in the United States, to the dairy community of Trenholm, Virginia. I was trying to combine a

---

1. Chapter 5 is adapted from MaryKate Morse, "Leading from the Center." Copyright © 2012 by Karen A. Longman. Used by Permission of Abilene Christian University Press.

business trip with a visit to relatives. I flew into Charlotte from Portland, Oregon on the West Coast, picked up my rental car, set my GPS device for the journey, and started on my way. I left the airport at five in the evening and misjudged the distance between those two places, so it was getting darker and darker as I drove. Just before dusk, I arrived in Farmville, Virginia. I had no idea I would be driving through Farmville, Virginia. I hadn't consulted a map. I had just let the GPS lead the way.

Going through the downtown center of Farmville and not expecting it, especially in the mixed light and grey of evening, stirred in me intense waves of emotions and memories. I had gone to college at Longwood University in Farmville. I moved there from Heidelberg, Germany, where I left my dad and four siblings and the grandmother who did the housekeeping and made sure we didn't kill each other. I didn't know anyone when I arrived. And though I sat in classes and did well academically, it wasn't the campus I remembered now but the town.

As I drove through Main Street, I felt anew the offense of seeing young men in Confederate uniforms marching through the center of town with a Confederate flag, just as they did every Saturday morning at ten. I passed the street on the right, lined with buildings, where I had an ecstatic spiritual experience involving a ragged and bent-over beggar, and the wonder of it filled my soul. I shuddered as I drove past the church on the left with its impressive white columns, where the pastor got too friendly after I went to him for spiritual counsel. It was the same church where, after I had invited a black female student to Sunday service, the elders came to the college on Monday, met with her in the President's office, and asked her not to return. They were uncomfortable with her worshiping with them. Then one long block down on the same side was the African American church where I had begun worshiping the following Sunday, and where I had been welcomed like a long-lost child. I had been overwhelmed with their embrace.

It wasn't just my mind going back. My whole body remembered these forgotten things. The anger, the wonder, the confusion, and the belonging all flooded my adult sensibilities. Though the people were long gone, and the town and Longwood were not at all like they were in my college days, the place was etched on my body. Out of those experiences, many of my leadership passions—for healthy spiritual leadership, for justice, and for the marginalized—took initial form. My call was shaped by the place of Farmville, Virginia, and the person I was in that place, and I was remembering.

In this chapter, I want to focus on the intersection of body and place in leadership. Our bodies—our physical beings that house our instincts, thoughts, and feelings—are shaped by the environments—the culture, characteristics, and history—of places where we work and live. The relationship of body and place has particular import for Christian leaders, precisely because of our belief in the central role of Jesus Christ in our lives. There is an overlay of the body and place of Jesus on our bodies and places. He came in the flesh to first-century Palestine and through his death and resurrection he made possible our new life. He lived out of his body a relationship of love and mission to those who yearned and hoped for more. People experienced his physical presence in specific places when he taught, healed, prayed, and served.

This chapter is based on the underlying premise that Christ calls us to lead like him in body and place. As we are images of the Triune God placed on earth in fleshly form, it is reasonable to assume that our flourishing happens best when we are integrated selves in our places. We show up fully as the embodied presence of Christ to a particular place and people. The mission of God is this hope that we in human form express in community the love and grace of God. We have a desire to conform to the life and character of Jesus in our bodies and in the places we serve. As Christian leaders, we have Christ's indwelling presence. We have at a central place in us, "Christ in you, the hope of glory" (Col 1:27 NRSV). It's more than having a positive spirit toward our work, defined by Goldsmith (named one of the most influential business thinkers by Forbes) as a feeling starting on the inside and radiating out.[2] For us, that positive spirit comes from our investment in and calling to Jesus Christ. Christ in us is Christ with us, braided into our natures. We are partners. Leading with Christ at the center of our physical beings and at the center of our workplaces requires a particular attention to our own physical beings in our workplaces. I will begin by unpacking the relationship of our bodies and places to our calls. I will then propose three types of places and physical behaviors that are vital to leading like Jesus.

EMBODIED LEADERSHIP: THE CALL TO BODY AND PLACE

We are called to lead like Christ. Call constitutes the universal possibilities innate in each person. We desire to do meaningful work that contributes to God's purposes in the world. In his book *Courage and Calling*, Gordon T. Smith, president of reSource Leadership International, distinguishes between a general call to follow Jesus and a specific call that is a person's unique vocation and contribution to God's mission.[3] An individual's specific call is reflected in the collection of his or her gifts, life experiences,

---

2. Goldsmith, *Mojo*.
3. Smith, *Courage and Calling*.

and passions that get expressed in a meaningful vocation. Arthur Miller, the founder of People Management International, and Bill Hendricks, founder of the Hendricks Group, make the point that we are designed for unique contributions and not for becoming anything we want.[4]

Calls that come out of prayer, personal and communal discernment, and a desire to serve others, often result in individuals living courageously and honestly in today's complex and challenging world. Steger, Shin, and Dik, in the *Journal of Career Assessment*, wrote, "Recent scholarship indicates that persons who view their work as a calling are more satisfied with their work and their lives."[5] The leaders who are most effective in addressing the many community and global needs of our day are those who have a sense of purpose and calling.

One of the reasons that we are designed for *unique* contributions is that our calls are influenced by who we are in our bodies and by where we are in differing places. Our calls unfold in places that shape and define us. Body and place are inextricably woven together like the filaments of a spider's web. Movement in any one area affects the entire web and alerts the spider to a change. Like the spider, the human brain is constantly assessing all the incoming information and adapting the body's response to the environment. But the world is hectic, and the brain has to make sense of large volumes of information in short time periods. Without an organizing process, the brain gets overwhelmed and doesn't function rationally and clearly. Focus is necessary. A call provides focus.

Elite performers know this well. A high-caliber athlete does not want to "freeze," be distracted or overwhelmed by the challenges of the environment or the limitations of his or her body. Therefore, athletes want to move from *explicit learning*, the craft and knowledge associated with one's sport, to *implicit learning*, learning practiced so often, over and over, that it physically becomes second nature. The body knows the skill without conscious thought. The skill is embedded in the unconscious and in the midst of pressures, the body re-enacts these skills. In the same way, the leader who senses the call of God *implicitly* in his or her body has a focus to lead like Jesus in any type of situation.

As leaders in churches and Christian institutions, being mindful of the role place and body play in our calls will help us lead more like Christ. As the brain assesses incoming information, the more we *lead implicitly* as Christ, the more effective we will be. Churches, educational institutions, non-profit organizations have unique demands and challenges placed on

---

4. Miller and Hendricks, *Power of Uniqueness*.
5. Steger et al., "Calling in Work," 82.

them, ranging from responding to a rapidly changing world, to developing sustainable financial practices in a stressed economy, to paying attention to the myriad of constituents and stakeholders in the churches and institution's mission. The constant onslaught requires an implicit response from our beings. Otherwise, the stressed, distracted, or overworked leader often begins to function from inner survival mechanisms rather than from the living presence of Christ.[6] "The call" becomes "the grind." The leader moves from "I love this" to "I can handle this."[7]

The brain as an organ of information and decision-making is constantly gathering three kinds of information and assessing it: information about the environment, information about the body, and information about the connections between the two, both good and bad.[8] Our brains are always and unconsciously discerning if our bodies are safe or unsafe. Our most primal response is ensuring our safety. Our environments—place—includes location and people, culture, and events. Our bodies include external features such as race and gender, and internal features such as personality and strengths. All of our bodily realities influence how we manage ourselves in various places.[9]

Call and Body

Call is influenced by one's body. A person's ethnicity impacts his or her perspective on call in different places. Ethnicity shapes a person's understanding of belonging. The dominant group shapes the collective consciousness about how things "should" work. Therefore, the non-dominant group is less likely to be heard; a person's perspective within that group is less likely to be sought out or valued. Primarily, the persons most in positions of power, with a collective force, assume that the way they see the world is the only reality. Often, they are not intentionally shutting out other possibilities; they don't know other possibilities exist; they don't even know to look.

In my opening story, the pastor of the church was a very influential and charismatic leader. He was beloved by his congregation. My experience of him revealed a dark side to his character. I don't think I would have been believed at the time if I had complained to the elders. My black student friend also experienced a dark side to this church's leadership, an assumption of the threat of black people.

6. Norfolk, *Stress Factor*; Lundberg and Cooper, *Science of Occupational Health*.
7. Muller, *On Being, Doing, and Having Enough*.
8. Gonzales, *Deep Survival*, 32.
9. Morse, *Making Room for Leadership*.

Gender, too, affects a person's calling and direction. "It's a boy," or "it's a girl" tends to be the first news heard after the birth of a child. Then the place, the cultural setting of the child's life, further structures the arch of possibilities as he or she grows. For example, in traditional cultures, females are *defined by their bodies* and by their role as nurturers, and males are *defined by their minds* and by their roles as competitors and providers.[10] These conceptual frames impact the leadership options that men and women have and recognize.[11] Women leaders and men leaders have differing challenges as to even the possibility of what they hear as a call. Women usually are encouraged, networked, and mentored less, and take fewer risks than men, not necessarily because they are risk-averse but because there is more at stake if they should fail.[12] One's male or female body often impacts one's imagination about the potential or possibility to fulfill certain roles. Therefore, women sometimes don't think of themselves as executive-level leaders as easily as men might.

Whether they are socialized into a specific understanding of gender roles or not, men's and women's experiences are influenced by their gendered bodies. The very constructions of the body, the rhythms of the body's cycles for men and women, the hormones that wash male and female brains, all bend us toward particular tendencies.[13] More testosterone compels a person to be more competitive, and more oxytocin compels a person to be more caring. All human bodies have both testosterone and oxytocin, but the amount varies from person to person. Thus, these and other physical features of our gendered bodies will take in the world and interpret varying responses. Because we are shaped by the experience of our body, we bring different things to leadership.[14] Since men and women are made in the image of God, both reflect God's nature.[15] Good leadership is focused and competitive as well as encouraging and empowering of others.

---

10. The field of gender studies disagrees on whether gender differences are primarily nature or nurture. Books that support physical differences include Moir and Jessel, *Brain Sex*; Blum, *Sex on the Brain*; Barash and Lipton, *Gender Gap*; and Sykes, *Adam's Curse*.

11. McKay, "Gendering the Body."

12. Fels, "Do Women Lack Ambition?"; Frankel, *Nice Girls Don't Get*; Jaschik, "Too Nice to Land"; Eagly and Carli, "Women and the Labyrinth."

13. Van Leeuwen, *Gender and Grace*; Gurien, *Wonder of Boys*; Gurien, *Wonder of Girls*.

14. Rosener, "Ways Women Lead"; Helgesen, *Female Advantage*; Cunningham and Hamilton, eds., *Why Not Women?*; Freeman et al., *Women on Power*; Helgesen and Johnson, *Female Vision*.

15. LaCelle-Peterson, *Liberating Tradition*.

Understanding the impact of body and place can contribute important perspectives on leadership challenges, especially in our call. Our bodies, which reflect gender and culture, impact the world we experience and the leadership opportunities we have (or don't have) and our approach to leadership. There are other ways in which our bodies influence our perception of our call, such as physical features, physical and mental capacities, and our natural personalities. Ethnicity and gender are the most obvious.

Call and Place

Formation of our sense of self and our call is also a place phenomenon. Our identities are formed by how safe or unsafe we feel in physical environments. If a person feels safe, he or she will be more open and relaxed and more likely to grow and interact. When a person feels unsafe, he or she is more likely to withdraw and protect or react. We know who we are by where we are. This is why family homes, towns or farms, churches and places where we work all are part of the shaping force of our sense of self. Whenever we spend time in a place with smells and sights, touch and sounds, we are inevitably shaped. We are conformed to our world. This is not necessarily good or bad; it just is. Physical place limits and defines us, but it also gives us a place from which to move out.

The brain keeps track of the environment around it. Our sense of well-being is shaped by how safe and known we perceive ourselves to be in a physical environment. People create a mental map that is grounded between the place, their emotional well-being, and the capacity to stay rational despite the circumstances. The power of physical place is made clear by what happens when people are alone in an unfamiliar location. Persons who get lost in the woods can enter into such a state of panic that within forty-eight hours they are dead, even with clothing and resources at their disposal to survive.[16] Neuroscientists have found that the brain becomes inordinately confused when it doesn't recognize anything in the surrounding environment.[17] The body is unable to connect to anything familiar. People who are overwhelmed by this confusion may not survive.

In the same way, leaders can become disoriented when challenges overwhelm them or they are in unfamiliar territory. There can be an internal panic, and even though the body is present and engaged, the internal emotional systems may run amok. Leaders can rise to these challenges and manage their emotions only when there are *implicit responses* ingrained

---

16. Gonzales, *Deep Survival*, 51.
17. LeDoux, *Emotional Brain*; LeDoux, *Synaptic Self*.

in their physical beings. Implicit responses are instinctive because the response has been internalized through constant repetitive practice. The response becomes automatic. When a leader moves from anger or frustration to responding authentically, like Christ, then the response is usually implicit. Or at least the leader will backtrack and admit mistakes or ask for forgiveness. Otherwise, an angry, uptight, or reactive leader has allowed his or her environment to subvert the call from vocation to survival.

Environments add another level of complexity to the experiences of females and males in leadership. Girls who tend to have had small environmental spheres, limited to their homes and safe places, carry the impact of that world in their sense of self and their sense of possibilities. Boys, on the other hand, who are more often allowed to roam, wander free, and try new things, will tend to grow up to have a much more expansive vision of their call.[18] The freedom to be dominant in one's environment, take risks, and explore, shapes the person's imagination for the possibilities of leadership. Though a challenge, the nature of the environment does not limit a woman's capacity for leadership. Taking risks and imagining possibilities are not character traits but learned skills. Anyone limited by his or her environment might actually have a possible leadership advantage. Since power is not a privileged expectation for such people, they see and often empower those in lesser positions of influence. This action has positive spiritual, economic, and social implications.

Assumptions about how environments work, such as the example above, illustrate the nature of mental models. They are useful, but they can also have limitations. Because of the complexity of the world, we create mental models of an expected reality to help us respond in perceived appropriate ways. This strategy is not only natural, but necessary. However, sometimes leaders are wrong. Sometimes leaders get lost. The mental map often needs adjustment when the environment has changed, and if the leader doesn't adjust his or her mental map but persists in the path chosen, disaster usually follows for the leader, the church, or the institution. People get lost, leaders get lost, because they refuse to retrace their steps. They've constructed a new reality that is so compelling they push ahead to a point where they are unable to return. They don't go back to the fundamentals. Calls of individuals and organizations are important precisely because they remind us where we started and what we value most.

---

18. Sebba, "Girls and Boys"; Carr-Ruffino, *Promotable Woman*; Van Norstrand, *Gender-Responsible Leadership*; Ibarra and Obodaru, "Women and the Vision."

Body and Place Together

As leaders who are connected with a high sense of mission and calling—such as churches, Christian colleges, and non-profits—an awareness of the impact of body and place on our leadership is necessary. Both body and place influence the sphere of our call and our response to the challenges we face. Next, I want to suggest three types of body behaviors and spaces that will help us lead implicitly with Christ at the center: (1) the body and intimate/private space; (2) the body and social space; and (3) the body and public space.

Body and Intimate/Private Place—"It's About God"

As leaders called to serve in Christian churches and institutions, our relationship with God is a fundamental aspect of our identity and our work. Search committees, elders, boards, congregants, and constituents often care that an applicant for a position is a person of faith and a person committed to the faith values of the institution. Persons with whom leaders will work expect a certain level of integrity and authenticity in the expression of their leaders' faith. Because most Christian churches and institutions have deep historical roots in a particular religious tradition, leaders who do best are those who also have deep personal roots in God. Therefore, effective leaders find ways to nurture their faith in concrete and regular ways, and their relationship to God becomes implicit.

The first and primary commandment in the Old Testament is "I am the Lord your God . . . you shall have no other gods before me" (Exod 20:2–3 NRSV). In the New Testament, Jesus's radical obedience put God and God's call before everything else, even to the point of death on the cross (Phil 2:5–10). In John 5, Jesus proclaims his equality with God and his dependence on God for judgments, actions, and healings. To lead from the center as Christ led, we too must have no other gods before us and must depend on God for our judgments and actions. To live in that extreme place of dependence requires an intimate place for being with God. All our life and work comes out of that place. From that place, we learn that it's all about God.

Edward Hall, a ground-breaking anthropologist who died in 2009 at age ninety-five, coined the term *proxemics* and wrote about the impact space has on animals and people.[19] Hall believed that communication was the core of life and that we need to have intimate and personal relationships

---

19. Hall, *Hidden Dimension*.

to stabilize our bodies. He distinguished four different types of physical spaces: intimate, personal, social, and public:

1. Intimate space occurs when bodies are between zero and eighteen inches apart, as between a husband and wife, or parent and child, or the closest of friends.

2. Personal space is between eighteen inches and four feet 18, which occurs between good friends, such as when they are having coffee together.

3. Social space is a distance between four and ten feet and occurs when persons are together for a common purpose, such as in worship, meetings, and on project teams.

4. Public space is the preferred personal distance of ten feet or more from strangers, such as on a beach or in a restaurant.[20]

In this section, our focus is on intimate and personal space—particular in the spiritual context of intimacy with God. This close proximity suggests safety and honesty. The body in this distance with others tends to be authentic. With these distances, if there is frustration or anger, the body instinctively moves apart, and the reverse is true if there is affection. The more intimate a person is to someone else, the more physical contact is desired.[21]

The result of such intimacy is transformative. The psychologists who authored *A General Theory of Love* came to the same conclusion, writing, "Who we are and who we become depends, in part, on whom we love."[22] The development of a loving relationship only happens when real time and space are designated for interactions. Intimate and personal space depends on proximity and privacy. Therefore, to become like Christ and to grow in Christlikeness demands time and space dedicated to that purpose.

Jesus himself regularly went off to pray alone or with a small group of devoted followers. After those times of prayer, he came back energized for next steps, he discerned decisions, he refocused, and he was affirmed and comforted. Jesus told his disciples to abide in his loving and redemptive presence (John 15:1–11). Such primal trust can only happen when our bodies have a place for regular personal and intimate attentiveness to Christ.

Reflective space, both physical and linear, is needed daily and weekly. Many find benefit in taking thirty minutes to an hour each day for prayer,

---

20. Hall, *Hidden Dimension*.

21. Persons can also use proximity for aggressive and self-serving purposes such as how an abuser or narcissistic leader might move in close to assert authority. However, the instinct on the part of the one "attacked" will be to move back. If he or she cannot move back physically, the instinct will be to move back internally and to close off.

22. Lewis et al., *General Theory of Love*, 144.

reflection, and study. Weekly space, the day each week we are called to Sabbath-keeping, may seem an extraordinarily strange command alongside those such as "do not murder and steal" and "do not create graven images."[23] Yet since the rhythm of creation and daily life from sun-up to sun-down is intimate space with God, Sabbath-keeping prepares the leader to embody Christ in a thoughtful, nonreactive way. Furthermore, since we are shaped by place, physical space is as important as time. The creation of a sacred space that quickly draws a leader into God's presence can help establish the value of intimate space: "To survive, you need a sanctuary where you can reflect on the previous day's journey, renew your emotional resources, and recalibrate your moral compass."[24]

I don't know of any other behavior that has a more stabilizing, Christ-in-us effect than non-legalistic daily time for reflection, study, and prayer and observing a weekly Sabbath. Rest is directly connected to the well-being of our bodies. The busy leader has a busy body and, more often than not, a stressed body. Our cognitive capacities, and thus how we think and interpret the world around us, are directly related to how rested our bodies might be. Under stress, the body releases cortisol to help the body handle extreme moments of pressure and danger with a clarity that allows for the possibility of survival. However, the constant release of cortisol eventually has the opposite effect and begins to impair cognitive function, though most times the person doesn't recognize the shift. Such a person sees less, hears less, and makes poorer decisions than when he or she is rested. Eventually malformed perceptions create new realities for a leader and lead to tragic mistakes, often the type that hurt others.[25]

In *Leadership Ethics*, Terry Price, professor of leadership and philosophy at the University of Richmond, makes the point that leaders at the top are more likely to make colossal moral mistakes because their brain rewires to exclude important reality-checking information.[26] Because they see themselves as unique, they don't need to follow the standards that guide others. They believe that somehow, they will escape the fate that others might expect. Therefore, they begin to make small immoral decisions that lead to larger mistakes. For leaders to thrive, they must first have regular immersion in times and places dedicated to communion with Christ precisely

---

23. Many books have been written on this commandment, including *Sabbath* by Wayne Muller, who served as a senior scholar at the Fetzer Institute.
24. Heifetz and Linsky, "Survival Guide for Leaders."
25. Campbell et al., "Why Good Leaders."
26. Price, *Leadership Ethics*.

so they do not wander away from reality-checking their call and character. Sacred space replaces hectic space.

Body and Social Place—It's About Others

The next critical space where body and place shape a leader's call and identity is social space. Edward Hall, remember, described this distance as between four and ten feet. Social space consists of those settings where a group of individuals are interacting with each other around a common purpose or are engaged together in a common event such as worship. The closer the physical space, the more sensory data is picked up by the body, which means more opportunities for an emotional exchange and thus for a relationship. Leadership author Sally Helgesen has written, "Identity is inseparable from relationship."[27] The embodiment of a leader's character and call are experienced more clearly in social settings, especially when individuals are seated around a table or are in a small group setting. When Jesus allowed the sinful woman in Simon's house to touch him in social space (Luke 7:36–50), he communicated volumes about the people he valued, the people he came to serve. Leaders typically talk a lot, but how a leader functions in social space communicates more than the leader's words.

I recall attending a small retreat at which an internationally-known, charismatic leader presented. When he was not up front speaking, he was on his phone and reading books on his Kindle. He would leave the room often and was not available to engage the attendees. In contrast, I recently attended another small retreat that trained leaders from all over the world. The attendees were from countries including Latvia, India, Russia, Philippines, Nigeria, Kenya, and Mexico. The training was designed to create spiritual mentoring communities to invest in and sustain the next generation of catalytic Christian leaders. The four trainers all held doctorates and had served in significant leadership environments nationally and internationally. The trainers were not introduced beyond their first and last names. When they were not presenting, they were participating with the attendees.

On the fourth day, a woman from Kenya said, "I don't get who you people are. Who are you?" She could not comprehend how persons of social status and achievement would assume positions of identification with the attendees. The message of the trainers' presence was one of interest, partnership, and value. She was confused that they sat next to the attendees and spent time with them, even giving up their free time to listen and pray with participants. She commented, "What has changed me most is the experience

27. Helgesen, *Web of Inclusion*, 16.

of these important leaders taking time for me. I can do this for others in my country." These busy persons of influence embodied Christ-centered leadership that was relational and other-centered.[28] The first retreat leader was not present; the second leaders were. When a leader is physically present in social space, the capacity for influencing others is greatly enhanced.

Meals are especially important social space opportunities. Jesus ate with sinners. He took time to engage with persons the culture had labeled as outsiders. Leaders who take time to eat socially with their staff can expect to see and hear more than they ever would from a report. As Helgesen observes, "Eating and drinking with others cements an elemental bond and implies a basic trust. . . . I could not help but note how often vital exchanges occurred in informal but comfortable communal spaces that defined the true image people had of the organization."[29] When a person of less role influence has a meal with someone of more—especially when the leader spends the time listening, asking questions, and simply getting to know the other person—the experience has great potential to build mutual trust.

There is a physical "wholeness" observed in community, not just by a handshake or smile but by the gift of focused time and a relaxed and attentive body, which communicates a message of value to the recipient. This whole physicality is dynamic, not fixed and stylized. Who a leader is behind closed doors in a meeting or in small gatherings is a more accurate portrayal of how that leader lives out his or her call than a mission statement written on a website. Therefore, in small social spaces, the effective leader brings a body that is rested, attentive, and focused on serving others and the institution.

Body and Public Place—It's About the Mission

The final place where a leader's call is embodied is in public space. Hall describes public space as occurring when the preferred distance is ten or more feet. Public settings include large events where the leader is expected to speak or represent the institution. Public space is powerful in institutional life. In the fall of 2008, our university experienced an ugly racial incident when four students hung a cardboard cutout of then-presidential candidate Barack Obama from a campus tree. Within a few hours, our campus was inundated with reporters and camera vans, and the story made international headlines. One of our highest values at George Fox University is racial reconciliation, and we had worked with focus to create an ethnically

---

28. Wright, *Relational Leadership*.
29. Helgesen, *Web of Inclusion*, 256, 257.

diverse campus. By the time of the incident, we had managed to attract a student body that was 25 percent people of color (the university was located in a small town that was mostly white). The "prank" hurt many students on our campus, particularly our African American students; it also shamed our university. The university president, Robin Baker, gathered the local community for a public statement to the press, the students affected, and to us. The resolute public presence and words of our president clearly and eloquently renounced the act and affirmed our mission. He met over and over in public venues with local African American leaders to listen and learn and to affirm our commitment to diversity. Because of his heartfelt public response, our humiliation led to a determination to work harder to have a safe and diverse campus.

Though the public arena for a leader is extremely important, especially in times of crisis and change, it has limits to how authentically a leader is known. The authentic inner self is primarily known in more personal relational settings. This is obvious with the many stories of major public figures, especially pastors, who surprise us with moral failure. Communicating powerfully is a gift, but it does not guarantee integrity. Face-to-face encounters are more authentic expressions of Christ-like leadership. Therefore, embodying one's call in a public place is helped greatly by walking around and engaging the random people one might meet. Public space can be turned into social and personal space simply by walking from the stage to an office space or table in the eating area. Jesus did a lot of ministry in public space, yet he was unique as a rabbi in that he traveled. Most rabbis would establish themselves in a specific location, but Jesus was itinerant. He went to the people.

In earlier years, I had a dean who had a habit of walking around and outside the seminary visiting faculty, staff, and the various persons who served seminary students. He would go downstairs and check in with Sheila, our beloved admissions counselor, and ask her how things were going and how she was doing. He would drop in on faculty and share his thinking and wondered what each one thought. He would connect regularly with the provost, outside of required meetings, simply to touch base and visit. For busy leaders, casual walking-around visits can seem like a luxury. I argue that it is a necessity.

Tom Peters popularized "management by walking around" in the 1980s. Walking around became important in that decade because leaders felt that they were becoming more and more isolated from their employees, customers, and constituents. It was found to be an extremely effective leadership practice. Peters called the practice the "technology of the obvious." By walking around and engaging a wide variety of persons impacted by the company—or for us, a church or Christian institution—a leader would get a more accurate picture of the actual state of affairs.[30]

This practice is even more important in our technology-rich environment where emails and Zoom sessions are the common means for getting things done. Technology probably saves hundreds of work hours. However, churches are faith-based organizations that should model the mission of the institution by being the presence, the "face," of it to others. Pastors or leaders who walk around and talk to employees, faculty, volunteers, congregants, and people who live in the community embody the caring and purposeful mission of the institution. Vital exchanges that occur in informal public spaces are meaningful for the leader as well as for those benefiting from the leader's time.

Resistance to "walking around" in public space often comes down to two concerns—not having enough time and wanting to avoid the trap of "blame and complain." The best way to manage time is to tame it. Walking around does not need to take much time. If a leader were to allow for informal fifteen-minute conversations two or three times a week, it would make considerable difference in the long run. To minimize getting caught in those inevitable "blame and complain" conversations, leaders can begin conversations with a focus on the other person's family and interests, and then ask what is meaningful and what is challenging with their life and work. Some things leaders will hear do need to be fixed. Other times encouragement is needed. Sometimes things can be redirected. Most of the time, though, people feel respected when a leader or pastor listens to them.

When my dean walked around, using public space for personal encounters, the students, faculty, and staff experienced his energy, his love of the seminary, and his pastoral touch. In these types of conversations, the leader embodies the mission and values of the institution.

EMBODIED LEADERSHIP—TYING IT TOGETHER

Thriving in uncertain times is often defined more by outward success, but for Christian believers it is also defined by a deep conviction that Christ is the source and the reason for why we do what we do. We are *Christian* pastors, educators, and leaders. We have a holy calling. We are engaged in a holy vocation. We lead from the center of Christ in us.

This type of leadership is more than following Jesus's teachings. It is a life lived out of an inner conviction of the indwelling presence of Christ. Therefore, ours is a uniquely embodied leadership, and even more so when

---

30. See Serratt, "Managing by Walking Around."

our work is in institutions that are shaped by faith convictions. We must live out our callings in specific physical ways and in specific places. Jesus came in the flesh to physically express the nature of God and God's work in the world. By routinizing our physical behaviors in physical spaces, we can lead more *implicitly* like Jesus. These behaviors are central to effective leadership and inspire hope within us and with others, especially during difficult times.

BIBLIOGRAPHY

Barash, David, and Judith Lipton. *Gender Gap: The Biology of Male-Female Differences.* New Brunswick: Transaction, 2002.

Blum, Deborah. *Sex on the Brain: The Biological Difference between Men and Women.* New York: Penguin, 1997.

Campbell, Andrew, et al. "Why Good Leaders Make Bad Decisions." *Harvard Business Review*, Feb. 2009. https://hbr.org/2009/02/why-good-leaders-make-bad-decisions.

Carr-Ruffino, Norma. *The Promotable Woman.* Belmont: Wadsworth, 1993.

Cunningham, Loren, and David Joel Hamilton, eds. *Why Not Women?* Seattle: YWAM, 2000.

Eagly, Alice H., and Linda L. Carli. "Women and the Labyrinth of Leadership." *Harvard Business Review*, Sep. 2007. https://hbr.org/2007/09/women-and-the-labyrinth-of-leadership.

Fels, Anna. "Do Women Lack Ambition?" *Harvard Business Review*, Apr. 2004. https://hbr.org/2004/04/do-women-lack-ambition.

Frankel, Lois. *Nice Girls Don't Get the Corner Office.* New York: Warner Business, 2004.

Freeman, Sue, et al., eds. *Women on Power: Leadership Redefined.* Boston: Northeastern University Press, 2001.

Goldsmith, Marshall. *Mojo: How to Get It, How to Keep It, How to Get It Back If You Lose It.* New York: Hyperion, 2010.

Gonzales, Laurence. *Deep Survival: Who Lives, Who Dies, and Why.* New York: Norton, 2003.

Gurien, Michael. *The Wonder of Boys: What Parents, Mentors, and Educators Can Do to Shape Boys into Exceptional Men.* New York: Penguin, 1997.

———. *The Wonder of Girls: Understanding the Hidden Nature of our Daughters.* New York: Penguin Putnam, 2002.

Hall, Edward T. *The Hidden Dimension.* New York: Anchor, 1966.

Heifetz, Ronald A., and Marty Linsky. "A Survival Guide for Leaders." *Harvard Business Review*, June 2002. https://hbr.org/2002/06/a-survival-guide-for-leaders.

Helgesen, Sally. *The Female Advantage: Women's Ways of Leadership.* New York: Currency Doubleday, 1995.

———. *The Web of Inclusion: Architecture for Building Great Organizations.* Washington, DC: Beard, 2005.

Helgesen, Sally, and Julie Johnson. *The Female Vision: Women's Real Power at Work.* San Francisco: Berrett-Koehler, 2010.

Ibarra, H., and O. Obodaru. "Women and the Vision Thing." *Harvard Business Review*, Jan. 2009. https://hbr.org/2009/01/women-and-the-vision-thing.

Jaschik, Scott. "Too Nice to Land a Job." *Inside Higher Ed News*, Nov. 10, 2010.

LaCelle-Peterson, Kristina. *Liberating Tradition: Women's Identity and Vocation in Christian Perspective*. Grand Rapids: Baker, 2008.

LeDoux, Joseph. *The Emotional Brain: The Mysterious Underpinnings of Emotional Life*. New York: Simon & Schuster, 1996.

———. *The Synaptic Self: How Our Brains Become Who We Are*. New York: Viking, 2002.

Lewis, Thomas, et al. *A General Theory of Love*. New York: Vintage, 2001.

McKay, Heather A. "Gendering the Body: Clothes Maketh the (Wo)man." In *Theology and the Body: Gender, Text, and Ideology*, edited by Robert Hannaford and J'Annine Jobling, 84–103. Exeter: Short Run.

Miller, Arthur, Jr., and Bill Hendricks. *The Power of Uniqueness*. Grand Rapids: Zondervan, 1999.

Moir, Anne, and David Jessel. *Brain Sex: The Real Difference Between Men and Women*. New York: Delta, 1991.

Morse, MaryKate. "Leading from the Center: Body and Place." In *Thriving in Leadership: Strategies for Making a Difference in Higher Education*, edited by Karen A. Longman, 59–78. Abilene, TX: Abilene Christian University Press, 2012.

———. *Making Room for Leadership: Power, Space, and Influence*. Downers Grove, IL: InterVarsity, 2008.

Muller, Wayne. *A Life of Being, Having, and Doing Enough*. New York: Harmony, 2010.

———. *Sabbath: Finding Rest, Renewal, and Delight in Our Busy Lives*. New York: Bantam, 2000.

Norfolk, Donald. *The Stress Factor*. New York: Simon & Schuster, 1979.

Price, Terry. *Leadership Ethics: An Introduction*. Cambridge: Cambridge University Press, 2008.

Rosener, Judy B. "Ways Women Lead." *Harvard Business Review*, Nov.–Dec. 1990. https://hbr.org/1990/11/ways-women-lead.

Sebba, Rachel. "Girls and Boys and the Physical Environment." In *Women and the Environment*, edited by Irwin Altman and Arza Churchman, 43–72. New York: Plenum, 1994.

Serratt, Olivier. "Managing by Walking Around." *Knowledge Solutions* 37 (2009) 1–2.

Smith, Gordan T. *Courage and Calling: Embracing Your God-Given Potential*. Downers Grove, IL: InterVarsity, 1999.

Steger, Michael F., et al. "Calling in Work: Secular or Sacred?" *Journal of Career Assessment* 18 (2010) 82–96.

Sykes, Bryan. *Adam's Curse: The Science That Reveals Our Genetic Destiny*. New York: Norton, 2004.

Van Leeuwen, Mary Stewart. *Gender and Grace: Love, Work, and Parenting in a Changing World*. Downers Grove, IL: InterVarsity, 1990.

Van Norstrand, Catherine Herr. *Gender-Responsible Leadership: Detecting Bias, Implementing Interventions*. Newbury Park: Sage, 1993.

Wright, Walter. *Relational Leadership: A Biblical Model for Influence and Service*. Philadelphia: Authentic, 2009.

Section II

Church Healing

Growing Communities That Restore and Transform

Chapter 6

Shepherding Well

Guiding a Theology of Interpersonal Power and Authority

CHRISTA L. MCKIRLAND

INTRODUCTION

THE METAPHOR OF GOD as Israel's Shepherd (Ps 23), leaders of Israel as shepherds of the people of God (both good and bad), Jesus as the Good Shepherd (and sacrificial lamb), the church as the flock that knows the Good Shepherd's voice, and New Testament leaders as undershepherds, provides a pastoral through line across the Christian Scriptures. But what is the relationship between the Shepherd, undershepherds, and sheep meant to be like today? How does this contribute to our being communities of hope? I will use the shepherd-sheep metaphor to guide how we think of interpersonal power and authority, proposing that each member of the flock is meant to hear the Shepherd's voice, but not in isolation. We need the flock, especially members of the flock that know the Shepherd well and are living a life worthy of imitation. These other flock members do not have authority *over* the flock or individual sheep, but they do have power to point other members to the Chief Shepherd. Importantly, *every* member of the flock has the *potential* to guide other sheep to the Chief Shepherd. Ultimately, we have hope for the church because, as the flock of God, the church is not our creation.

GOD AS OUR SHEPHERD AND MY SHEPHERD

The first explicit mention of the Lord as shepherd is Gen 48:15.[1] In Jacob's blessing on Joseph, he recounts how God has been his shepherd all his life: "The God before whom my ancestors Abraham and Isaac walked, the God who has been my shepherd all my life to this day." As Jacob, or Israel, was the father of the twelve tribes, naming God in this way, at the fountainhead of this nation, establishes a shepherd-flock relationship that will characterize God's people. What the Old Testament shepherd image provides is an enrichment to God's kingship of sovereign rule. A shepherd cannot shepherd from afar. They must be nearby and personally present. This is exactly what we see in how God engages with Israel—especially in times of crisis.[2] The Lord leads, corrects, assures, protects, and heals the flock.[3] Such actions are found throughout Israel's story even if explicit shepherd language (in the Pentateuch) is less frequent (Gen 48:15; 49:24; Num 27:17).[4]

Of course, the quintessential text about God as Shepherd is Ps 23:

> The Lord is my shepherd; I shall not want.
> He makes me lie down in green pastures;
> he leads me beside still waters;
> he restores my soul.
> He leads me in right paths
> for his name's sake.
> Even though I walk through the darkest valley,
> I fear no evil,
> for you are with me;
> your rod and your staff,
> they comfort me.

Here we can read of God's care, protection, and provision for us as the sheep of his pasture. This image evokes gentleness and care (Ps 23:2 and Isa 40:11). Such gentleness is also seen in God carrying Israel in Exod 19:4; Deut 1:31; 32:11; and Hos. 11:3. God is a guide for the flock on paths of righteousness. Comparing Israel's God with the surrounding nations' deities and leaders, we see a commonality for using this metaphor for those gods and leaders.

---

1. All Scriptures in chapter 6 are taken from the NRSV.

2. Chae notes how much the Lord is associated with shepherd imagery especially in the exodus and exilic narratives. Chae, *Jesus as the Eschatological*, 26.

3. For instance, Exod 13:21–22; 14:19–20, 23–25; 15:13; 15:25–27; 16:4–5, 11–16; 17:5–7; 40:34–38; Deut 7:17–24; 23:14; 32:10–12.

4. For a detailed treatment of this metaphor see Laniak, *Shepherds*, 77–93; and Chae, *Jesus as the Eschatological*. Laniak and Chae feature heavily in Quentin Kinnison's application of this metaphor to pastoral ministry in *Transforming Pastoral Leadership*.

Israel's neighbors would call their gods and rulers shepherds, however, what is unique for Israel is how the Lord guides the flock in the wilderness.[5] Timothy Laniak notes this distinctiveness: "The strong emphasis on guidance in the wilderness is unique. Guidance in battle and guidance by law were common. But the image of God leading his 'flock' purposefully in a historic journey across a desert towards a permanent pastureland is a novel use of the shepherd metaphor."[6] God shepherds the Israelites in the wilderness and the valleys. God, as king of the universe, desired to be Israel's sole shepherd and king, guiding, protecting, and caring for them.

KINGS AND RULERS AS SHEPHERDS

However, after being guided in the wilderness and settled in the pasturelands of Canaan, Israel eventually wanted to be like the other nations. They wanted a human king. In God's graciousness, Israel is given what Quentin Kinnison calls a "permissive allowance."[7] However, even in the appointment of the king, God set up this process and the expectations differently from the surrounding nations. Deuteronomy 17:14–20 is a striking text:

> When you have come into the land that the Lord your God is giving you and have taken possession of it and settled in it, and you say, "I will set a king over me, like all the nations that are around me," you may indeed set over you a king whom the Lord your God will choose. One of your own community you may set as king over you; you are not permitted to put a foreigner over you, who is not of your own community. Even so, he must not acquire many horses for himself or return the people to Egypt in order to acquire more horses, since the Lord has said to you, "You must never return that way again." And he must not acquire many wives for himself or else his heart will turn away; also silver and gold he must not acquire in great quantity for himself. When he has taken the throne of his kingdom, he shall write for himself a copy of this law on a scroll in the presence of the Levitical priests. It shall remain with him, and he shall read in it all the days of his life, so that he may learn to fear the Lord his God, diligently observing all the words of this law and these statutes, neither exalting himself above other members of the

---

5. Laniak, *Shepherds*, 86. "Spiritual leaders in the New Testament are later called to shepherd God's flock in a world that is not their ultimate home" (86). See also Mann, *Divine Presence and Guidance*, 236.

6. Laniak, *Shepherds*, 86.

7. Kinnison, *Transforming Pastoral Leadership*, 37.

community nor turning aside from the commandment, either to the right or to the left, so that he and his descendants may reign long over his kingdom in Israel.

We see that the king is chosen by the Lord (v. 15), who must be from among them (v. 15), and he is not to acquire many horses, many wives, or great quantities of silver and gold for himself (vv. 16–17). The way this ruler must live is through complete dependence on God's direction by writing out a copy of the law by his own hand and reading it every day (vv. 18–19). Finally, he is not to exalt himself over his brothers and sisters (v. 20). By being humble, not acquiring these things for himself, and by knowing and keeping the law of the Lord, his reign would last (v. 20). With these conditions and constraints in place, this kingship is "the only kind of human rule over other humans that the Old Testament approves.... [However, his] rule becomes tyranny the moment he forgets that the horizontal relationship of brother/sisterhood is primary, kingship secondary."[8] So, while Israel does want to be like the other nations in having a king, Israel is not meant to be like the other nations in terms of how the king understood himself in relation to the people.

We should also pause to reflect on the all-powerful God's graciousness. That the Lord would permit a co-shepherd to share the responsibility of guiding Israel, the Davidic king, demonstrates God's humility and willingness to share power.[9] Returning, then, to Ps 23, while a passage of comfort for many, was first a psalm of the king of Israel, likely King David. While we cannot be sure that David was the author of this text, "there are important links between its lyrics and the life of the king who personally embodied the story of Israel."[10] What we see here and elsewhere in Pss 32 and 51 is that the human with the greatest authority in Israel submits his leadership to the Lord. The king is also a representative for the nation of Israel, and thus, it is appropriate to think of this psalm as applying to the whole nation (and to us as the expanded people of God today). Thus, we, too, can take comfort when we see the intimacy of relationship between the Shepherd and the sheep. What begins in vv. 1–3 as a statement about the Lord as his Shepherd, turns to a second-person address in v. 4; from "he leads me beside still waters" to "you are with me."

---

8. Bauckham, *Living With Other Creatures*, 5. See also Kinnison, *Transforming Pastoral Leadership*, 37.

9. For more on the Davidic appointee acting as a co-shepherd see Chae, *Jesus as the Eschatological*, 26. For how we know this was not what God wanted, read 1 Samuel 8.

10. Laniak, *Shepherds After My Own Heart*, 114.

Such intimacy then inflects how the sheep experiences the tools of the shepherd. The rod and staff are a comfort to the king. The rod was used for defense of the flock and was a shorter, club-like tool, often made from a tree branch.[11] The staff, also wooden, typically had a crook on the end to help snag animals who were caught, redirecting sheep, and also for their protection.[12] Between them, we see them used for protection from without and keeping peace within. However, these tools could also be used for abuse and oppression as seen in Isa 9:4 and 10:24. Instead, with the Lord we see a Shepherd who cares and protects, so much so that there is no fear even in the darkest valley because of the Shepherd's presence (Ps 23:4).

In light of what we have seen so far, I propose that power was meant to work differently in Israel. The main reasons for this are, first, the God of Abraham, Isaac, Jacob, and David is unlike any other god seen by the fact that the I AM shares power. Second, this shared power is meant to be continually drawn upon as the king and all of Israel recognize a dependence upon the Lord. This is not a power apart from God, but a power from God that most clearly comes out through knowing and observing the law, setting them apart as a holy nation. Third, by living out radically different ways of relating to their God, to one another, and to creation (living creatures and land especially), Israel was meant to live into their corporate vocation of being priests to the nations, whereby all nations might be blessed (recalling the Abrahamic covenant of Gen 12) and know the one, true Shepherd King.[13]

However, while power was meant to work differently, it did not. The shepherd kings, rulers, and majority of Israel did not live in dependence on the True Shepherd.[14] We can see why God wanted to be the sole Shepherd by the time we are reading Ezekiel and Zechariah. There we see that the shepherd rulers care more for themselves than for the flock, entirely disregarding God's rule (Ezek 34:1–10; Zech 10:3; 11:4–17). As Laniak notes, "Israel's kings had to understand that being a member of the flock of God was more fundamental than being an appointed shepherd over that flock."[15] Lamentably, they forgot about their need for God as one of the people, ruling self-sufficiently over the people.

This abusive shepherding sets up an expectation for the Good Shepherd who "will be present with God's people, leading them in faithfulness

---

11. Laniak, *Shepherds*, 55.
12. Laniak, *Shepherds*, 55.
13. Middleton, *New Heaven*, 64.
14. Middleton, *New Heaven*, 66; Kinnison, *Transforming Pastoral Leadership*, 44.
15. Laniak, *Shepherds*, 114.

to God's rule, and caring for God's flock by restoring them to 'shalom.'"[16] This Shepherd "will have God's Spirit residing upon him (Isa 11:2; 42:1; 61:1–2; Mic 5:4) as foreshadowing for the outpouring of YHWH's Spirit on all God's people."[17] Further, Israel was still meant to be a royal, priestly nation by following the law (Exod 19:6). Thus, Israel's prophets exercise forthtelling far more than foretelling—they keep calling the nation back to its first love, their Shepherd King, through covenant faithfulness. Despite Israel's unfaithfulness, God still promises that a new covenant is yet to come, one which will bring an even more intimate relationship with God's own shepherding Spirit.[18]

JESUS AS CHIEF SHEPHERD

The messianic Shepherd King coming with a rod of iron (Ps 2:9) loomed large in the expectations of oppressed Israel. However, the Shepherd King comes first as the Lamb who was to be slain. Yet, he didn't have to come that way! As we know at the end of time, he will bring the iron rod of justice (Rev 2:27), coming in power and authority over all things. However, for his first coming, while still the all-powerful Son, he demonstrates the proper use of power, especially in a fallen context. This is the power of submission and self-sacrifice, power through vulnerability and weakness, while Jesus remains a fully volitional agent.[19] For instance, in John 10, we see Jesus pulling heavily on shepherding language—he is the good shepherd. The sheep know his voice and he is willing to die for his sheep. In calling himself the "good shepherd," Jesus is likely contrasting himself from the bad shepherds from Israel's past (Ezek 34:1–10; Zech 10:3; 11:4–17). Looking at Ezek 34:2–6 as an example,

> Prophesy against the shepherds of Israel; prophesy and say to them: "To the shepherds—thus says the Lord God: 'Woe, you shepherds of Israel who have been feeding yourselves! Should not shepherds feed the sheep? You eat the fat; you clothe yourselves with the wool; you slaughter the fatted calves, but you do not feed the sheep. You have not strengthened the weak; you have not healed the sick; you have not bound up the injured; you

---

16. Kinnison, *Transforming Pastoral Leadership*, 40, and citing Chae, *Jesus as the Eschatological*, 93–94.

17. Kinnison, *Transforming Pastoral Leadership*, 39.

18. Num 11:29; Isa 59:21; Jer 31:31–33; Joel 2:28–31; Hag 2:4; See also Studebaker, *Lord Is the Spirit*, 191, 201.

19. For more, see McKirland, "Jesus, Agency," 762–82.

have not brought back the strays; you have not sought the lost, but with force and harshness you have ruled them. So they were scattered because there was no shepherd, and scattered they became food for all the wild animals. My sheep were scattered; they wandered over all the mountains and on every high hill; my sheep were scattered over all the face of the earth, with no one to search or seek for them."

In contrast, Jesus refuses to leverage his rightful power over all things, submitting even to the power of death.[20] He is the good shepherd who will lay down his life for his flock. Yet he does this as a completely volitional agent: "No one takes it [my life] from me, but I lay it down of my own accord. I have power (*exousian*) to lay it down, and I have power (*exousian*) to take it up again. I have received this command from my Father" (John 10:18). Interestingly, while the NRSV translates this as "power," most other translations state this as "authority" since that is the standard translation for the *exousia* word group.[21] Regardless of which word is used, power or authority, this is a reflexive description of the power or authority that Jesus has over himself. Jesus is a full agent who chooses to submit himself to the will of the Father. Jesus, who is both fully God and fully human, epitomizes perfect human submission to the Father through the Spirit.

The centrality of the Holy Spirit cannot be overstated. In the Old Testament, starting with the leadership of Moses, we see the need for the Spirit's presence on that person (Num 27:18; Josh 1:5).[22] We see this especially in Isa 11:1–5 with the foretelling of a coming Davidic king.[23] The same Spirit who was linked with the Old Testament texts about the Great Shepherd is now the one empowering and anointing Jesus. Jesus is both the Shepherd of Israel and the way by which this flock is expanded, by being also the Lamb who was slain.[24]

---

20. Kinnison, *Transforming Pastoral Leadership*, 45. See also Kearsley, *Church, Community, and Power*: "In the Spirit Jesus showed a special power not represented in Foucault's list of power strategies—the transgressive truth of self-denying love. Early Christian texts expected this self-denial to defuse self-interested, coercive power in the community and its power behaviours" (222).

21. Typically, when *dunamis* is used, "power" is the translation.

22. Laniak, *Shepherds*, 91.

23. Laniak, *Shepherds*, 120.

24. Kinnison, *Transforming Pastoral Leadership*, 45–46.

ASPIRATIONAL UNDERSHEPHERDS

While Israel has been the Lord's flock throughout the Old Testament, turning to the New Testament, the expanded people of God are now called God's flock. However, instead of a merely human shepherd-king, we now have the fully divine and fully human Shepherd King who has given us his Spirit. The Spirit constitutes this flock. This Spirit enables us to know his voice. So, any function of "undershepherds" is in service to the flock to know the true Shepherd's voice. For instance, we have one explicit mention of human shepherds (in a noun form) in Eph 4:11—apostles, prophets, evangelists, shepherds (*poimen*), teachers, and as a function (in a verb form) of elders and overseers in Acts 20 and 1 Peter. Timothy Laniak's monograph on shepherds across that biblical canon brings all these undershepherd references together. He explains,

> The elders are to shepherd (*poimainō*) God's flock under their care.... Paul urged the Ephesian elders, "Keep watch over yourselves and all the flock of which the Holy Spirit has made you overseers. Be shepherds of the church of God, which he bought with his own blood." In both contexts [Acts 20:28 and 1 Pet 5:1–4] the association between shepherding and careful oversight is clear. In Acts the "overseers" (*episkopoi*) are expected to guard or pay close attention to (*prosechō*) the needs of the flock (in the context of wolves; v. 29). Similarly, leaders in Hebrews 13:17 "watch over" (*agrypneō*) your souls as they serve the "great Shepherd of the sheep" (Heb. 13:20). In 1 Peter 5:2 the elders are to oversee (*episkopeō*) the flock. This is the flock of "the Shepherd and Overseer [*episkopon*] of your souls" (2:25). Watching, noted frequently in this study, is a comprehensive summary of shepherding tasks. It is the vigilant attention to threats that can disperse or destroy the flock. As in Acts 20:28, the sacrifice of the Shepherd-Lamb is the source of motivation for this vigilance.[25]

Looking especially at Acts 20:28, notice that these undershepherds are to *be vigilant over themselves first* (as they are not the Chief Shepherd). As the shepherds from Ezek 34:3 and 1 Tim 6:5–6 fed on the flock, these undershepherds must instead be mindful of their own tendency to use the flock for their own gain—something the Great Shepherd would never do. We, on the other hand, must reckon with the reality that *a potential tyrant and predator lives in all of us*. Second, *the Holy Spirit is the one who makes these*

---

25. Laniak, *Shepherds*, 232–33. Acts 20:17 and 20:28 draw all three terms for leadership ("elders," "overseers," "shepherds") together, seeming to equate them. See also Kinnison, *Transforming Pastoral Leadership*, 47.

flock members overseers—not a particular gender, not a title, not a degree, not an ordination, or a status. Third, *the flock is not a human's possession but God's*, purchased with God's own blood.²⁶ The value of the flock cannot be underscored more powerfully—and there is no sense of a human being owning "my flock," or "my congregation." Fourth, while less clear in the English prepositions, *these leaders are undershepherds from among the flock*. Fifth, *there is no singular leader of the church who is merely human*, there is always a group—these are not shepherd kings. And finally, while not explicit in this text, the theme throughout all of the leadership texts we might examine in the New Testament *is on living an exemplary life* (1 Pet 5:3; Titus 2:7).²⁷ This is consistent with their Spirit-empowerment that should be evidenced by the fruit of the Spirit.

Thinking in terms of authority and power, these leaders would have had some form of recognized epistemic and exemplary authority. Epistemic authority is to have more knowledge than another in a specific context, in this case, knowledge of sound teaching. Exemplary authority is to be worthy of imitation in how one lives, in this case, character that looks like Jesus through the empowerment of the Spirit. These kinds of authority are nonexecutive and do not carry with them the power to compel obedience—they are not powers over others. Instead, they are always testable, and this was likely much easier to do as the leaders would have been known within their communities and also would have likely met in more intimate settings and known those they led. They were tasked with caring for their communities and care is powerful. To care well, one must know what the needs of the other are, which means these undershepherds are trusted. The responsibilities of teaching, protecting, guiding, and caring for the community would have flowed from their legitimate nonexecutive authority. Such authority would involve power, but not a power *over* others but a power *to* bring life. This is because the primary role of leaders is to help equip the body to grow into their true source of life—their Chief Shepherd—Jesus Christ. In humility, undershepherds know that they are only instruments for God's purposes, serving God's flock.²⁸ Finally, due to that humility and because serving as leaders is the function given by the Spirit, these people can distinguish

---

26. "Some interpret this phrase to mean 'his own [Son's] blood' (see Eph. 2:13; Col. 1:20; 1 Pet. 1:18–19; Rev. 5:9). The grammar of the text suggests that it refers to God's blood, which gives prominence to how much it cost to redeem the church." Garland et al., *Acts*, 212.

27. Kinnison, *Transforming Pastoral Leadership*, 47–48, 52.

28. Kearsley, *Church, Community and Power*: "Caring here is not a tactic for gaining control but is itself a form of power and therefore a disinterested one. It is a genuine 'power to' rather than 'power over'" (115).

between their identity as children of God and their function to the body. If the flock shrinks, or a flock member disagrees or even disparages the undershepherd flock member, the undershepherd can remember that this is not their flock but God's. Such an understanding allows them to serve out of weakness, which is not powerlessness, but "sharing in the self-renouncing, servant-like, faith centered on God and on drawing down God's power."[29] Such power will look like vulnerability, humility, and love.

ESCHATOLOGICAL LAMB AND SHEPHERD-KING

When all is made right and heaven has come down to earth, the royal priesthood will reign *with* the Shepherd King (1 Cor 6:1–3; 2 Tim 2:12; Rev 5:10; 20:4–6).[30] This priesthood is from every tribe and tongue—a rich fulfillment of the Abrahamic covenant, and even before that—the royal-priestly calling given to all humanity as those made in God's image.[31] In Rev 7:17, we see Jesus as the Lamb who is also the Shepherd: "For the Lamb at the center of the throne will be their shepherd, and he will guide them to springs of the water of life, and God will wipe away every tear from their eyes." As Kinnison notes, "In this particular shepherd motif, Jesus is a loving, guiding shepherd who cares for those who have suffered and been martyred for following the lamb (Rev 6:9–11; 7:14–16; 1 Pet 2:19–25; 5:10–11). However, in the remaining usages of ποιμαίνω [*poimainō*] the lamb 'rules' over the nations as judge and king against a 'preying' enemy."[32] Thus, the seemingly unmet messianic expectations for the first coming are now fully realized as Jesus's justice and righteousness now reign. Notably, *poimainō* is never used as "rule" when referring to human-to-human relationships at any point in the New Testament.[33] Thus, I close with some implications and exhortations as we use shepherd imagery today.

---

29. Kearsley, *Church, Community and Power*, 223. Kearsley explains, "Paul himself came to see his unwanted powerlessness as a hidden power so that the divine efficacy ('power to') may also spring from that same site" (224).

30. "Indeed, the church will one day be conformed to the full likeness of Christ (1 John 3:2), which will include the resurrection of the body (1 Cor. 15:49) and reigning with Christ on earth (2 Tim. 2:12; Rev. 22:5)." Middleton, *New Heaven*, 69.

31. Middleton, *New Heaven*, 70, 282.

32. Kinnison, *Transforming Pastoral Leadership*, 46.

33. Kinnison, *Transforming Pastoral Leadership*, 44, 46.

IMPLICATIONS AND EXHORTATIONS

In my experience of hearing the shepherd metaphor growing up, it was rarely set in the larger context of the Chief Shepherd's rule, guidance, and care. The pastor-shepherds were often seen as in authority *over* the flock, and, given our tendency to think of greater and lesser value, the *human* shepherd is seen as superior to the *animal*-sheep. I have even heard pastors jokingly talk about how dumb sheep are, with clear implications about their own congregations! Yet, leaders are from among the flock and they cannot forget this.

Helpfully, theologian Quinten Kinnison notes shepherding is also done by following the flock or even moving within the flock. So, while I acknowledge that what I am about to say is a metaphor of a metaphor, in today's context (especially as far removed as most of us are from pastoral contexts), I think this can be helpful.

Because shepherding is about both protection of the flock from without and maintaining unity within, one of the main ways flock cohesion is strengthened in some Bedouin shepherding practices is through the use of bell sheep. This practice is when the shepherd chooses sheep that "willingly and lovingly follow the shepherd" and the shepherd puts bells on them.[34] As these sheep follow the shepherd, the rest of the flock hears their bells and have an example to follow. Given what we have seen from Acts 20, these leaders "lead by example from within the flock as they passionately follow the Chief Shepherd, with their lives 'clanging' for others to follow as well."[35] Perhaps modifying our understanding of undershepherds to be "clangers" (in a good way) to draw attention to the Chief Shepherd's leading can constructively contribute to an understanding of leadership that de-elevates the leader and re-centers the true Leader. Additionally, such an understanding opens up the responsibility of each member of the flock to participate in becoming bell sheep no matter our place in the flock. The congregation does not get off the hook as the leader is de-centered, but the flock is also expected to participate in flock life—maturation into Christ-likeness.

A flourishing flock will witness to its otherwordly ground of existence. To me, that is hope. One feature of such a hopeful witness is that, regardless of status or particularity, each member of the flock can be a bell sheep, not to increase their own status but to point people to the true Shepherd, who is the content of our hope. Thus, I believe we need to address our structural barriers—which are often conditioned by our understandings of authority

---

34. Kinnison, "Shepherd or One of the Sheep," 68.
35. Kinnison, "Shepherd or One of the Sheep," 89.

and power—so that every member of the flock will be able to live into the hope of her calling. This will require leaders to move from enabling to equipping the flock and for the flock members to confront their own consumerist expectations. Bell sheep do not do for other sheep what those sheep should do for themselves.

I wanted to conclude with landing this in lived experience of how some Baptist communities are seeking to equip more bell sheep. In a survey of Baptist leaders and non-leaders in Aotearoa New Zealand, I asked the question "What practices do you or those in leadership use to ensure power is used in healthy ways?"[36] Of the 103 responses to that survey, thirty-two participants could identify practices that supported the agency of those gathered in their local church—31 percent![37] These practices included listening, creating contexts of belonging, having open elder's meetings, prayer, discussion, disagreement, debate, free-for-all, questioning, sharing the pulpit, transparency in board/elder meetings, being OK with diverse views, everyone being able to speak and contribute, going slowly, those with power not always getting their way, being open to criticism, giving leadership away, making decisions across multiple mediums (like small groups), considering the vulnerable highly, having term limits for elders, having accountability of leadership to members and members to members, accepting you could be wrong, and having mechanisms for anonymous feedback. My favorite response was from a self-identified leader who said, "There is always an expectation that God can and does speak through anyone." By critically examining how we conceive of authority and power, I believe we can embody the hope of "walking together and watching over each other."[38]

CONCLUDING PRAYER

Such walking together and watching over one another requires a posture of dependence on the one who is our hope. Thus, to conclude, I would like to end with a prayer for anyone who considers themselves a sheep of Jesus's flock, especially those who lead within it:

---

36. This survey was approved by Carey Baptist College's Ethics Committee and participants consented to have this content used in my book on authority, as well as to help our leaders and churches become safer in light of abuses of power and authority. This chapter is seeking to help local churches become safer and also to flourish.

37. This could be further broken down into self-identified "leaders" and "non-leaders" with twelve of forty-two non-leaders identifying those practices, and twenty of sixty-one leaders being able to identify them.

38. Haymes et al., *On Being the Church*, 116.

Shepherd King, thank you for loving me. Thank you that with you, I have no lack. Please remind me that by resting in you, I have nothing to fear. Guard my heart against pride and the perpetual temptation to use my rod and my staff for rulership instead of care. Help me to keep watch over myself and to be receptive to others who see ways in which I am missing your voice and pointing more to me than to you. Please give me patience with members of your flock who may rub me the wrong way. Please give me humility to listen to other sheep who also know your voice, who hear you differently and sometimes even better than I do. It is only by your Spirit that I am enabled to serve this flock; please don't let me forget that. Help me to live a life that looks like yours, so that by seeing my life, they catch even a glimpse of you, the true Shepherd. Amen.

BIBLIOGRAPHY

Bauckham, Richard. *Living With Other Creatures*. Milton Keynes: Paternoster, 2011.

Chae, Young S. *Jesus as the Eschatological Davidic Shepherd: Studies in the Old Testament, Second Temple Judaism, and in the Gospel of Matthew*. Tübingen: Mohr Siebeck, 2006.

Garland, David E., et al. *Acts*. Grand Rapids: Baker, 2017.

Haymes, Brian, et al. *On Being the Church*. Studies in Baptist History and Thought 21. Milton Keynes: Paternoster, 2008.

Kearsley, Roy. *Church, Community, and Power*. London: Routledge, 2008.

Kinnison, Quentin. "Shepherd or One of the Sheep: Revisiting the Biblical Metaphor of the Pastorate." *Journal of Religious Leadership* 9 (2010) 59–91.

———. *Transforming Pastoral Leadership: Reimagining Congregational Relationships for Changing Contexts*. Eugene, OR: Wipf & Stock, 2016.

Laniak, Timothy S. *Shepherds After My Own Heart: Pastoral Traditions and Leadership in the Bible*. New Studies in Biblical Theology. Downers Grove, IL: IVP Academic, 2006.

Mann, T. W. *Divine Presence and Guidance in Israelite Traditions: The Typology of Exaltation*. Baltimore: Johns Hopkins University, 1977.

McKirland, Christa L. "Jesus, Agency, and the Life Led Well." *Studies in Christian Ethics* 36 (2023) 762–82.

Middleton, Richard J. *A New Heaven and a New Earth: Reclaiming Biblical Eschatology*. Grand Rapids: Baker Academic, 2014.

Studebaker, John A., Jr. *The Lord Is the Spirit: The Authority of the Holy Spirit in Contemporary Theology and Church Practice*. Eugene, OR: Pickwick, 2008.

Chapter 7

Compassionate Realism
Reclaiming the Church's Core Identity as a Hope-Filled Community of Healing and Restoration

Karen M. Kemp

INTRODUCTION

The life-giving way of life that is God's promise and provision itself emerges precisely in the midst of . . . concrete and specific locations, where it unsettles, comforts, disrupts, and reconfigures persons and communities through the gift of new creation.

—Dorothy C. Bass and Craig Dykstra

Practical theology arises from theological reflection on concrete situations and requires a level of personal engagement. As both a practical theologian and minister in a denomination that has been exposed by a New Zealand Royal Commission of Inquiry as a place that has enabled serious harm, I am especially motivated to unpack the hope-filled dimension of the church as a community of healing and restoration.[1]

It is fair to say that the current narrative around the church in Aotearoa poses a question mark over our identity as a community of healing and restoration. From the earliest days the church worldwide has been known as a place of refuge, healing, and restoration.[2] However, as Bass and Dykstra infer, it is not possible to talk about the church as a healing community without probing the current reality of a church that has become known as a place, in New Zealand and the United Kingdom at least,[3] where the very things that traditionally made it a haven for the wounded have tragically enabled harm. This chapter posits that at the heart of the current disruption lies the hope-filled possibility to recenter our true identity as Christ's reconciled and reconciling community.

So, the question is, how does a harm-enabling church reclaim its core identity as a community of healing and restoration? How does a church mired in "bad news" become hope-filled good news again? Healing and restoration lie at the very heart of what it means to be the people of God. We cannot talk about hope in a vacuum—hope only makes sense in the presence of brokenness. The good news of the church is less that it is free of brokenness, but rather that it embodies a healing gospel with compassionate realism in the midst of its own imperfect humanity.

This chapter explores this topic across three sections. First, it probes the conditions that contribute to the current state of affairs in Aotearoa, while recognizing that moral failure and harm are part of the human condition and have been present from the outset. Second, it locates the church in God's bigger story of reconciling all things in Christ Jesus. The litany of moral failure, toxic leadership, and abuse challenges the church to reclaim its core identity and purpose, and to embody both collective and individual dimensions of that calling in ways that engender hope and healing. This section explores what reconciliation is and is not and suggests that restorative practice is a necessary precursor to the transformation we seek both individually and collectively. The final section realigns both the posture and

---

1. The Royal Commission of Inquiry into Abuse in Care found that "instead of receiving care and support, children, young people and adults in care were exposed to unimaginable physical, emotional, mental and sexual abuse, severe exploitation and neglect. Abuse and neglect were widespread throughout the Inquiry period in State and faith-based care institutions." Royal Commission of Inquiry, "Executive Summary," 1–2.

2. Sittser, *Water*, 50–71.

3. In November 2024, Archbishop of Canterbury Justin Welby resigned in the wake of his ineffectual response to allegations of abuse against Anglican clergy. Aikman and Farley, "Archbishop of Canterbury Resigns."

practices of church ministry away from triumphalism toward a compassionate realism in recognition of the key role that leaders play in cultivating the church's faithfulness and fruitfulness in relation to its identity and calling as a restorative community.

BEING HERE NOW

In his book *Deep Survival: Who Lives, Who Dies, and Why*, Laurence Gonzales identifies the key to survival in a crisis is to "be here now,"[4] that is, to pause, look around and notice the landscape, the climatic conditions, the people, and resources at hand. If the church is to reclaim its core identity as a place of healing and restoration, it must begin with accurately naming this moment in place and time. To move forward the church needs to be clear where it is and how it got here.

The church in Aotearoa New Zealand is mired in stories of toxic leadership and sexual abuse.[5] The 2024 report of the Royal Commission of Inquiry into Abuse in Care sheds light on key dynamics that enabled the harm of vulnerable people in faith-based institutions. At the heart of these dynamics is a failure of leadership. Charlotte Cummings offers a sobering analysis of the church contexts that enabled the abuse: a lack of appreciation for the risks of unexamined, poorly differentiated power and contexts which were low in both accountability and support. This power was exercised within opaque and ambiguous hierarchies that fostered the "othering," which ultimately enabled harm. In addition, low cultural competence led to racism and a failure to uphold the personhood of those being served, creating a distance between those serving and those being served. Finally, a lack of diversity in leadership exacerbated tacit attitudes towards women, those with disabilities, and LGBTQI+ people.[6] While not all churches have

---

4. Gonzales, *Deep Survival*.

5. These stories are common across the Western church, but this chapter consciously locates itself in Aotearoa New Zealand.

6. The Royal Commission of Inquiry into Abuse in Care spanning the years 1950–1999 details a litany of harm enabled by structural and leadership failure to care for the most vulnerable. Charlotte Cummings offers a summary of the inquiry findings and implications for churches and faith-based charities in Rhema Media, "Wilberforce Foundation." Cummings locates responsibility for care with leaders at all levels. This responsibility includes ensuring training and accountability for those engaged in caring for vulnerable people. Cummings concludes, "This is our time as the church in New Zealand to go well beyond sorry. No matter who caused the harm, we as the people of the church of New Zealand all have a place in making it right. If you're a leader of a Christian charity you can be part of that effort. The effort to restore trust in the church in this nation, to give assurances of our commitment to the safety and wellbeing of

been implicated in the Royal Commission's report, most denominations are enacting the Commission's recommendations around external supervision of leaders, complaints processes, and staff screening and training. Many churches are also seeking ways to better honor Te Tiriti o Waitangi[7] and be more hospitable to non-European peoples. The challenge is that the church, the people of God, an alternative community embodying the in-breaking kingdom, is called to so much more than mere compliance with secular recommendations!

The 2023 Wilberforce Faith and Belief Survey provides a broader snapshot of the church in Aotearoa. The survey report paradoxically locates declining church attendance, nominalism, and poorly-embodied discipleship in a broader societal context of spiritual curiosity and openness to the Christian faith. The report shows the church in Aotearoa making well-received efforts to relieve suffering and a new generation that are warm to Christianity. It seems people both in and beyond the church long for a positive future but struggle to paint a picture of what that looks like. This lack of clarity communicates that Christians lack both transparency and congruence with their Christian values. It appears that people are not rejecting Christianity as much as the church's dissonant and poorly-embodied discipleship.[8]

Read together, these two reports paint a picture of a church, conditioned to see the wounded "out there," being confronted with the reality of its own brokenness and need for repentance, healing, and restoration. It is a time for self-examination, for humility in reckoning with the uncomfortable realization that, at its worst, "Christendom was a parody—a triumphalist caricature of who the church is called to be."[9] This is akin to a high-ropes trapeze moment, where the church must let go of its idealized version of itself and grasp the nettles of what's been exposed.[10] Here, Dietrich Bonhoeffer's caution is salutary:

> Those who love their dream of a Christian community more
> than the Christian community itself become destroyers of that

---

all people, and to minister to those impacted by abuse." Rhema Media, "Wilberforce Foundation," 11:32–12:02.

7. New Zealand's founding document: The Treaty of Waitangi.

8. Wilberforce Foundation, "Faith and Belief," 37.

9. Christopher Marshall, personal communication to author, Apr. 30, 2024. Quoted with permission.

10. At the very least, what's been exposed is a persistent Platonic dualism that continues to open the door to the duplicity running through our communities and leaders—a duplicity that has enabled harm.

Christian community, even though their personal intentions may be ever so honest, earnest, and sacrificial.[11]

And the Christian community, the church itself, is a "community of differents"[12] on a good day, and a "fellowship of the unformed . . . a community of unrefined, unfinished, conflict-loving, trouble-causing, sin committing, cranky hypocrites"[13] on a bad day. Furthermore, the church does not exist in isolation from the world. The cultural "soil" the church is planted in is itself poisoned by an ethic of growth and unbridled development that colludes with the messianic tendencies common to church leadership.

So, just how did the church get to this moment? A combination of the long reach of Platonic dualism in the Western church and its propensity to foster a disembodied discipleship, male-dominated heroic patterns of leadership, and attractional church models whose *telos* is growth, all contribute. Furthermore, Broughton's 2021 study of the Anglican Church in Australia identifies leader isolation, vocational insecurity, and the rise of virtual connection over in-person communication as contributors to "individuals whose ministry life is turned in on itself—[Augustine's] *incurvatus in se*."[14] The outcome is a deepening "spiritual anaemia and systemic anxiety"[15]— significant barriers to becoming a restorative community. If the church is to be a place of healing for its own and beyond it must address these issues.

This moment challenges the church to weigh the tensions between the sacred calling of life in Christ and the need to work this calling out in the presence of brokenness and sin; between the propriety of victims' cries for justice, and the gospel imperative to restore *contrite* offenders;[16] between necessary lament and undaunted hope in the transforming power of the gospel. How the church holds these tensions is key to both unity in Christ and the capacity to become a place of healing and restoration for those seeking wholeness and open to the gospel but wary of the church.

---

11. Bonhoeffer, *Life Together*, 36.
12. McKnight, "Church as a Community."
13. Carlson and Leuken, *Renovation of the Church*, 107.
14. Broughton, "Pastoral Supervision," 182.
15. Broughton, "Pastoral Supervision," 182. For a closer look at systemic anxiety see, Friedman, *Failure of Nerve*; and Friedman, *Generation to Generation*.
16. Contrary to recent examples of perpetrators claiming repentance and being both "forgiven" and "restored" by their superiors with little or no contact with their victim(s), Scripture is clear that true repentance means an active turning away from harmful behavior (Luke 15:11–32), forgiveness is always and only the prerogative of the victim, and restoration the outcome of a robust restorative process. See Matt 18, nuanced by the Levitical law where a woman raped was to be believed despite the absence of witnesses (Deut 22).

HEALING, RESTORATION, RECONCILIATION, AND TRANSFORMATION EXPLORED

Healing and restoration are not unique to the church, but a Christian understanding is particular. Any discussion of healing and restoration needs to be located in the church's call to be a reconciled and reconciling community. The apostle Paul is unequivocal:

> So, from now on we regard no one from a worldly point of view. Though we once regarded Christ in this way, we do so no longer. Therefore, if anyone is in Christ, the new creation has come: The old has gone, the new is here! All this is from God, who reconciled us to himself through Christ and gave us the ministry of reconciliation: that God was reconciling the world to himself in Christ, not counting people's sins against them. And he has committed to us the message of reconciliation. We are therefore Christ's ambassadors, as though God were making his appeal through us. (2 Cor 5:16–20 NIV)

So, what is the connection between reconciliation and restoration and healing? Three questions nuance a response. First, just what is being healed and restored? We cannot talk about healing without exploring the notions of sin and shalom. Much more than peace, shalom encompasses the notion of right relationship across the whole of life: "the webbing together of God, humans, and all creation in justice, fulfilment, and delight" in a *"universal flourishing, wholeness, and delight."*[17] Ultimately, shalom is "the way things ought to be."[18] Here, peace is not merely the absence of conflict, nor the removal of an enemy, but the fruit of relational healing and restoration: reconciliation.

Sin on the other hand, is essentially "wrecked relationship"[19] or a "vandalism of shalom."[20] Cornelius Plantinga describes what this "vandalism" looks like:

> [Sin] is the missing of a target, a wandering from the path, a straying from the fold. Sin is a hard heart, and a stiff neck. Sin is blindness and deafness. It is both the overstepping of a line and the failure to reach it—both transgression and shortcoming. Sin is a beast crouching at the door. In sin, people attack or evade or neglect their divine calling. . . . Sin is disruption

---

17. Plantinga, *Not the Way*, 10; italics in original.
18. Plantinga, *Not the Way*, 10.
19. Brown Taylor, *Speaking of Sin*, 57.
20. Plantinga, *Not the Way*, 7.

of created harmony and then resistance to divine restoration of that harmony. Above all, sin disrupts and resists the vital human relation to God.[21]

This brings us to the second question: What does biblical reconciliation entail? Reconciliation is ultimately the restoration of wrecked relationships. While many in the helping professions seek to support the "wellbeing" of their clients, a biblical understanding says healing is not complete until relationships are reconciled and shalom is restored. Reconciliation is an arduous journey during which identity is questioned, deep wounds are probed, and behavior is changed. It stretches the imagination in an exercise of hope. Geoff Broughton's restorative exploration of Jesus's post-resurrection reinstatement of Simon Peter in John's Gospel[22] plots four key moments on the journey which are especially pertinent to the discussion:

1. *The restoring Jesus reveals Peter's failings and failure—relationally, in the context of hospitality.* Peter's denial is seen as a three-fold relational failure: of loyalty to Jesus, of vocation, and of leadership in relation to his fellow disciples.[23]

2. *The restoring Jesus remembers failings and failure—rightly.* Remembering rightly depends on hospitality, and recognition of the presence of Christ. Only then can the courageous task of re-telling the stories of failure truly begin.[24]

3. *The restoring Jesus interrogates failings and failure—rigorously.*[25] In the context of abundance and generous welcome Jesus's questions intensify to get to the heart of what has gone wrong. Here, Jesus steps Peter through shame that might seek to hide failure, down to the deeper hurt of relational breakdown. It is only here that true forgiveness and reconciliation is possible.

4. *The restoring Jesus resurrects fidelity and following—reparatively.*[26] Here, on the beach, it is "reconciliation and reinstatement. Peter's faith in Jesus, his calling as a disciple, and his commission as an apostle is

---

21. Plantinga, *Not the Way*, 5.
22. John 21: 15–25.
23. Broughton, *Practical Christology*, 103.
24. Schreiter, *Ministry of Reconciliation*.
25. Broughton, *Practical Christology*, 105.
26. Broughton, *Practical Christology*, 107.

restored and re-created."[27] Seen in this way, reconciliation is a genesis event because it negotiates and inaugurates a new relationship.[28]

This brings us to the third question: What is the connection between restoration and transformation? Transformative moments, like Simon Peter's, provide fresh insight, shift thinking and position in relation to key issues, and change behavior, responses, and outcomes—in short, the person emerges both in a different place and as a changed person.[29] Seen in this way, the church's task to seek the restoration of shalom through the pursuit of reconciliation is critical to the ongoing transformation of both church and society, in its vision to be part of the in-breaking shalom of the kingdom of God, a sign of hope in a fractured world.

This all sounds inspiring, but as noted earlier, reconciliation—healing and restoration—is an arduous journey that will test both imagination and resolve, especially in a climate of cynicism, spiritual anemia, and anxiety. Clearly, more than inspiration and good intentions is needed to embody the hopefulness of the reconciled and reconciling community of Paul's letter to Corinth.[30] Plantinga highlights the need to grasp both the pervasive enormity of sin and God's limitless resolute grace:

> To speak of sin by itself, to speak of it apart from the realities of creation and grace, is to forget the resolve of God. . . . But to speak of grace without sin . . . is to trivialize the cross of Christ. . . . For the sober truth is that without full disclosure on sin, the gospel of grace becomes impertinent, unnecessary, and finally uninteresting.[31]

We turn now to the heart of this discussion—to enjoin a compassionate realism as *habitus*,[32] shaping both the posture and practice needed to hold this tension, foster healing, and embody the gospel of grace and hope in the current climate.

---

27. Broughton, *Practical Christology*, 107.
28. Kemp, "Transforming Congregational Conflict."
29. Weld, *Practical Guide*, 37,
30. 2 Cor 5:11—6:13.
31. Plantinga, *Not the Way*, 199.
32. The Aristotelian idea of *hexis* or *habitus* suggests that "character is a set of dispositions molded, fixed, and crystallized through repetition." Deary, *How We Are*, 181.

COMPASSIONATE REALISM

Compassionate realism is not a term that's been applied in the church before; it is a new term that this chapter conceives. However, two related terms are useful here. First, Oxford philosopher Colin Marshall's "compassionate moral realism" is a response to core questions in both normative ethics (Why should we be moral?) and metaethics (What is morality itself?).[33] Second, New Testament scholar Chris Marshall's "compassionate justice" comes from reading the parables of the Good Samaritan and the Prodigal Son through a restorative justice lens.[34] With these two connections in mind, we explore both compassion and realism before bringing them together to inform posture and practice in response to the current moment.

Colin Marshall's philosophical naturalistic[35] metaethic of compassion locates morality at the place where both compassion and reality meet: "Being moral partly involves being in touch with certain aspects of reality, and being in touch is an irreplaceable epistemic good . . . compassionate reactions are a way of being in touch in [this] sense." Furthermore, "Being good involves seeing the world as it really is and failing to be good involves a kind of perceptual failure."[36] While this naturalistic view is not grounded in Christian understandings of compassion, it does connect ways of seeing and being in touch with the world, with the capacity to be compassionate in our responses to it. This is significant for the discussion at hand. But first, to a thicker understanding of compassion.

Chris Marshall identifies key New Testament terms for compassion: *splangchna* (a deep affective distress felt in the pit of the belly) and *eleos* (the act of performing mercy):

> "Having compassion" designates the emotional reality and "doing mercy" its practical outworking, and it is the combination of the affective and the ethical that signals the Samaritan's exemplary character. . . . Compassion may be defined as *an experience of emotional pain and moral concern occasioned by the awareness of, and identification with, another subject's suffering or unhappiness.*[37]

---

33. Marshall, *Compassionate Moral Realism*.

34. Marshall, *Compassionate Justice*.

35. "Moral naturalism" is a term with a variety of meanings in ethics, but it usually refers to the version of moral realism according to which moral facts are natural facts. Lutz, "Moral Naturalism."

36. Blanchard, Review, 92.

37. Marshall, *Compassionate Justice*, 253; emphasis in original.

This emotional pain is participatory, a suffering-with that brings the pain home as if it were one's own. This participation is not possible without a conscious and costly awareness—an imaginative entering in, a decision to identify even at personal cost to oneself. Marshall contends that such identification is constrained by our limited human capacity to enter into another's inner world,[38] but it's only by doing so that we can "begin to grasp the other person's needs and try to meet them." Significantly, genuine compassion "remains focused on the welfare of the sufferer, not on one's own empathetic discomfort."[39] Marshall concludes that compassion is "more than a vague *caring about* human suffering in general; it is a positive response of *caring for* concrete instances of pain and misery."[40]

A biblical understanding of compassion must also include the Hebrew notion of *ḥesed*, commonly translated as steadfast kindness and mercy. With no English equivalent, it is easy to overlook the richness of this term. Routledge connects *ḥesed* to *raḥămîm* (kindness) but notes that *ḥesed* "is more than the emotional, benevolent response to the need of another; it also includes loyalty and obligation: a sense of duty and faithful commitment to do what is right."[41] This *běrît* (covenant) dimension of *ḥesed* is especially pertinent to instances of harm within the church:

> As well as being God's lovingkindness expressed towards those who stand in right relationship with him, *ḥesed* is also of vital significance as that in accordance with which God forgives those who have broken the terms of the relationship and by which he ensures that the breakdown is not permanent. This corresponds to the two-way link between *ḥesed* and *běrît* in which *ḥesed* both derives from the relationship and is the means by which the relationship is enabled to continue even though, because of the unfaithfulness of one party, it might properly be terminated.[42]

Significantly, Routledge goes on to say that "members of God's covenant community are to show the same *ḥesed* in their relationships with

---

38. And I would add, by our postmodern propensity to see ourselves through social media projections—either glossed over to present a successful image or gilding the lily for effect—this capacity to see ourselves as we truly are needs to be reignited. The primary way we do this is in community—the church.
39. Marshall, *Compassionate Justice*, 254.
40. Marshall, *Compassionate Justice*, 254.
41. Routledge, "Prayer, Sacrifice, and Forgiveness," 19.
42. Routledge, "Ḥesed as Obligation," 192.

one another."⁴³ God's *ḥesed* is to be embodied in the life of the covenant community as a foretaste of the coming Messianic age.⁴⁴

This understanding of *ḥesed* nuances the question of what, epistemologically, constitutes grounds for compassion. Drawing on Nussbaum's work,⁴⁵ Chris Marshall identifies three epistemological components: "an assessment of seriousness, a judgement about culpability, and a consciousness of common participation in the frailties of the human condition."⁴⁶ These three components make sense in stimulating compassion for victims of abuse. The Parable of the Good Samaritan enjoins such compassion even when contrary to social scientists' observations of the biases inherent in the "bystander effect,"⁴⁷ the victims are either unknown to us or outside our social grouping. However, Marshall's study of the Parable of the Prodigal Son connects with our understanding of *ḥesed* in its thicker, costly, and more demanding compassion for the contrite perpetrator who ultimately, carefully, also needs to be restored. If the church is to be a healing community, it must be so for all who would genuinely seek it—without prejudice—while also maintaining safety for the flock.

If compassion for the victim requires a deep awareness of *their* plight in relation to the three epistemological dimensions noted earlier, compassion for a contrite offender can only come from a deep awareness of one's own brokenness, including but not limited to one's part in what's happened. In other words, this awareness can occur when the three epistemological components of compassion are applied to oneself with an unflinching realism about one's own condition.⁴⁸ Taken in turn, an assessment of serious-

---

43. E.g. Hos 12:6(7); Mic 6:8; Zec 7:9. Routledge, "*Ḥesed* as Obligation," 195.

44. Isa 16:5.

45. See Nussbaum, "Compassion"; and Nussbaum, *Upheavals of Thought*.

46. Marshall, *Compassionate Justice*, 261.

47. Marshall, *Compassionate Justice*, 102–6. Marshall helpfully summarizes research findings on the unwillingness to get involved associated with the "bystander effect" in cases of public victimization: (1) a concern for personal safety and fear of retaliation; (2) ambiguity around whether the victim needs or deserves help, often exacerbated by biases associated with dissimilarity of race, class, rank, religion, or physical appearance; (3) a "diffusion of responsibility" brought on by the presence of other people, (4) anonymity; and confrontingly, (5) hurry, especially that associated with relentlessly "competing demands on one's attention and resources."

48. Jesus's statement in Matt 7:1—"Do not judge, so that you may not be judged" (NRSV)—is less an instruction to suspend judgement, and more a precursor to what follows: Jesus uses the ludicrous image of someone trying to remove a speck from another's eye while having their own vision obscured by a log to underscore the importance of self-judgement before judging others. Clearly, seeing others truthfully requires us to rightly see ourselves first. When we see ourselves truthfully before God, we realize our need for God's mercy and compassion and more readily see this need in others. In

ness requires that we locate ourselves in a church which has fallen far short of the calling to be a healing and restorative community. Our shortcomings here not only impact our common life but our witness before a fractured world.[49] When it comes to a judgement about culpability, Udine Kayser's broad definition of what constitutes an "offender" is confronting because it incorporates the perpetrator, victimizer, bystander,[50] and those who benefit from the system.[51] Seen in this way, we who call ourselves the people of God are all in some way implicated in the church's current predicament. Finally, a consciousness of common participation in the frailties of the human condition requires that we be realistic and truthful about our own brokenness. Only when we grasp the reality of our own humanity can we mitigate the tendencies to self-righteous indignation, judgmentalism, and vindictiveness. This leads us to the realism dimension of this discussion.

Colin Marshall's dual assertion—that compassionate reactions are a way of being in touch with reality and that our capacity for goodness is tied to our capacity to see the world as it really is[52]—suggests that, from a worldview which centers Christ as the ultimate reality, a truthful sense of our own standing before God and others is key to our embodiment of compassionate realism. But here the notion of realism becomes more complex than even Colin Marshall asserts because we cannot talk about seeing ourselves truthfully without confronting the reality that all our seeing is contingent on not only the limitations of being human but the distortions of our own sinfulness. The limitations of our humanity are demonstrated by the Johari Window[53]—there are things about myself others know because I choose to disclose them, there are things about myself I'm unaware of but that others clearly see, there are things I know about myself that I choose to keep hidden, and finally, that there are things neither I nor others know about me—these can only be discovered in relationship with God and neighbor.

---

much the same way as the unforgiving servant in Matt 18 was unable to show mercy because he failed to realize the magnitude of his own debt and the corollary overabundance of the king's mercy and compassion, so our capacity to show compassion is tied to a truthful estimation of ourselves.

49. Stanley Hauerwas's challenge comes to mind when he notes that if those of us who say we follow a reconciling God fail to be reconciled to one another, then the broken world looking on and longing for an alternative can be forgiven for concluding that the God we follow is in fact a false god who doesn't deliver. Hauerwas, "Peacemaking," 325.

50. See note 16 above for a description of the "bystander effect." [x-ref]

51. Kayser, "Creating the Past."

52. Blanchard, Review, 190, 92.

53. Luft and Ingham, *Group Processes*.

This "discovering" of who we are and who God is never ends because as Miroslav Volf and Matthew Croasmun note,

> There is "unknowing" in all our knowing of God, and there is "untruth" in all our legitimate truth claims about God. . . . We can know and articulate in positive terms the Christian vision of a flourishing life—and the truth of God and the truth of Jesus Christ, as well—only in a broken, unknowing kind of way, stretching ourselves toward something we see "in a mirror, dimly," and "know only in part" (1 Cor. 13:12).[54]

When it comes to confronting the reality of our brokenness, Catholic theologian Robert Schreiter's work with victims of torture in Central America raises questions about the roots of the human capacity to injure others.[55] Echoing the notion of Satan as the father of all lies,[56] Schreiter sees sin as the decision to embrace and enact Satan's "narrative of the lie"—a distortion of the truth of who we are in relation to God and others. In other words, sin is essentially relational so part of the "reality" we must confront is our propensity to justify our actions by choosing to believe a lie about others; to "dehumanize" the other by "demonizing" them so that the seriousness of our actions and our own culpability is diminished, and, critically, our own humanity is compromised.[57] If Colin Marshall is right, the way to break this vicious cycle is through acts of compassion that require first and foremost an identification with the truth of the "other" as a fellow human being made in the image of God.[58]

What then is the shape of this "realism" that we must cultivate? How do we construe ourselves and the world rightly, in such a way that compassion is not only felt but enacted? Living as we do within the tension of the in-breaking kingdom, construing the world rightly, according to Volf and Croasmun, involves living with the tensions of a good world created by God, yet "malformed" by sin; of a world indwelled by Christ yet incompletely being redeemed; and of a world infused with the hope of eschatological consummation that paradoxically brings a "sober awareness of our

---

54. Volf and Croasmun, *Life of the World*, 94–95.

55. Schreiter, *Reconciliation*.

56. John 8:44.

57. Schreiter, *Reconciliation*, 29–38.

58. Drawing on the story of Jacob's and Esau's reconciliation and his own peacebuilding work in Central American war zones, Mennonite peacebuilder and scholar John Paul Lederach argues that forgiveness and reconciliation begins with looking for and finding "that of God in the face of the other." Lederach, *Journey Toward Reconciliation*.

incompleteness."[59] Volf and Croasmun conclude that "awareness of these tensions makes it possible to willingly accept certain limitations to flourishing without giving up on the vision of its fullness."[60]

Having identified the contours of a *posture* of compassionate realism, we turn to the practices that support its embodiment. How might compassionate realism contribute to our capacity to accept the limitations within which we seek our own and others' flourishing without allowing these limitations to diminish the hope of the peaceable Kingdom? Compassionate realism is not something that can be legislated, although safeguarding policies and restorative processes are an essential communal outworking of it. Compassionate realism is cultivated in spaces where people are seen, heard, and connected to others in community.

First, the need to be seen: people need to know they are seen for who they are; that their identity is not narrowed to the shame of either their experience of being harmed or of causing harm. Chronicling stories of survivors of abuse, journalist Aaron Smale says, "I didn't 'break' the story. It had been hiding in plain sight for decades"—we chose not to see![61] "Seeing things as they really are" here means being present to what's happened and entering into the suffering with its attendant mystery. Presence—the act of being with the sufferer—says Sam Wells, is mostly wordless and empty-handed. It means

> being close, showing up, not being deterred or scared away, making a journey to see with one's own eyes, not flinching from the new reality . . . taking time to let it sink in, dwell on its unique features, begin to witness the bifurcation of the story that would have been without it . . . and what seems, at least initially, to be the smaller and more impoverished story that ensues from it.[62]

Being with the sufferer is primarily about taking time, as long as it takes for the person to experience being seen and recognized as a human being gloriously created in God's image yet impacted by sin.

It takes time to come to terms with what's happened: the victim needs time to grasp their own powerlessness, to "discover how to function despite it," and the contrite offender must come to terms with "the power they have and the damage they've proved capable of."[63] It is only in the context of be-

---

59. Volf and Croasmun, *Life of the World*, 163.
60. Volf and Croasmun, *Life of the World*, 163.
61. Smale, "State Care."
62. Wells, *Incarnational Ministry*, 168–69.
63. Wells, *Incarnational Ministry*, 147.

ing accompanied, of being seen, that the story of what's happened can begin to be re-narrated and the possibility of healing—of memories, of victim, of wrongdoer—can be contemplated. This brings us to the need to be heard if compassionate realism is to grow.

Second, the need to be heard: once again, Aaron Smale's report of meeting with survivors is confronting:

> There was a deathly silence. About forty Māori men, all of them gang members, had gathered at a marae.[64] The silence wasn't hostility, it was vulnerability. Because these men had been silenced since childhood and didn't know how to articulate the trauma that had dominated their lives ever since. They didn't know what to say in response to someone acknowledging, even obliquely, what had happened to them.[65]

The opportunity to be not only genuinely seen but also heard relies on honest self-examination in relation to wounds received and inflicted. Time-full, accepting, grace-filled spaces where the truth of what has happened can be recalled with "radical candor"[66] in ways that capture its meaning for both the present and the future, without unduly constraining the possibilities of either.[67] This is essentially how we hold the tension between the harsh realities of harm and the hopeful possibility of healing and restoration. Here, Colin Marshall's compassionate moral realism resonates with Dietrich Bonhoeffer who said, "telling the truth is not solely a matter of moral character; it is also a matter of correct appreciation of the real situations."[68] This, too, is nuanced because, as Schreiter notes,

> Situations that need to be addressed in reconciliation have often been distorted by lies told about the victims and the wrongdoers and by a pall of silence thrown over the wrongdoing to hide or disguise it and its effects. Part of rebuilding the narrative and restoring the agency of victims involves speaking the truth about what has happened . . . [so that] a future can be built that overcomes the suffering of the past.[69]

---

64. Māori meeting ground.

65. Smale, "State Care."

66. A term coined by Kim Scott: to care personally and challenge directly—to speak plainly and truthfully—without judgment. Interestingly, Scott also uses the term "compassionate candor," which "engages the heart (care personally) and the mind (challenge directly)." Scott, *Radical Candor*, pref.

67. Schreiter, "Reconciliation and Prophetic Dialogue," 129–30.

68. Bonhoeffer, *Ethics*, 363.

69. Schreiter, "Reconciliation and Prophetic Dialogue," 130.

Getting to the truth of what's happened, or as Christine Pohl puts it, "the numerous aspects of truth . . . operative in most communities," requires not only "speaking hard things, but discerning the whole picture with gentleness, humility, and patience."[70] Truthfulness is about "more than reliability and factual accuracy,"[71] it involves an acknowledgment that the truth—the whole picture—is co-narrated by all the actors in the story. That "behind every behavior lies a story, and every story cries out for grace."[72] This is especially hard in situations where harm has occurred, and compassionate realism functions here as both prerequisite and fruit of such co-narration. It is in the truthful telling and retelling of the story in the presence of others and of "the other" that the contours of harm can be acknowledged, lamented,[73] and contained. This is the place where toxic power and self-interest is disrupted,[74] trust can begin to be restored, and relationships reconfigured.

Remembering truthfully acknowledges the harm done to the victims and the propriety of their anger and distress and discharges the self-blame and shame they often carry.[75] But remembering truthfully also allows contrite offenders[76] to accept responsibility both for the harm caused and the obligation to put things right so that their wrongdoing is contained and they are kept from being either demonized or dehumanized in the retelling. More than this, accepting responsibility makes room for the offender's "disordered desires [to be] transformed toward friendship across lines of estrangement."[77] Seen in this way, being heard is essential to both victim and offender's capacity to contemplate partnering together for the sake of imagining a future where the harm no longer dominates.[78] This leads to the

---

70. Pohl, *Living into Community*, 115.

71. Pohl, *Living into Community*, 116.

72. McKnight and Barringer, *PIVOT*, 195.

73. Walter Brueggemann sees lament as the antidote to denial and cover-up—only grief expressed in lament permits healing and newness. Brueggemann, *Hopeful Imagination*, 131.

74. Katongole and Rice, *Reconciling All Things* 105.

75. Marshall, *All Things Reconciled*, 125.

76. It's important to stress that offenders must be genuinely contrite—restorative practice requires careful preparation of all concerned to ascertain readiness for these risky conversations.

77. Katongole and Rice, *Reconciling All Things*, 102.

78. The very process of restoring the penitent offender is an exercise in compassionate realism and an embodied reminder of the reality that we are on a journey of transformation—a *haerenga* (journey) that relies on compassionate realism both to hold us together in the solidarity of the broken and reconciled and to keep us from harming each other.

third dimension of cultivating compassionate realism, the need for people to be connected in community.

Third, the need to be connected: being connected is both precursor to and fruit of being seen and heard truthfully. In an age where the language of covenant is all but lost, life is governed by contracts that reinforce the prevailing consumer mindset—contracts have out clauses and courts of appeal for when things go wrong. But whenever promises are broken, the relationships are devalued, diminished, and undermined.[79] It follows, then, that a key to staying connected in community is *hesed*-like relational fidelity—the commitment to stay at the table even when things are difficult.[80] If cultivating compassionate realism includes people feeling seen for who they are and heard in the context of truth-telling, then communities of relational fidelity are the space where this can happen.

Covenant *hesed*-shaped communities are built on faithful relationships, but because covenants are dependent on volitions beyond our control,[81] there are tensions. In the absence of a contract, a commitment to stay connected for the sake of a shared vision can open the way for abuses of power.[82] Moreover, high mobility and fragmented lifestyles with competing demands for both time and attention make both the rootedness and attentiveness that covenantal relationships require hard to maintain. In this context, a compassionate realism accepts the tensions and anticipates that commitments will go unmet, people will falter, and disappointments will come. Compassionate realism is once again precursor and fruit: precursor to seeing things as they really are but also the fruit of finding ways to stay connected that ameliorate the tensions.

Here, Sam Wells's reframing of both contract and covenant embodies a compassionate realism:

> Care and detail over contracts is a form of love towards those we don't know very well. It's a recognition that life is full of unexpected pitfalls, and contracts are a way of holding one another to honesty and honour in the face of temptation and distraction. Contracts give us security and trust. We should always aspire for

---

79. Pohl, *Living into Community*, 78.

80. Staying at the table for Christians includes the Lord's Table, the Eucharist. It is beyond the scope of this discussion, but there's much to be learned from reflecting on the ways Communion can hold community strong even in the midst of disagreement and pain. For an exploration of what this might constitute, see Porter, *Spirit and Art*.

81. Wells, *Learning to Dream Again*, 41–42.

82. For a recent example, see Dine, "Independent Review"; and NZ Herald, "Founders of Arise Church."

every relationship to become a covenant, but we should never let any relationship fall below the level of a contract.[83]

Seen in this way, contracts are a way of being attentive to the safeguarding of our most vulnerable members—including those who are susceptible to harming others. Restorative Circles have much to offer here. Circles involving whole communities impacted by harm ask: What has happened? How have you been impacted? What do you think needs to happen to make things right? What part are you willing to play?[84] All voices are heard, and solutions are negotiated and owned. The Royal Commission's recommendations are important but only as a starting point on which to build covenantal relationships.

CONCLUSION

This chapter began by asking what a compassionate realism might contribute to a church called to be a community of healing and restoration, to a place where the "life-giving way of life that is God's promise and provision" can emerge to "unsettle, comfort, disrupt, and reconfigure persons and communities through the gift of new creation."[85] Compassionate realism requires a posture of humility and openness to the contrite other, regardless of how they are located in relation to the community. Compassionate realism requires adopting a posture that doesn't deny the realities of our shared human condition but finds solidarity in it and the will to persevere in the hope of the eschaton—especially in tough times.

However, this posture must be cultivated if it is to support such a hopeful reconfiguring. Our capacity for compassionate realism grows whenever people are seen for who they truly are, when the truth of their lives is heard, and when they understand themselves to be connected through relationships of fidelity and trust. When, as realism anticipates, such relationships are damaged, compassionate realism functions as a foil for the inevitable shame that accrues, as a transforming initiative.[86] It is something we exercise that breaks the vicious cycles we so easily get into. As such, compassionate realism is both precursor and outcome of people knowing they are seen, heard, and connected, especially in the midst of brokenness. It has the

83. Wells, *Learning to Dream Again*, 44.

84. For practical examples of a restorative framework applied in faith communities, see Vennen and Braganza, "Can We Talk."

85. Bass and Dykstra, eds., *For Life Abundant*, 356.

86. This term was introduced by Glen Stassen and David Gushee in their book on the Sermon on the Mount, *Kingdom Ethics*.

potential to unite us in the solidarity of the broken and reconciled and keep us from further harming each other. And here ultimately is the hope-filled good news of the gospel. It is through such authentic, paradoxical, costly, and compassionate realism that the shalom of God's kingdom continues to leaven our relationships, our communities, and our world.

BIBLIOGRAPHY

Aikman, Ian, and Harry Farley. "Archbishop of Canterbury Resigns over Church Abuse Scandal." BBC, Nov. 13, 2024. https://www.bbc.com/news/articles/c4gvpyzxvjp0.

Bass, Dorothy C., and Craig Dykstra, eds. *For Life Abundant: Practical Theology, Theological Education, and Christian Ministry*. Grand Rapids: Eerdmans, 2008.

Blanchard, Joshua. Review of *Compassionate Moral Realism* by Colin Marshall. *Journal of Moral Philosophy* 18 (2021) 190–93. https://brill.com/view/journals/jmp/18/2/article-p190_190.xml.

Bonhoeffer, Dietrich. *Ethics*. New York: MacMillan, 1955.

———. *Life Together and Prayerbook of the Bible*. Translated by Daniel W. Bloesch. Edited by Geffrey B. Kelly. Dietrich Bonhoeffer Works 5. Minneapolis: Augsburg Fortress, 2004.

Broughton, Geoff. "Pastoral Supervision for Safe Churches." *Journal of Anglican Studies* 19 (2021) 181–92.

———. *A Practical Christology for Pastoral Supervision*. Explorations in Practical, Pastoral and Empirical Theology. Abingdon: Routledge, 2021.

Brown Taylor, Barbara. *Speaking of Sin: The Lost Language of Salvation*. Cambridge, MA: Cowley 2000.

Brueggemann, Walter. *Hopeful Imagination: Prophetic Voices in Exile*. Philadelphia: Fortress, 1986.

Carlson, Kent, and Mike Leuken. *Renovation of the Church: What Happens When a Seeker Church Discovers Spiritual Formation*. Downers Grove, IL: IVP, 2011.

Deary, Vincent. *How We Are: The Force of Habit and the Work of Change*. Dublin: Penguin, 2015.

Dine, Jonty. "Independent Review Paints Damning Picture of Arise Church Abuse Allegations." RNZ, Aug. 17, 2022. https://www.rnz.co.nz/news/national/472998/independent-review-paints-damning-picture-of-arise-church-abuse-allegations.

Friedman, Edwin H. *A Failure of Nerve: Leadership in the Age of the Quick Fix*. New York: Seabury 2007.

———. *Generation to Generation: Family Process in Church and Synagogue*. New York: Guilford, 1985.

Gonzales, Laurence. *Deep Survival: Who Lives, Who Dies, and Why*. New York: Norton 2003.

Hauerwas, Stanley. "Peacemaking: The Virtue of the Church (1985)." In *The Hauerwas Reader/Stanley Hauerwas*, edited by J. Berkman and M. Cartwright, 318–26. Durham: Duke University Press, 2001.

Katongole, Emmanuel, and Chris Rice. *Reconciling All Things: A Christian Vision for Justice, Peace, and Healing*. Downers Grove, IL: IVP, 2008.

Kayser, Udine. "Creating the Past—Improvising the Present." Honors thesis, University of Cape Town, 1998.

Kemp, Karen M. "Transforming Congregational Conflict: An Integrated Framework for Understanding and Addressing Conflict in Christian Faith Communities." MA thesis, Victoria University Wellington, 2010.

Lederach, John Paul. *The Journey Toward Reconciliation*. Scottdale, PA: Herald 1999.

Luft, Joseph, and Harry Ingham. *Group Processes: An Introduction to Group Dynamics*. Palo Alto, CA: National, 1955.

Lutz, Matthew. "Moral Naturalism." Stanford Encyclopedia of Philosophy, Jun. 12, 2024. https://plato.stanford.edu/entries/naturalism-moral/.

Marshall, Christopher. *All Things Reconciled: Essays on Restorative Justice, Religious Violence, and the Interpretation of Scripture*. Eugene, OR: Wipf and Stock, 2018.

———. *Compassionate Justice: An Interdisciplinary Dialogue with Two Gospel Parables on Law, Crime, and Restorative Justice*. Eugene, OR: Cascade, 2012.

Marshall, Colin. *Compassionate Moral Realism*. Oxford: Oxford University Press, 2018.

McKnight, Scot, and Laura Barringer. *Pivot: The Priorities, Practices, and Powers That Can Transform Your Church into a Tov Culture*. Carol Stream, IL: Tyndale, 2023.

McKnight, Scott. "The Church as a Community of Differents." Paper presented at the Mission of the Church in the 21st Century conference, Laidlaw College, Auckland. New Zealand, May 7-8, 2014.

Nussbaum, Martha C. "Compassion: The Basic Social Emotion." *Social Philosophy and Policy* 13 (1996) 27-58.

———. *Upheavals of Thought: The Intelligence of Emotions*. Cambridge: Cambridge University Press, 2001.

NZ Herald. "Founders of Arise Church Resign amid Abuse Allegations." *The New Zealand Herald*, May 26, 2022. https://www.nzherald.co.nz/nz/founders-of-arise-church-resign-amid-abuse-allegations/MMSYFEMRKJOOYLQLR6WG226AAI/.

Plantinga, Cornelius. *Not the Way It's Supposed to Be: A Breviary of Sin*. Grand Rapids, Michigan: Eerdmans, 1995.

Pohl, Christine D. *Living into Community: Cultivating Practices That Sustain Us*. Grand Rapids: Eerdmans, 2012.

Porter, Thomas W. *The Spirit and Art of Conflict Transformation: Creating a Culture of Just Peace*. Nashville: Upper Room, 2010.

Rhema Media, "Wilberforce Foundation." Jul. 31, 2024. Vimeo, 12:17. https://vimeo.com/993101021.

Routledge, Robin. "Ḥesed as Obligation: A Re-Examination." *Tyndale Bulletin* 46 (1995) 179-96.

———. "Prayer, Sacrifice, and Forgiveness." *European Journal of Theology* 18 (2009) 17-28.

Royal Commission of Inquiry. "Executive Summary." Abuse in Care. https://www.abuseincare.org.nz/reports/whanaketia/preliminaries/executive-summary.

Schreiter, Robert. *The Ministry of Reconciliation. Spirituality and Strategies*. Maryknoll, NY: Orbis, 2006.

———. "Reconciliation and Prophetic Dialogue." In *Mission on the Road to Emmaus: Constants, Context and Prophetic Dialogue*, edited by Cathy Ross and Stephen B. Bevans, 123-35. London: SCM, 2015.

———. *Reconciliation: Mission and Ministry in a Changing Social Order*. Maryknoll, NY: Orbis, 1992.

Scott, Kim. *Radical Candor: Be a Kick-Ass Boss Without Losing Your Humanity*. New York: St. Martin's, 2019. Kindle.

Sittser, Gerald L. *Water from a Deep Well: Christian Spirituality from the Early Martyrs to Modern Missionaries*. Downers Grove, IL: IVP, 2007.

Smale, Aaron, "State Care Has Key Role in Creating Violent Gang Members," 1News, July 24, 2024. https://www.1news.co.nz/2024/07/25/state-care-has-key-role-in-creating-violent-gang-members-submission/.

Stassen, Glen H., and David P. Gushee. *Kingdom Ethics: Following Jesus in Contemporary Context*. Downers Grove, IL: IVP, 2003.

Vennen, Mark Vander, and Morgan E. Braganza. "Can We Talk but Still Stay Together: Using Restorative Practice to Address Conflict in Faith Communities." *Social Work and Christianity* 49 (2022) 87–105.

Volf, Miroslav, and Matthew Croasmun. *For the Life of the World: Theology That Makes a Difference*. Grand Rapids: Brazos, 2019.

Weld, Nicki. *A Practical Guide to Transformative Supervision for the Helping Professions: Amplifying Insight*. London: Jessica Kingsley, 2011.

Wells, Samuel. *Incarnational Ministry: Being with the Church*. Norwich: Canterbury, 2017.

———. *Learning to Dream Again: Rediscovering the Heart of God*. Norwich: Canterbury, 2013.

Wilberforce Foundation, "Faith and Belief." Nov. 2023. https://faithandbeliefstudynz.org/wp-content/uploads/2023/11/willberforce-report-2023-digital-2.pdf.

Chapter 8

The Church Body as a Healing Sacrament

Watiri Maina

INTRODUCTION

> People travel to wonder
> at the height of the mountains,
> at the huge waves of the seas,
> at the long course of the rivers,
> at the vast compass of the ocean,
> at the circular motion of the stars,
> and yet they pass by themselves
> without wondering.
> —Saint Augustine

THIS CHAPTER WILL FOCUS on the church body as a healing sacrament using examples from Tumaini Church. "Tumaini" is the Swahili word for hope. This church is a composite of various churches in New Zealand. The chapter will highlight how Tumaini Church has been a healing sacrament, bringing healing and restoration as a beacon of hope. I will explore who we are as the body of Christ and will then explore why it is important that we are a people of healing and hope. The church body is called and chosen to convey restoration, reconciliation, hope, and transformation through its sacramental actions. The church's role as a healing sacrament includes addressing, not only physical ailments but also social, relational, and spiritual brokenness. It seeks to restore *shalom* and establish a healthy relationship with God, people, and creation.

The church as a sacrament can be understood as *sanctifying, social, and subversive*, borrowing from the categories derived from 1 Cor 11 by Robert Mulholland in his article *Discerning the Body*.[1] I will use this framework as a metaphor to explore how the church body, like the Eucharist or baptism, functions as a sacrament. I will examine how healing happens and how this healing sacrament brings hope to the body. Therefore, it is a sanctifying, social, and subversive sacrament that gives hope to its members and is a witness of God's healing presence in the world. It can be what it is called to be through taking steps to heal itself when troubles arise.

THE CHURCH BODY AS A HEALING SACRAMENT

The church is not merely a physical building or institution; it is a living, breathing community of believers united by faith in the crucified and risen Christ. This community of Christ's followers partners with God in his mission in the world, empowered by the Holy Spirit. This communal aspect forms the foundation of the church's role as a healing sacrament. A sacrament is a sacred, tangible, symbolic act that mediates God's grace to us, offering spiritual, emotional, relational, and sometimes physical healing. Augustine describes a sacrament as "an outward and visible sign of an inward and invisible grace."[2] Examples of sacraments are the practices of baptism and Eucharist. The church body not only offers sacraments to its members, but it is also a sacrament itself, one that integrates faith in God, the healer, who mediates divine healing through the community of believers to bring about restoration and transformation for individuals, communities, and even creation, all for the glory of God.

The church body, therefore, becomes another visible sign of God's grace. This invisible reality is made visible through the relational interactions within the community of believers and their witness in the world. Through the divine presence and the redeeming power active in individuals and the community, unity and healing are expressed as believers share God's Word, pray, confess, repent, support one another, and live in interconnectedness. They become a healing community set apart as holy. As 1 Peter reminds us,

---

1. Mulholland, "Discerning the Body," 20–26.
2. Diocese of Westminster, "What Is a Sacrament?"

> But you are a chosen people, a royal priesthood, a holy nation, God's special possession, that you may declare the praises of him who called you out of darkness into his wonderful light. (1 Pet 2:9 NIV)[3]

These chosen people—the church—become an expression of hope and the light of God's healing presence to each other and to the world.

The church body, chosen and broken, mirrors the Eucharist, in which the body of Christ is offered for the healing (*sozo*)[4] of the world.[5] As members of the body of Christ, Christians are called to participate in Christ's work of healing and renewal. The church, as a healing body, is a *wounded healer*[6]—one that has suffered much and yet brings hope and healing to individuals, communities, and the world. This analogy is significant because no one can bring healing unless they truly understand what it means to be wounded. Thus, the church becomes a compassionate healer to the world. As 2 Cor 4:7–12 reminds us, the body is broken, yet through its brokenness, it ministers healing.

The concept of the church as the body of Christ and a healing sacrament is deeply rooted in the New Testament. The early church was understood as both the universal body of Christ and the local gathered community, particularly in Paul's first Letter to the Corinthians. The Corinthian church faced numerous challenges that hindered its growth and its witness in the world. In 1 Cor 12, Paul reminds the believers in Corinth that they are one in Christ, united by him, and dependent on one another. Each person in the church is important—no one is indispensable, and no one is inferior or superior. Each member plays a role in nurturing a healthy community of believers. Paul uses the metaphor of the human body to describe the church:

> The human body consists of many parts, yet these parts come together to form a single whole body. Similarly, in the Body of Christ . . . we have all been baptised into one body by one Spirit, and we all share the same Spirit. (1 Cor 12:12–13 NLT)

---

3. All biblical references in this chapter are taken from the NIV, unless explicitly noted.

4. The Greek word *sozo* in the New Testament points to the holistic nature of salvation. It is not just about spiritual forgiveness but also includes physical healing and wholeness. In the Gospels, Jesus frequently uses *sozo* to describe the comprehensive nature of salvation. For example, sometimes he said, "Your faith has saved (*sozo*) you" (Luke 7:50, Luke 18:42), indicating that salvation included not just spiritual salvation but also physical and emotional healing—wholistic healing.

5. Liebscher and DeSilva, *SOZO: Saved Healed Delivered*.

6. Nouwen, *Wounded Healer*.

For the body to function in wholeness, each part must be recognized as essential, and placed there by God's design. Verse 27 reminds us: "All of you together are Christ's body, and each of you is a part of it" (NLT). God has given different gifts so that the body may flourish, but love is the uniting heart of the body.

While being a healing sacrament means showing love, it also means being real about what needs to change. As an adage states, "Hope has two daughters: their names are anger and courage. Anger at the way things are and courage to see that they do not remain as they are." This quote, attributed to Augustine, captures how hope can mean being angry at what is not right and what is unjust[7] and also the courage to take action to change things for the better.[8] The church requires both anger and courage—anger to confront what is undermining hope and courage to rekindle it. To be a healing sacrament starts with the church healing itself first. This might involve being angry about the things that are creating dysfunction within its own body and having the courage to make the necessary changes for its healing presence to have efficacy.

When I joined Tumaini Church, I felt that my calling was to engage in what God was doing as the community aimed to reignite hope and reclaim its identity as a healing community. Tumaini Church had faced numerous challenges that made it difficult to become the body it aspired to be. While the community experienced anger, it also showed the courage to confront its brokenness and pursue reconciliation, hope, and healing, enabling it to serve as a healing balm for the world. When a community is divided and fights among itself, it forgets that it is a sacramental body set apart for God's service. When the body is unified, as Ps 133 reminds us, God commands a blessing when brothers and sisters live together in harmony. In this way, we must not overlook the spiritual aspect of our identity as a sanctifying sacrament together. We dishonor Christ when we dishonor each other, and this brings shame to Christ's body.

As noted above, in the New Testament, the Greek word *sozo* encompasses salvation, healing, deliverance, restoration, and wholeness. The church is a *sozo sacrament* because it embodies Christ's ongoing work of saving, healing, reconciling, and restoring all things. The body of Christ—the

---

7. Psalm 89:14: "Righteousness and justice are the foundation of your throne; love and faithfulness go before you." See also Ps 97:2; Isa 32:17; Jas 3:18.

8. Restoring *shalom*—righteousness (Hebrew *ṣedeq*) reflects God's moral perfection and faithfulness to what is right. Justice signifies fairness, equity, and restoring balance. Peace (*shalom*) arises where righteousness and justice coexist—it embodies the holistic well-being that flows from God's order. All these done with loving kindness that comes from God.

church—is not just a dispenser of grace; it is a living sign and active participant in God's redemptive mission.

As well embodying *sozo* through baptism and the Eucharist, the church also continues Jesus's ministry of healing and deliverance through its healing ministries. Anointing with oil, prayer, and the laying on hands are tangible expressions of Christ's compassion and power (Matt 10:8; Jas 5:14–15). Within its community life, the church becomes a space of mutual love, forgiveness, and restoration, where relationships are healed, and souls are nurtured in belonging (Acts 2:42–47).

One example of this healing ministry is the role of healing prayer ministry. Prayer ministry takes multiple forms, including spiritual healing, inner healing, and physical healing. Physical issues are sometimes healed. However, the slow and deep recovery from sometimes severe chronic health problems is indeed remarkably evident in communities that embrace holistic perspectives of healing. John Swinton observes, "Healing is not the same as cure. Cure refers to the removal of symptoms; healing refers to the restoration of meaning in the face of suffering."[9] Still, unfortunately, many people suffering from chronic illness report feeling pressured to claim they are better when nothing has changed, which prevents them from seeking prayer. However, accepting people for who they are, regardless of the baggage they carry, recognizing the service they can offer, and showing the unconditional love of God through ordinary people who are willing to sit, listen, and pray with them seems to lead to a healing of mind and soul.

This healing resembles "the peace of God that passes all understanding" (Phil 4:7) even when bodily troubles persist. John Swinton notes, "Healing happens when people are heard, respected, and recognized as valuable members of the community—regardless of whether their condition changes."[10] This kind of healing is believed to be due to the nonjudgmental attitudes of church members, who are not upset by unusual behavior or the presence of a service dog for example. This healing can happen when the community is protective of vulnerable individuals who feel uncomfortable for any reason and cares for them, welcoming them to the community in loving ways.

Finally, the church embodies *sozo* in its mission and pursuit of justice. Through advocacy, acts of compassion, and work toward the transformation of unjust systems, the church joins in God's desire to bring wholeness to individuals and societies. In all these ways, the church serves as both a

---

9. Swinton, *Spirituality and Mental Health Care*, 21.
10. Swinton, *Dementia*, 179.

sign and instrument of God's *sozo*—a living sacrament of Christ's saving presence in the world.

In summary, the church body is sacramental, meaning it is a visible sign of an invisible, grace-filled reality that brings glory to God. I now describe more specifically how the body of Christ, as a sacrament, is *sanctifying*—set apart for God's worship and witness in the world. It is also *social*, as it forms a connected community where love is shared and expressed, bringing about healing, restoration, and transformation. Finally, it is *subversive*, resisting cultural narratives that distort relationships and instead embodying the countercultural love, justice, and grace of Christ.

THE CHURCH BODY AS A SANCTIFYING SACRAMENT

Sanctification occurs through a deeper union with Christ and one another. The church can symbolize and actualize the reconciliation of sinners with God and each other. This reconciliation emerges through love for God when members of the church community embrace vulnerability, share their lives, extend forgiveness, and strive for unity. The healing power of God can be present, restoring and nurturing wholeness, with divine grace mediated through the community, through which people can experience healing. However, conflict can sometimes lead to fragmentation and pain, creating a collective wound that affects the community. Nonetheless, forgiveness offers a pathway to restoration.

Healing begins when individuals listen to one another and share their stories of pain and sorrow. Sharing these narratives can enable individuals and the community to reclaim and remember their vision—their identity and their calling. The spiritual journey of healing takes place under the church's authority, where ministers facilitate deeper conversations and allow divine wisdom to guide the process.

A solemn assembly exemplifies this practice, where individuals share their pain in the presence of God, guided by Scripture. In these gatherings, language rooted in Christ's teachings nurtures hope and encouragement. Additional practices such as confession, lament, and the pursuit of emotional and relational reconciliation play vital roles. Abiding in prayer and Scripture, various healing practices may be integrated in the services as necessary. God's healing encompasses holistic salvation—not just spiritual redemption but also relational, emotional, and even physical restoration. This process may involve repentance, confession rituals, or the application of Scripture, as illustrated in Neil Anderson's work,[11] where biblical truth

---

11. Anderson, *Bondage Breaker*.

is spoken into wounded places, bringing freedom. Neil Anderson says, "Freedom from spiritual conflicts and bondage is . . . a truth encounter."[12] Deliverance prayers, where God's compassionate word is read, may assist those burdened by oppression, despair, or spiritual bondage. In some cases, medical support, including medication and professional care, is necessary. Inner healing processes, where Christ is invited to ease pain and facilitate transformation, are also significant. Often, the presence of a compassionate listener unlocks deep pain, fostering a sense of liberation within a caring and loving community that nurtures hope.

In 2019, the Tumaini Church consisted of individuals eager to restore its former vibrancy. However, the church had endured a significant period of conflict, leaving many members disillusioned, divided, and discouraged. Despite this, a desire for renewal lingered. Those who remained were reluctant to address the issues that had caused the unrest, and the resulting factions bred distrust and sorrow. The leadership embraced new ministers, aiming to support a community in need of healing.

Engaging with the congregation made it clear that unresolved wounds were hindering progress. Many felt lost and uncertain about the potential for restoring unity. In the latter part of 2019, discussions with congregants uncovered a strong need for public acknowledgment of past pain, collective lament, and a structured healing process. Many expressed frustration over a history of unresolved conflicts and showed a readiness to tackle them. The senior minister was consulted about the possibility of convening a church-wide meeting to openly discuss the recent challenges.

The Role of Solemn Assemblies

A solemn assembly was envisioned, inspired by Ezra's gatherings, where individuals engaged in mourning, honest dialogue, and scriptural discernment to determine a path forward. The Hebrew term for a solemn assembly, 'ăṣārâ, signifies a "sacred assembly" or "holy meeting."[13] Biblical examples include the eighth day of the Feast of Booths, the seventh day of Passover, and the dedication of the temple. During solemn assemblies, the community was sanctifying and instructed to "do no work" as a sign of ritual holiness.

In contemporary practice, these sacred gatherings offer a chance for reflection, dialogue, and a shared commitment to God. This reflects the efforts to restore the church body to health, acknowledging the necessity for spiritual renewal and guidance. The aspiration continues to manifest the

---

12. Anderson and Mylander, *Setting Your Church Free*, 112.
13. Ezra 9–10; Lev 23:36; Neh 29:35; Acts 2:1–4.

prayer of Jesus in John 17:17–23, where he requests the Father to sanctify his people through his truth, bringing them together in divine love so that the world may see his glory. Having a solemn assembly presented an opportunity for deep reflection on the church's identity as the body of Christ and its need for healing and restoration. Scripture and prayer guided the process, while open conversations were facilitated using restorative narrative frameworks.[14] Each individual was encouraged to share their perspective, the impact of past events, and their hopes for the future. These discussions were honest, challenging, and sometimes painful, yet they fostered a renewed sense of being heard, reconnection, and a shared desire for unity. The church's vision, once threatened by conflict, was reaffirmed.

This event marked the beginning of a healing process. Fractured relationships and spiritual wounds started to mend. Those on the brink of departure found a measure of renewed hope and chose to stay. Individuals who had faced discord showed the courage to seek reconciliation and offer forgiveness. A new energy flowed through the community, reigniting a longing for deeper communion with Christ. The re-establishment of trust took time, but gradual progress was clear.

Storytelling

Storytelling within the Tumaini Church community has also been a powerful medium for healing and fostering connection with God and with one another. By sharing narratives of pain and longing, individuals revisited past wounds, allowing suppressed emotions to surface and facilitated healing. Susan S. Phillips highlights the profound role of storytelling in shaping lives, as it weaves together four connected parts: memory, meaning, ethos, and mending. Through storytelling, experiences are not only recalled but also given depth and significance, fostering both personal and communal transformation.[15]

---

14. Winslade and Williams, *Safe and Peaceful Schools*. Within the therapeutic approach of narrative therapy, narrative restorative practices include circle conversation and restorative conferencing. These restorative practices address the harm created by an offense so as to build community of care that allows for all voices to be heard in a welcoming way and helping to facilitate healing processes that restore identity and foster hope and flourishing in the church community and individuals. These restorative practices promote accountability, emotional healing, and reconciliation, shifting from judgment to restoration and assisting the congregation in moving forward with grace and peace.

15. Philips, "Telling Our Stories."

Memory plays a crucial role in this process, as stories evoke emotions that embed experiences deeply within individuals. At Tumaini, the act of remembering—both moments of grace and seasons of pain—has allowed the community to confront past traumas. In doing so, they have opened themselves to renewal through the Spirit, allowing healing to take root in their collective journey. Beyond memory, storytelling constructs meaning, shaping a spiritual framework of grace and restoration. As individuals share their narratives, they strengthen their connection with God and one another, reinforcing a communal identity rooted in faith and hope. Storytelling also nurtures ethos, the moral and spiritual fabric of a community. Jesus himself used parables to communicate divine truth, and within the church, storytelling continues to fortify its foundations. Through shared narratives, the community is encouraged to persevere, discern wisely, and uphold integrity in their faith journey. Finally, storytelling serves as a means of mending or healing. Narrative reflection allows individuals to process and organize anxious emotions, contributing to their spiritual and emotional well-being. Just as the disciples on the road to Emmaus encountered Christ in the midst of their grief (Luke 24:13–35), storytelling becomes a sacred space where pain is met with grace, and brokenness is transformed into healing. These are practices of remembering.

Remembering

Remembering, deeply rooted in Jewish and Christian traditions, can act as a transformative practice for healing and wholeness within church communities. In Jewish thought, to "remember" is to engage with an event so profoundly that it shapes present and future realities.[16] This concept is echoed in Christ's command during the Eucharist: "Do this in remembrance of me" (1 Cor 11:24–25).

Memory plays a key role in hindering or facilitating healing processes. Miloslav Volf aptly states, "Memory is a double-edged sword. It can heal or it can wound. Communities that have suffered trauma must decide whether to remember the past in a way that restores life or to forget it, only to be haunted by the unhealed wounds. The challenge lies in remembering rightly—not forgetting the wrongs, but not letting the wrongs define the community's future."[17] When things are remembered in a way that facilitates identity formation and restoration, they bring about healing to communities and individuals in it. This can be done through collective storytelling.

16. Exod 2:24; Exod 12:14; Josh 4:6; Ps 105:8.
17. Volf. *End of Memory*, 25.

Collective storytelling is described by Leah Salter as follows: "Storytelling can be conceptualized as a verbal or written process of putting words to experience—'real' or 'imagined'—or in its widest form it can be considered as a way of talking and engaging in everyday life." She goes on to say that "storytelling can also be conceptualized as a resource for transformation and as a mechanism for systems thinking to create 'social change.'"[18]

This kind of "narrative collective storytelling" is participatory as people are invited to cocreate and share stories to make sense of their shared experiences, values, identity, or social realities. All personal and shared memories can be collectively harnessed to bring about healing. Walter Brueggemann observes that "the memory of the community, especially the community of faith, is shaped by the recurring acts of God that define the identity and vocation of that community. Memory is not an abstract mental activity; it is the active recollection of God's interventions in history that shape how the people of God understand their present calling and their future hope."[19] Healing and reconciliations can take place as remembered stories are told. Volf asserts that "reconciliation is a form of healing in which the memory of past injuries is not suppressed but is instead reframed, acknowledged, and reconciled with the future. Memory does not vanish in reconciliation, but its power to divide is dismantled as the community collectively embraces a new narrative of shared humanity and mutual restoration."[20] Through storytelling and remembering, the church functions as a sanctuary of restoration, embodying the sanctifying presence of Christ in the world.

THE CHURCH BODY AS A SOCIAL SACRAMENT

The Eucharist, as emphasized by Kenneth Leech and Robert Mulholland, is fundamentally a social sacrament, embodying active communal participation and profound relational dynamics. Leech describes Christian spirituality as inherently eucharistic, rooted in the communal liturgy of eating and drinking, reflecting both an active encounter with God and a shared experience within the faith community.[21] Mulholland highlights the call to "discern the body" (1 Cor. 11:27–30), stressing that the Eucharist challenges individuals and communities to confront brokenness in relationships, and the broader world. This involves recognizing areas where the church fails to embody the peace, justice, and shalom that God desires.

---

18. Salter, "Stories 'Matter,'" 44–67.
19. Brueggemann, *Prophetic Imagination*, 15.
20. Volf, *End of Memory*, 135.
21. Leech, *Experiencing God*.

It is essential to examine our relationships and unity with Christ, who sacrificed himself on the cross. This understanding calls the church to be an agent of healing and reconciliation, embodying God's restorative mission through its relationships with individual members and structural practices. A church body must be cognizant of the relational depth that shapes human interactions and nurtures spiritual growth. Relational depth is essential for promoting both personal and community transformation, allowing the church to fulfil its role as a healing sacrament. Relational depth refers to profound, authentic connections in which individuals experience complete understanding, acceptance, and safety. It involves vulnerability, mutual understanding, and a sense of belonging.[22] Relational depth is essential for promoting both personal and community transformation, allowing the church to fulfil its role as a healing sacrament. This concept provides a framework for fostering relationships that embody divine communion and channel God's grace. In a church context, relational depth aligns with the sacramental principle of grace expressed through tangible relationships. It is nurtured through practices like small groups, spiritual direction, and pastoral care, fostering an environment conducive to healing and growth.

When the church embodies relational depth, it models God's love, providing safe spaces, facilitating reconciliation, and enabling divine encounters. This is realized through communal liturgical practices, nurturing community life, and forming leaders who embody empathy and active listening. By cultivating these principles, the church becomes a transformative, grace-filled community that embodies God's healing presence through relational and sacramental life. This is exemplified through practices such as passing the peace during the Eucharist, where individuals stand before one another in openness, ready to confess, receive grace, and move forward. It also includes collaborative decision-making guided by Scripture and fostering resilience. When the church functions as a space of healing for individuals and the broader community, it strengthens relationships and nurtures hope. Sharing testimonies allows the gospel to be experienced as a living truth—tangible and near—encouraging believers to trust in God's real and abiding presence.

The body of Christ was particularly tested during the COVID-19 pandemic, a time of heightened anxiety and division. The act of passing the peace, inviting confession, repentance, forgiveness, and reconciliation became vital in urging believers to embody Christ's presence in a fragmented world. Mulholland warns against harboring bitterness, manipulating others,

---

22. Cooper and Mearns, *Relational Depth in Therapy*.

neglecting the marginalized, or harming the environment, as such failures undermine the wholeness of the body of Christ.[23]

In early 2020, shortly after a church general meeting, COVID-19 arrived at Tumaini church as an unforeseen challenge. Lockdown forced the church to find new ways to stay connected. The pastoral team developed a strategy to maintain communication with all members by allocating pastoral ministry resources to different individuals. Many experienced not only physical isolation but also social and spiritual disconnection. In response, the church initiated online prayer meetings, incorporating short services and social interactions on Zoom. Initially chaotic due to inexperience with virtual platforms, the meetings soon became spaces of deep connection. When in-person gatherings resumed, it became evident how much people had longed for face-to-face fellowship, Bible study, and corporate worship.

The lockdown underscored the deep need for community, pastoral care, and spiritual nourishment. A subsequent lockdown in August 2021 introduced further challenges, particularly with the rollout of the COVID-19 traffic light system and vaccine mandates. Navigating these restrictions required wisdom and discernment. Some members were unable to be vaccinated due to medical, ideological, or faith-based reasons, raising questions about inclusion and hospitality. The elders of Tumaini Church, guided by historical church responses to crises, sought to balance public health concerns with the call to community. Learning from the early church's model of house churches, the decision was made to form small home-based congregations. Each was led by a designated shepherd responsible for guiding spiritual formation and weekly worship. Vaccinated and unvaccinated members were accommodated through separate but inclusive arrangements, ensuring that all had a place within the faith community.

Pre-recorded sermons and service outlines facilitated engagement, while regular Zoom meetings maintained a sense of corporate unity. Congregational feedback was actively sought through surveys and pastoral check-ins, ensuring that the approach remained responsive to the needs of the community. Ultimately, this strategy proved effective in maintaining spiritual and relational cohesion during a highly stressful season. This model not only sustained engagement but also strengthened relationships within the church. New leaders emerged as small group settings provided opportunities for individuals to practice leading prayers, reading Scripture, and offering pastoral support. When corporate worship resumed, the church was well-equipped with a revitalized roster of lay leaders. Many praised God

---

23. Mulholland, "Discerning the Body," 24.

for keeping the community united and healthy during a very challenging season.

Through these experiences, several key lessons emerged: godly hospitality is a costly but necessary part of Christian discipleship; fear can be paralyzing and divisive; a fear-based approach to life creates barriers to relationships and communication; language can unite or divide; one must avoid vilifying individuals based on vaccination status and also to withhold judgment; spiritual nourishment is essential in times of crisis; journeying together in faith strengthens resilience; and finally, celebrations are vital for community healing and renewal.

To foster healing and deeper connections, Tumaini Church embraced celebrations as a vital aspect of communal life. In April 2022, an Easter service marked the return to in-person worship, followed later by a church anniversary celebration. Drawing from African traditions of communal festivities, these gatherings fostered a shared sense of belonging, unity, and restoration. Celebrations serve as powerful tools for strengthening bonds, promoting inclusivity, and enhancing collective well-being. Just as African festivals provide space for reconciliation and gift-sharing, church celebrations can restore relationships and nurture connections. They also serve as a means of cultural expression, preserving faith traditions while fostering creativity and spiritual growth.

Great care was taken to foster a culture of respect and mutual understanding throughout these times. Sermons addressed the dangers of labelling or making assumptions about others, emphasizing Christ's call to honor and welcome all. Acts of reconciliation were encouraged, fostering a spirit of grace and unity within the body of Christ. By prioritizing hospitality, intentional community-building, and celebration, the church can become a space of healing, embodying God's reconciling love in tangible ways.

THE CHURCH BODY AS A SUBVERSIVE SACRAMENT

The church also needs to challenge the power structures of the world, proclaiming God's kingdom of justice, peace, and healing. It needs to resists division, greed, and injustice, offering a vision of a world made whole through Jesus's redemptive work. As a healing sacrament, the church is subversive in that it acts as God's instrument of restoration, not only in the lives of individuals but also within society as a whole. In a culture that frequently embraces cancellation, intolerance, individualism, and separation, the church seeks unity, mercy, and expressions of love, justice, and kindness. It aims to be a *TOV* church, as Scott McKnight and Laura Barringer describe in their books *A Church Called TOV* and *PIVOT*—a church where goodness is its *modus operandi*. A subversive church expresses difference and resists entrenched, unhealthy, and oppressive systems through its ethos, language, and practices.

"Church is not a spectator sport; it is a gathering around the Word and Sacrament, cradled in prayer, where God's people participate in this world as an outpost of God's kingdom," writes Zachary Jones in his article "How to Become a Subversive Church."[24] He emphasizes that attending church breaks self-idolatry, offering an alternative community where grace transforms people. Here, believers learn to love even when it is difficult, without permitting harm, because the church is meant to be a place of safety.

Romans 12:1–2 encourages Christians to transform their thinking and be wary of conforming to worldly patterns. Likewise, the writer of Hebrews calls the church to prioritize gathering for worship, urging believers not to neglect their assembly:

> Let us hold tightly without wavering to the hope we affirm, for God can be trusted to keep His promises. Let us think of ways to motivate one another to acts of love and good works. And let us not neglect our meeting together, as some people do, but encourage one another, especially now that the day of His return is drawing near. (10:23–25 NLT)

This passage encourages the church to persevere in hope, consistently gathering in love and service, all with an eschatological awareness. Much of this is countercultural and subversive. In his book *Subversive Kingdom: Living as Agents of Gospel Transformation*, Ed Stetzer writes, "If God has a mission, it should also be the church's mission.... The church doesn't *have* a mission; the mission has a *church*. God, who by nature is on purpose and on task, has invited people like us, gathered in churches like ours, to join him in fulfilling his chief desire. And that mission is this: for God to be glorified."[25] For God's mission is his glory. He is creating a kingdom for his glory; he saves people through the gospel for his glory; his purposes will all be accomplished for his glory, and he has placed us in the church to participate in his mission to bring him glory. God's subversive mission, as expressed through the church, involves proclaiming the gospel and demonstrating it in word and deed.

One of the issues the global church (the body of Christ) has found challenging to deal with is mental illness within the congregation and in the community. The Lausanne Movement notes that

24. Jones, "How to Become."
25. Stetzer, *Subversive Kingdom*, 166.

there is a growing global mental health movement around the world today; and the global church is beginning to recognize mental health problems, which are the leading cause of disability worldwide—more disabling than such conditions as heart disease, stroke, or diabetes—as a major ministry priority. Mental health problems are usually the result of a combination of many factors, including family environment, biology, personality, spirituality, and challenging community contexts, including poverty and violence. Increasingly, the impacts of traumatic events such as childhood abuse, interpersonal violence, or natural disasters are being recognized as major causes of mental health problems. Churches, as communities of faith where people can find safety and help in times of need, can have a key role.[26]

Tumaini Church has been seeking to impact its community by addressing mental health challenges with intentionality and sensitivity. Through a welcoming and hospitable atmosphere, the church has fostered an environment where people can find healing and feel genuinely included. By embracing individuals without discrimination and by caring for each person holistically, Tumaini has created a space of belonging and restoration.

A significant cultural shift occurred within the church regarding mental health. In the past, individuals facing mental health challenges were often excluded from ministry opportunities. However, the congregation has come to understand that mental health exists on a spectrum and that no one is immune to difficulties. Swinton, in his book *Finding Jesus in the Storm: The Spiritual Life of Christians with Mental Health Challenges*, concurs with this view. He asserts, "Mental health is not a fixed state. It is a spectrum that includes both struggles and flourishing, and people can move between these states at different points in their lives."[27] Instead of making assumptions about a person's abilities, the church has adopted a stance of listening and discernment, enabling individuals to contribute according to their capacity.

I was aware that a member of Tumaini Church had a long history of clinical depression, triggered by circumstances. Although they functioned well, they needed significant support. A large part of their recovery was due to the supportive, inclusive, and non-pushy nature of Tumaini Church. While still feeling shell-shocked, nothing was expected of them; however, as they grew stronger, their gifts and training were fully utilized and further developed, and this continues to be the case. John Swinton has said, "Mental illness does not disqualify someone from ministry. Quite the opposite:

26. Mwiti and Smith, "Turning the Church's Attention."
27. Swinton, *Finding Jesus*, 52.

experiences of suffering can become deep wells of compassion, wisdom, and insight into the human condition."[28]

Over the years, others arrived at the church in various states of chronic unwellness and found the same acceptance, quiet support, encouragement, and immensely reassuring, Christlike lack of judgment. One example is a member who had been diagnosed as having Dissociative Identity Disorder (DID) and was previously excluded from participating in church life. For six years, Tumaini Church has been a place of love, acceptance, and healing for this member. Initially invited by a friend during a period of severe anxiety and spiritual attacks—exacerbated by harmful exorcism attempts—this individual found unconditional support within the church community, even being allowed to bring a comfort dog.

Encouraged to serve in ways previously thought impossible, they became involved in youth and children's ministries and received health and safety training. They were later diagnosed with a degenerative neurological condition as well as facing serious mental illness. Unlike past experiences where their struggles were dismissed as mental illness, both hospital staff and the church family responded with respect and understanding. This support strengthened their confidence and self-worth. Through this journey, they reconciled with their family, learned to accept physical limitations, and developed the trust to ask for help. By listening to them and allowing space for their contributions, the church saw their confidence grow, their sense of belonging deepen, and their well-being improve. They later testified that the community had "loved them into healing." This reminded me of Swinton's challenging words: "To assume that people with mental illness are unable to offer care, ministry, or friendship is to misunderstand both their humanity and the nature of God's call."[29] He further explains, "The Spirit calls all people to participate in the life and mission of the church—including those whose lives may not conform to standard notions of rationality or ability."[30]

Tumaini Church has become a second family for many, offering joy, love, and truth—elements that have been vital to its healing. Its hope is that others will also come to know that all are welcome in God's community. This transformation is just one of many. By welcoming individuals in all their complexity, the church has embodied the social sacrament of healing, fostering peace both within itself and among its members. This is practicing biblical hospitality. Biblical hospitality, deeply rooted in Scripture, serves as a healing sacrament within the church community. As argued above, just as

---

28. Swinton and Innes, *Mental Health*, 43.
29. Swinton, *Resurrecting the Person*, 92.
30. Swinton, "From Inclusion to Belonging," 172–90.

sacraments such as baptism and the Eucharist are outward signs of inward grace, so hospitality shares God's grace with the community, providing a tangible experience of his love. By welcoming the stranger—those who differ culturally, socially, or personally—the church actively participates in God's redemptive work. In the Old Testament, hospitality was a divine mandate, urging God's people to remember their own experiences as strangers and extend care to the marginalized. Abraham's encounter with God through three strangers at Mamre exemplifies this sacred hospitality (Gen 18). Likewise, in the New Testament, the Emmaus story (Luke 24:13–35) illustrates how hosting the risen Christ revealed his presence, restoring hope and strengthening faith.

The Greek term *philoxenia* (love of the stranger) contrasts with *xenophobia* (fear or hatred of strangers). This reciprocal relationship shifts roles between host and guest, fostering mutual care and dignity. As theologians like Amos Yong suggest, hospitality mirrors the Trinitarian nature of God's redemptive economy, embodying unconditional welcome.[31] For the church, hospitality is a conduit of grace, healing isolation, alienation, and brokenness. By embracing *philoxenia*, the church mirrors the Trinitarian relationship of mutual love and welcome. This dynamic act of hosting and being hosted transforms both the giver and the receiver, making God's presence tangible.

Biblical hospitality invites all—whether estranged from God, others, or themselves—into a community of care, trust, and dignity. By advocating for the marginalized and creating inclusive spaces, the church enacts God's restorative love. Through this sacramental practice, the church body not only reflects God's kingdom but also becomes an instrument of his healing, offering divine hospitality and hope to a broken world.

CONCLUSION

The church is and can be a healing sacrament where God infuses the community with hope for the present and the future. As restoration can take place through relational connections, here spiritual growth can happen. This chapter presents a call for action to cultivate practices of hospitality, patience, prayer and presence; an opportunity to align ourselves to God's vision of *shalom*, to bring healing to both individuals and communities. It is therefore essential for the church as the body of Christ to discern the more profound significance of its life as a sacrament and to live it out in ways that bring healing and restoration, reconciliation and transformation

---

31. Yong, *Hospitality and the Other*.

to individuals and the broader community. We can do this by honoring the body of Christ in the sacraments and one another, through not only baptism and the Eucharist but offering hospitality and welcome to all. Through this, the church becomes a place where God's healing grace is made visible, fostering peace, unity, and transformation in a broken world. In conclusion, the church body as a healing community offers hope for the present and the future as a sacred space or place cultivated for encountering Christ individually as faith communities to be witnesses to the world.

BIBLIOGRAPHY

Anderson, Neil T., and Charles Mylander. *Setting Your Church Free: A Biblical Plan to Help Your Church*. Ventura, CA: Regal, 1994.

Augustine. *Confessions*. Translated by Henry Chadwick. Oxford: Oxford University Press, 1991. https://ccel.org/ccel/augustine/confess/confess.

Aquinas, Thomas. *Summa Theologica*. Translated by Fathers of the English Dominican Province. 2nd ed. New York: Benziger Bros., 1947.

Brown, Robert McAfee. *Spirituality and Liberation: Overcoming the Great Fallacy*. Philadelphia: Westminster, 1988.

Brueggemann, Walter. *The Prophetic Imagination*. 2nd ed. Minneapolis: Fortress, 2001.

Catechism of the Catholic Church. 2nd ed. Vatican City: Vatican, 1997.

Cooper, Mick J., and Stephen Mearns. *Relational Depth in Therapy: Understanding the Transformational Power of Connection*. 2nd ed. London: Sage, 2016.

Diocese of Westminster. "What Is a Sacrament?" https://rcdow.org.uk/att/files/faith/catechesis/baptism/sacraments.pdf.

Jones, Zachary. "How to Become a Subversive Church." Anglican Compass, Sept. 5, 2019. https://anglicancompass.com/how-to-become-a-subversive-church/.

Leech, Kenneth. *Experiencing God: Theology as Spirituality*. San Francisco: Harper & Row, 1985.

Liebscher, Teresa, and Dawna DeSilva. *SOZO: Saved Healed Delivered: A Journey into Freedom with the Father, Son, and Holy Spirit*. Shippensburg, PA: Destiny Image, 2016.

Maier, Francis X. "Hope and Her Daughters." *First Things* 311 (2021) 19–22.

Marshall, Ellen Ott. *Though the Fig Tree Does Not Blossom: Toward a Responsible Theology of Christian Hope*. Eugene, OR: Wipf & Stock, 2015.

Mulholland, Robert. "Discerning the Body." *Weavings: Journal of the Christian Spiritual Life* 8 (1993) 20–26.

Mwiti Gladys, and Smith, Bradford. "Turning the Church's Attention to Mental Health." Lausanne Global Analysis, Nov. 2018. https://lausanne.org/global-analysis/turning-the-churchs-attention-to-mental-health.

Nouwen, Henri J. M. *The Wounded Healer: Ministry in Contemporary Society*. New York: Image, 1979.

Phillips, Susan. "Telling Our Stories: Spiritual Direction, Healing Gift." Conversatio, Fall 2012. https://conversatio.org/telling-our-stories/?collection=12532.

Salter, Leah Karen. "Stories 'Matter': Storytelling As Community Learning Within a Whole Systems Approach to Recovery." *Murmurations: Journal of Transformative*

Systemic Practice 3 (2020) 44–67. https://murmurations.cloud/index.php/pub/article/view/97.

Slocum, Robert Boak, ed. *A Heart for the Future: Writings on the Christian Hope.* Eugene, OR: Wipf and Stock, 2018.

Snyder, C. Richard, ed. *Handbook of Hope: Theory, Measures, and Applications.* San Diego: Elsevier Science and Technology, 2000.

Stetzer, Ed. *Subversive Kingdom: Living as Agents of Gospel Transformation.* Nashville: B&H, 2012.

Swinton, John. *Dementia: Living in the Memories of God.* Grand Rapids: Eerdmans, 2012.

———. *Finding Jesus in the Storm: The Spiritual Lives of Christians with Mental Health Challenges.* Grand Rapids: Baker Academic, 2016.

———. "From Inclusion to Belonging: A Practical Theology of Community, Disability and Humanness." *Journal of Religion, Disability and Health* 16 (2012) 172–90.

———. "The Healing Power of Story: Theology, Narrative, and People with Mental Illness." Lecture presented at Duke Divinity School, Durham, NC, Oct. 3, 2013.

———. *Raging with Compassion: Pastoral Responses to the Problem of Evil.* Grand Rapids: Eerdmans, 2007.

———. *Resurrecting the Person: Friendship and the Care of People with Mental Health Problems.* Nashville: Abingdon, 2000.

———. *Spirituality and Mental Health Care: Rediscovering a "Forgotten" Dimension.* London: Jessica Kingsley, 2001.

Swinton, John, and Jeanine Innes. *Mental Health: The Inclusive Church Resource.* London: Darton, Longman, and Todd, 2014.

Tillich, Paul. "Right to Hope." *Neue Zeitschrift Für Systematische Theologie Und Religionsphilosophie* 7 (1965) 371–77.

Volf, Miroslav. *The End of Memory: Remembering Rightly in a Violent World.* Grand Rapids: Eerdmans, 2006.

Yong, Amos. *Hospitality and the Other: Pentecost, Christian Practices, and the Neighbor.* Maryknoll, NY: Orbis, 2008.

Winslade, John M., and Michael Williams. *Safe and Peaceful Schools: Addressing Conflict and Eliminating Violence.* Thousand Oaks, CA: Corwin, 2012.

Section III

Church Flourishing
Sustaining the Healing Power of the Church

Chapter 9

At a Loss for Words

How the Spirit Prays When the Children of God Can't (Romans 8:18–27)

Geoff New

ROMANS 8:18-27

I consider that our present sufferings are not worth comparing with the glory that will be revealed in us. For the creation waits in eager expectation for the children of God to be revealed. For the creation was subjected to frustration, not by its own choice, but by the will of the one who subjected it, in hope that the creation itself will be liberated from its bondage to decay and brought into the freedom and glory of the children of God.

We know that the whole creation has been groaning as in the pains of childbirth right up to the present time. Not only so, but we ourselves, who have the firstfruits of the Spirit, groan inwardly as we wait eagerly for our adoption to sonship, the redemption of our bodies. For in this hope we were saved. But hope that is seen is no hope at all. Who hopes for what they already have? But if we hope for what we do not yet have, we wait for it patiently.

In the same way, the Spirit helps us in our weakness. We do not know what we ought to pray for, but the Spirit himself intercedes for us through wordless groans. And he who searches our hearts knows the mind of the Spirit, because the Spirit intercedes for God's people in accordance with the will of God. (NIV)

INTRODUCTION

IN 2012 I ATTENDED a small conference of preachers and pastors in Auckland, New Zealand.[1] The keynote speaker was Ajith Fernando, the teaching director of Youth for Christ, Sri Lanka. Ajith's Christian ministry involved extensive global experience. After completing theological study in the US, he returned to his home country to serve the church during the Sri Lankan civil war (1983–2009) rather than pursue a prestigious teaching career in the US. During the conference in 2012, he briefly commented on an aspect of Christian spirituality—it was almost an aside. Yet those few words have agitated in my heart since. He said:

> First Corinthians 1:2–3 speaks of God's comfort. However there can be a battle to come to the place of experiencing God's comfort. The key in it all is "groaning." We need to be skilled in the groaning as described in Romans 8:17–23. Frustration is normal in ministry. Lament. Develop the kind of friends to whom we can groan—but remember they are not God. If we learn the discipline of groaning, we can cope with frustration. And we will come to realize frustration is part of life. And we will discover groaning is an alternative to quitting.

The biblical text in view, Rom 8:18–27, has the sequence of frustration and groaning. Embedded in this sequence is a pulsating message of hope (vv. 24–25). The positioning of this message of hope is significant; it appears between the description of creation's and the children of God's groaning, and then the Spirit's groaning. These words of hope (vv. 25–25) speak of promise and, at least in part, fulfilment. Such promise and fulfilment rests on the effect of the Spirit's intercession; the God who knows the human heart and all that grieves it, is represented by the Spirit's ministry in accordance with God's will (v. 27). Hence, the dramatic testimony of Rom 8 is hope complemented both by the need to wait patiently *and* by the Spirit's divinely accurate intercessory ministry. Amid frustration and groaning we are not *left* to a hope and a prayer as much as we are *accompanied* by hope

---

1. The conference was convened by Carey Baptist College (Auckland, New Zealand) as part of their School of Preaching.

and the Spirit's prayer. The Spirit's intercessory prayer *is* hope and the illumination of this gift from God assures us that we are not alone. We are assured that all that causes us to groan is presented to God by the Spirit in accordance with God's will. So, a crucial aspect of living in patient hope and relying on the intercessory ministry of the Spirit, is our practice of groaning inwardly (v. 23) knowing that this groaning connects us with the Spirit's intercessory and hope-full groaning.

Without an awareness of the Spirit's place in the sequence of frustration and groaning, Ajith Fernando's warning about quitting becomes a real prospect. The context for this Spirit encounter is creation and the church, and that context is described in present terms of futility, bondage, decay, labor pains, and groaning. Yet, the context is also described in future terms such as glory, freedom, redemption, and hope. At times the experience of pain reduces these latter words to merely a promise-in-print rather than what they are; a living description of the hoped-filled activity of the Trinity in the here-and-now.

In this chapter, we will linger in the place of what it means to be ministering in times of frustration and feeling overwhelmed. We will consider the contours of the burden of Christian leadership and the potential outcome of prayerlessness. The gift of Rom 8:18–27 is how it reveals that our groaning *is* a form of prayer. We will see that our groaning can be an expression of hopeful spirituality. This kind of prayer has perhaps passed the attention of many a church leader. This chapter will illustrate and itemize the wondrous effect and infusion of hope the church can enjoy through the expression of prayerful groaning both by the disciples of Christ and the Spirit of Christ.

We will look at how our first admission needs to be that we are weak. We will consider how an acknowledgement of our weakness positions us to be attuned to the intercessory ministry of the Holy Spirit. With this acknowledgement we are placed to perceive the biblical pattern of discipleship of suffering then glory. In response to this, we discover that groaning is a legitimate and necessary spirituality. We do not know how to pray as we ought, and we are exhorted to groan and in our weakness to discover that the Spirit groans in intercession. We will see how Rom 8:18–27 describes both creation and the church groaning as they struggle with flawed limitations. Mysteriously, this groaning is the raw material for the Spirit to intercede when "we do not know what we ought to pray for" (v. 26).

We will then reflect on the passage's use of the word "groan" in the exodus tradition. The Spirit's intercession is majestically faithful in the tradition of God's exodus presence and work. Due to the Spirit's intercession, God hears, sees, and acts for us in our suffering and groaning. The trajectory of Rom 5:2–5 provides insight into the relationship between suffering, groaning, and hope. But our frustration can be compounded because the Spirit's intercession can be inaudible to the ear and incomprehensible to the mind. We will therefore draw on the story of Martha (Luke 10:38–42) and an example from creation to help orientate us to the reality of the Spirit's prayer.

The invitation then, if not challenge, to the church and her leaders is to embrace the divine power of God's mystery and apparent silence by ceasing frenetic human activity, and mistakenly thinking God is absent and inactive. Human incomprehension about the Spirit's intercession does not equate to divine inactivity. The Spirit helps us in our weakness with groans too deep for words. The outcome is hope fulfilled by virtue of the Spirit's intercessory prayer being answered by the God who searches the human heart and knows the Spirit's mind which is in accordance with God's will (v. 27). In all this, our posture is one of patient hope (v. 25). The point of this chapter is that the experience of hope requires engaging in the discipline of groaning and encountering the resultant intercessory ministry of the Spirit, which is in accordance with God's will. Let's then delve into considering the human experience of difficulty and see how Rom 8 resurrects that experience into hope.

WE DO NOT KNOW HOW TO PRAY AS WE OUGHT ... OR GROAN

In considering the spirituality (suffering and groaning) as described in Rom 8 and the Spirit's response, we need to consider the grim reality of those times when ministry overwhelms. An honest admission that all is not well is our starting point. The experience of Christian leaders and disciples can be prayerlessness born out of suffering. Notwithstanding the hope of the Christian life, the burdens of Christian leadership can erode and weaken the most robust of church leaders. In 2 Cor 11:21–28, Paul presents his curriculum vitae of suffering for Christ. The length of the catalogue of his suffering is only matched by the variety of the ways in which he suffered. His articulation of suffering is also complemented by the revelation that it demonstrates how Christ is experienced and discerned:

> The kind of weakness and suffering Paul describes is not in itself conducive to flourishing. However, his weakness has its own efficacy, as it were, as it provides the climate for Christ's power to reach its zenith, or telos, in him.[2]

---

2. Nicol, "Flourishing in Frailty."

Yet, without experiencing the divine agency described in Rom 8, perhaps contemporary pastors do not share Paul's spiritual expertise as seeing suffering, not as the death throes of ministry but the birth of new life in Christ. By way of example, the final entry of Paul's list in 2 Cor 11:21–28 has the sense of "and as if all that is not bad enough . . . 'Besides everything else, I face daily the pressure of my concern for all the churches'" (2 Cor 11:28). For those in primary pastoral leadership positions, especially vocational positions, the weight of the daily burden of the church can only be experienced rather than described. I well recall attending a two-day gathering of experienced ministers who had invited the likes of myself—younger and inexperienced ministers who would benefit from mentoring. However, at the commencement of the gathering the question was asked, "What are you reading?" The most common answer from the experienced ministers was "situations vacant" for non-ministry positions. I was both impressed and dismayed with their confession. I was impressed with their honesty and vulnerability; I was dismayed that things had got to the point that they wanted to do anything other than lead the church. As the years passed by in ministry, I began to understand the sense of weakness that underlay such a confession, and I, too, found myself frequently wondering about life other than pastoral ministry.

Like Paul, any contemporary pastor could compile their own version of 2 Cor 11:21–28, itemizing what they have suffered. Such a list is not to suggest a lack of love of God or desire to serve his people, but it is a comment on a diminishing capacity to keep going and a growing sense of weakness. Yet, regardless of what features in the list, perhaps the most unnerving of all "weaknesses" is when a pastor no longer knows "what we ought to pray for" (v 26):

> Prayer in the context of suffering is in some sense both the easiest and the hardest thing for Christians to practice. It is easy because we are so needy, so fragile, so cognizant of our weakness and our mortality. It is hard for the same reasons. But it is also hard because we often truly do not know how or what to pray.[3]

Even more unsettling, is when the community of faith looks to their pastor to lead them in prayer, and the only response is "we do not know what we ought to pray for." The spiritual discipline in Rom 8 of groaning is an open secret that can be easily missed by many leading the church of Jesus Christ. However, hope abounds because the Spirit helps us in such times of weakness and continues a majestic biblical tradition—the tradition of the

---

3. Gorman, *Romans*, 214.

exodus. The exodus is predicated upon groaning and upon God noticing. Perhaps leaders often groan and yet are not cognizant of the fact that such groaning reaches heaven. Our "not knowing what we ought to pray for" and instead we groan, is wondrously taken as prayer by the Father of the exodus. Our Father in heaven sees his people's suffering and hears their cry for deliverance. In reading the Letter to the Romans, a principle is established. God is active in times and places that pre-empt human devotion and spirituality. For example, while we were still sinners, Christ died for the ungodly (Rom 5:6). Where sin abounds, grace abounds even more (Rom 5:28). Then here in Rom 8, when we groan in weakness, we discover that even in this there is the pre-eminence of the work and love of God. God is ready and waiting to respond to such depth of expression when at our weakest. In that moment, by the Spirit, he is poised to infuse robust hope into our lives.

ARE YOU WEAK ENOUGH?

The circumstances necessitating deliverance from bondage first need acknowledgement. Our human existence is not to be responded to by whistling in the dark; it is to be responded to by honest theological reflection. Romans 8:18–27 does this by assuming human weakness. We begin by not only acknowledging we are weak but realizing that weakness is the best place to start. Unless we share this assumption, the reader of Rom 8 will be unable to penetrate its message. In my role of training candidates for ordained ministry, the first question I ask the class is, "Are you weak enough to be a minister?" The inspiration for this question comes from an address by a Jesuit priest in the 1970's speaking at an ordination service. On that occasion, he went on to say,

> *Is this person weak enough to be a priest?* Is this man [sic] deficient enough so that he cannot ward off significant suffering from his life, so that he lives with a certain amount of failure, so that he feels what it is to be an average man? Is there any history of confusion, of self-doubt, of interior anguish? Has he had to deal with fear, come to terms with frustrations, or accept deflated expectations? These are critical questions and they probe for weakness. Why weakness? Because, according to Hebrews, it is in this deficiency, in this interior lack, in this weakness, that the efficacy of the ministry and priesthood of Christ lies.[4]

---

4. Buckley, "'Because Beset by Weakness,'" 125.

In concert with the intercessory texts in Hebrews (2:18; 4:15; 5:2), we have the majestic mystery of the Spirit's intercessory intervention of Rom 8:26. The Spirit's "wordless groans" (NIV), "sighs too deep for words" (NRSV), or "inexpressible groanings" (NET) can only be truly discerned by the Christian leader who is cognizant of their own weakness and acquainted with suffering. Such Christians who are weak enough to lead will model to their community a posture inclined towards hope in the promised help of the Spirit. This posture rests on the irreducible biblical and spiritual pattern of Christian discipleship: "suffering then glory."

We see this trajectory in the exodus story where the journey is from slavery to freedom, from a foreign land to a promised land, from groaning to a glorious relationship with their God. We see this spiritual dynamic in the beauty of the Servant Songs of Isaiah (42:1–9; 49:1–7; 50:4–11; 52:13—53:12), which speak of suffering and then vindication by God. We see it on the first Easter day on the road to Emmaus (Luke 24:13–35) where Jesus rebuked the two disciples asking, "Did not the Messiah have to suffer these things and then enter his glory?" (Luke 24:26 NIV). We see it in the shape of leadership for a scattered persecuted church (1 Pet 5:1–11), yet for whom the reward is a crown of glory from the Chief Shepherd. There is no other path for Christian leadership apart from suffering then glory. This is the Jesus-way of Gethsemane, to Calvary, to the tomb, to the Mount of Olives and ascension.

Such a vision of Christian leadership may be inspirational and aspirational, yet amid the vortex of ministry ofttimes it proves unattainable. Over time, the overwhelming and soul-destroying nature of negativity, opposition, criticism, and other assaults on the mind and spirit can destroy even the strongest sense of call to ministry. Within the trajectory of the biblical witness of suffering-then-glory, Rom 8 provides further evidence of this spiritual axiom by virtue of the promise of the Spirit's activity in response to the church groaning from a place of weakness.

Hence, our experience of frustration and suffering positions us to admit that we are fundamentally weak. From this position we hope and look to the Spirit to help us in our weakness. The path from weakness to the power of the Spirit as described in Rom 8:18–27 is by virtue of groaning.

BOTH CREATION AND THE CHURCH GROAN AND HOPE

Romans 8:18–27 conveys that groaning is legitimate spirituality that in turn leads to hope. This pericope in Rom 8 provides a kaleidoscope of theological wonder as it rehearses the interconnectedness between creation and the church; both groaning and both hope. The pain is described in terms of futility and bondage to decay (vv. 20–21) and the hope is described in terms of labor pains, first fruits, adoption, and redemption (vv. 22–23). This is Christian spirituality. The interconnectedness between creation and the church is also sequential: "For the creation waits in eager expectation for the children of God to be revealed" (v. 19) while in turn the church waits for "our adoption to sonship, the redemption of our bodies" (v. 23). During this time lag to fulfilment, a vacuum is formed in which the only way the church can breathe is by virtue of hope: "For in this hope we were saved. But hope that is seen is no hope at all. Who hopes for what they already have? But if we hope for what we do not yet have, we wait for it patiently" (vv. 24–25). On the other side of this vacuum of waiting, where hope is all we have, we read a stunning statement that is a breath of fresh Spirit air: "In the same way, the Spirit helps us in our weakness" (v. 26).

The weakness that v. 26 speaks of describes our state of groaning, waiting, and hoping *and* the fact that "we do not know what we ought to pray for" (v. 26). The nature of our weakness, especially for those in vocational Christian leadership, is aptly described by Michael Buckley:

> Weakness is the experience of a peculiar liability to suffering a profound sense of inability both to do and to protect, an inability, even after great effort, to author, to perform as we should want, to effect what we had determined, to succeed with the completeness that we might have hoped.[5]

In such weakness, before Rom 8 has a chance to reveal that we do not even know how to pray, our spirituality is described in terms of groaning. Such groaning is a longing for the limitations of this world to be replaced by the promise of all that is eternal and heavenly (2 Cor 5:1–5). We have had enough. We have been promised much and experienced little. And yet, the mention of "groaning" is couched in such a way that it is legitimatized as an appropriate spiritual response to futility, bondage, and labor pains.

We who groan are those who possess the first fruits of the Spirit (v. 23). Somehow, this groaning is a fruit of the Spirit; it contrasts with the moaning and complaining that has beset the people of God at various junctures of the

---

5. Buckley, "'Because Beset by Weakness,'" 126.

biblical narrative (e.g. Num 14) and church life. "Groaning is not so much faithlessness but faithfulness—a sign of those who have the first fruits of the Spirit. We groan because we have the Spirit rather than 'even though' we have the Spirit."[6] To quote Ajith Fernando again, "Groaning is an alternative to quitting."

Romans 8 redefines our conventional understanding of what constitutes prayer and spirituality; words are absent and groaning is present. Creation and the church mysteriously share this practice, and we are orientated to the Spirit out of our deep need and frustration. Hope abounds and yet perhaps for many, hope eludes. Such a spirituality can be elusive to grasp. The very nature of the conditions that birth such an expression of faith—suffering and groaning—can also be the very conditions that cause people to stumble in their faith. Our attention now turns to this tension.

GOD SEES, HEARS, AND ACTS

The exodus motif that threads throughout the biblical narrative lands here in Rom 8 and in our lives, if we have a heart and mind to see it. In Rom 8, the sequential and triple mention of groaning (vv. 22, 23, 26) of creation, church, and Spirit brings us to the climactic revelation that the Spirit shares our groaning and magnifies it.[7] This is an exodus moment. Through the Spirit's ministry, God sees, hears, and acts (v. 27). The Greek variant of groaning is found only here in v. 26 (with reference to the Spirit's groaning) and Acts 7:34 with reference to the Israelites' groaning as slaves in Egypt. Here we lean into the biblical tradition of human groaning, divine hearing, and an exodus response.[8] Abraham Joshua Heschel captures the divine activity eloquently:

> Dark is the world for me
> for all its cities and stars.
> If not for the certainty that God listens

---

6. Moo, *Romans*, 519.

7. "There is one Greek root that occurs three times, here and only here in Romans. That is the clue. . . . This repetition tells us how to read the passage." Wright, *Heart of Romans*, 142.

8. N. T. Wright itemizes the theme of the exodus in the chapters in Romans leading up to chapter 8. He likens Rom 6 with the crossing of the Red Sea, Rom 7 with arriving at Sinai, Rom 8 with being led to the promised inheritance, and the groaning in Rom 8 relating back to Exod 2 and slavery. This leads to his reflection on the already–not yet eschatological tension. Wright also places the weakness (Rom 8:26) and related experiences for pastoral leaders in the context of Jesus's passion. Wright, *Heart of Romans*, 138, 145–46, 150–51.

> to our cry,
> who could stand so much misery,
> so much callousness.⁹

Such an exodus response is fulfilled in Jesus's own exodus journey. Such an exodus journey is seen at his transfiguration and the discussion there with Moses and Elijah about his *exodon* from Jerusalem (Luke 9:30–31), to the darkness of Gethsemane (Luke 22:42–44) and his prayer of anguish, to the trauma of Golgotha (Mark 15:44) and his cry of abandonment, to his final cry of trust in committing himself to the Father (Luke 23:46). Our own exodus plight includes having the anguish of being enslaved and longing for release. Creation shares our anguish and longing. The Spirit picks up the tone of our weakness and intervenes for us in an exodus fashion. The Spirit's presence is a beautiful expression of incarnation for the purposes of intercession. The Spirit is both the God who hears and sees, and the God who takes up our cry at the point when "we do not know what we ought to pray for." The intricacy of this divine activity amid the church's groaning, weakness, and enforced silence is articulated superbly by Michael Gorman:

> Possessing the Spirit, however, is no protection against suffering; in fact, just the opposite is true. Having the Spirit connects us to the suffering creation and, by extension, to other people who suffer (cf. 1 Cor 12:26). For Paul, in fact, even the Spirit participates in this suffering; the Spirit groans while giving aid to, and interceding for, believers, who do not know how, or what (so NIV), to pray in the midst of suffering (8:26). This remarkable assertion becomes all the more noteworthy in the corollary that God (the Father) and the Spirit of God are of one intercessory mind and will (8:27), thus implying not only fatherly concern but even participation in the children's groans. And we will hear in 8:34 that Jesus also intercedes for us. *Communication about the welfare of God's children is characteristic of the communion among the persons of the Trinity.*¹⁰

Our groaning is not the last word on whatever situation is causing us frustration and a sense of futility. Our groaning is the means by which hope emerges and we are assured that "communication about the welfare of God's children" becomes the topic of conversation within the Trinity. Hope emerges from groaning because it is sanctioned by God. Earlier in Romans, we see some of the working parts that connect suffering to hope. According to Rom 5:2–5,

---

9. Heschel, *I Asked for Wonder*, 42.
10. Gorman, *Romans*, 207; emphasis in original.

And we boast in the hope of the glory of God. Not only so, but we also glory in our sufferings, because we know that suffering produces perseverance; perseverance, character; and character, hope. And hope does not put us to shame, because God's love has been poured out into our hearts through the Holy Spirit, who has been given to us. (NIV)

The starting point is suffering and the end point is hope. Romans 5:2–5 serves as a precursor to our Rom 8 text. The triad of suffering-perseverance-character (Rom 5) is the inner working of the coupling of suffering-groaning in Rom 8. The church's groaning in patient hope (Rom 8:26) is an expression of perseverance, a character trait, and an orientation to hope (Rom 5:3–5). Such hope is sure and confirmed by the gift and presence of the Holy Spirit. In this the people of God are sustained. We are sustained by the love of God poured into our hearts through the Holy Spirit and sustained by the experience, since the exodus onwards, that God hears his people's groanings. While the earth beneath us may be like iron, heaven is not like bronze (see Deut 28:23). Taken together, the texts from Rom 5 and 8, affirm that the DNA of our groaning is perseverance and character. We suffer and, by way of response, groan as an expression of perseverance and character. This DNA leads to fully-fledged hope. The love of God and intercession of the Spirit sustains us in it all because God responds to our groaning by ensuring it does not end with us but that our groans are taken up by the Spirit. This ministry is one way by which God sees, hears, and acts in response to his people's suffering.

Our groaning is the tuning fork in comparison to the Spirit's full symphonic version. The Spirit's symphonic groaning is in the hearing of the Trinity; and yet out of the range of our hearing. Abraham Joshua Heschel describes the ministry of the Old Testament prophet as one who "employs notes one octave too high for our ears. He experiences moments that defy our understanding. . . . Often his words begin to burn where conscience ends."[11] Here in Rom 8, the Spirit employs notes one octave too low "through wordless groans." The Spirit's intercession begins where human strength ends. Or rather, the Spirit's intercession begins where human weakness overwhelms. While what the Spirit prays is outside our ability to hear and comprehension to understand, we lean on the hope of vv. 24–25 insofar as "if we hope for what we do not yet have, we wait for it patiently" (v. 25). We wait and hope that God who searches the heart and knows the mind of the Spirit responds because the Spirit has interceded according to the will of God (v. 27). In this way, "Believers never have to worry about the efficacy of this intercession,

---

11. Heschel, *Prophets*, 12.

because it is born from God's own presence within them (8:27), working to bring about his purpose (8:28)."[12] So in true exodus tradition, God sees and hears the misery of his people and acts dramatically. We are too weakened and overwhelmed to know how we ought to pray, and into this vacuum of human activity the Spirit acts in the exodus tradition of "Let my people go!" We are not alone or abandoned. Our groaning is in harmony with the Spirit's groans and this reaches heaven. God the Holy Spirit groans and the Trinity responds.

"IS THAT ALL THE HELP WE GET?!"

As mentioned though, the divine activity is not immediately discernible by humanity. The Spirit's intercession is an octave too low for us to hear. This indiscernible divine activity in response to our groaning means there is one thing for us to do: nothing; "nothing" insofar as trying to *do* something to redeem the situation. Yes, we wait in patient hope. No, we don't take matters into our own anxious and active hands. We must do that which is not a natural response for churches anxious to move out of times of suffering: wait. Indeed, the posture of waiting is an honest admission of the enormity of the situation and the enormity of the promise of God:

> *Absolute hope* arises in the face of the *negativity of absolute despair*. It germinates close to the *abyss*. The negativity of absolute despair characterizes a situation in which action seems no longer possible. It germinates in the moment of the total collapse of the narrative that constitutes our life.[13]

However, our honest admission of the enormity of the situation and God's response still does not resolve the issue of not quite knowing precisely what the Spirit is praying. So, while it is distressing enough that we do not know how to pray, how is it of any help that we do not know what the Spirit prays in light of our prayer paralysis? The intercessory ministry of the Spirit, this Trinitarian deliverance from futility and pain, is a gift and challenge. It is a gift insofar as when the church is at its weakest, she is promised prayer will still take place. It is a challenge insofar as when the church is at its weakest, the gift of Spirit intercession means that it is FYI not DIY. Generally, in the presence of crisis, churches do not do well at doing nothing. Further, during a crisis, the admission of a pastor that she or he is at the end of themselves and that they do not know how they ought to pray would likely

---

12. Keener, *Romans*, 108.
13. Han, *Spirit of Hope*, 37; emphasis in original.

be ministry-ending. Surely that is ironic given that the biblical testimony of Rom 8 is that such an admission is Spirit ministry-beginning. Eugene Peterson incisively exposes the church's obsessiveness with human activity at the expense of divine agency:

> The church is understood almost exclusively in terms of function—what we can see. If we can't see it, it doesn't exist. . . . Church is an instrument that we have been given to bring about whatever Christ commanded us to do. Church is a staging ground for getting people motivated to continue Christ's work. This way of thinking—church as a human activity to be measured by human expectations—is pursued unthinkingly. The huge reality of God already at work in all the operations of the Trinity is left on the bench while we call timeout, huddle together with our heads bowed and figure out a strategy by which we can compensate for God's regrettable retreat into invisibility. This is dead wrong . . . this way of going about things has done and continues to do immeasurable damage to the [Western] church.[14]

For the weakened, anxious, and hyperactive pastor or church, the Spirit's intercessory "wordless groans" can be mistakenly construed as a form of God's "regrettable retreat into invisibility." The vocabulary of vv. 24–25 of hoping for the unseen and waiting for it with patience is as much activity as the church needs to do. Their groaning has been heard and taken up by the Spirit who helps in their weakness. The Greek word assigned to the Spirit's "help" (v. 26) is found only here in Rom 8 and in Luke 10:40: "But Martha was distracted by her many tasks; so she came to [Jesus] and asked, 'Lord, do you not care that my sister has left me to do all the work by myself? Tell her then to help me.'" The use of the word "help" in Luke 10 acts as an early warning system for what happens later in Rom 8. In a sense, Martha's prayer is answered a second time in Rom 8 where "help" is now given by virtue of the Spirit's intercession. If we take Martha as a representative of the weakened pastor or anxious church, the essence of what Martha needs to do remains the same as in Luke 10: recognize the center of gravity is the presence and agency of God, not our activity. Taken together, the two occurrences of "help" in the New Testament amount to the message of "sit" (Luke 10:40) and "allow God to speak" (Rom 8:26). Yet the implicit need conveyed from the context of Martha's story in Luke 10 is that she needs to sit and listen to Jesus as her sister has done. The apparent break in the connection and corollary, from the first use of "help" in Luke 10 to the second use in Rom 8, is that listening in Rom 8 is not as straightforward. Unlike Jesus in Luke 10,

---

14. Peterson, *Practise Resurrection*, 118.

what the Spirit is saying in Rom 8 is one octave too low. How is that "help"? Romans 8 frames this theological conundrum by first referring to creation's experience in this world of corruption and decay. Perhaps, then, an example from creation will help us rest in this mysterious ministry of the Spirit.

My place of ministry is situated on a campus amid a city green belt and close by are the city's botanical gardens. There is a large aviary in the gardens with an array of exotic birds. These caged birds squawk and it is a cacophony of cries. In contrast, the gardens attract a native bird of Aotearoa New Zealand: the tūī. The tūī has a distinct bird song. It is made up of a series of trills and scales, ranging from guttural sounds to melodious tunes. The tūī is also one of the few birds in the world that can mimic human speech with the added skill of being able to do so with a New Zealand accent. However, the tūī's song appears to be staccato. The bird song is punctuated with moments of silence. Yet what appear to be silent pauses are in fact a continuation of the tūī's song; the notes are beyond the human hearing register. The tūī's song is in stark contrast to the imprisoned birds. There we have a picture of bondage and freedom, of two kinds of calls. The tūī's combination and capacity to mimic human speech *and* to sing beyond the human aural register is analogous to the Spirit's "wordless groans." The Spirit both imbibes the caged human groaning (incarnational) *and* takes it to another level (intercessory). As mentioned earlier, the Spirit prays one octave too low for us to hear. Even though aspects of the Spirit's "wordless groans" might be beyond the human spiritual register, this incomprehensible intercession is a source of hope and wonder, not dismay and frustration. Whatever else the Spirit's relationship is with the church by way of guiding God's people into truth and taking what is Jesus's and making it known to his disciples (John 14:26; 16:13–15), there is an irreducible mystery and incomprehension concerning aspects of the Spirit's engagement with the world. While writing with the ministry of the Old Testament prophets in view, Abraham Heschel's reflection on the nature of God has currency in our reflection on the Spirit's intercession: "God's ways are just, right, wise, but neither transparent nor immune to misunderstanding. There is an unfolding and a shrouding, a concealing within a disclosing, consoling as well as confusing."[15] Biblically speaking, God does some of his best work in apparent concealment and in the ensuing silence due to spiritual activity happening beyond our ability to hear. And the church does some of its best work by faith-full listening and discernment when the Spirit helps us in our weakness with "wordless groans."

---

15. Heschel, *Prophets*, 224.

HUMAN INCOMPREHENSION DOES NOT MEAN DIVINE INACTIVITY

That we cannot necessarily comprehend, via the faculty of human speech, the Spirit's "wordless groans" does not invalidate the efficacy of the prayer. "Thus what we do not understand, we can be sure God does, because even if the 'groanings' are 'inarticulate' and therefore not understandable to our minds, Paul reassures his readers, they are not so to God. He knows the mind of the Spirit."[16] Paradoxically, and wondrously, the church's incapacity to know how to pray as we ought (v. 26) is answered by the experience of not knowing what the Spirit prays as a result. Our loss for words is complemented by a loss of comprehension; hence silence, mystery, and hope are inescapable aspects of being in relationship with God and experiencing redemption. Are the church's leaders weak enough to recognize that and offer this experience to their congregation as evidence of the intervention of God? Perhaps such a disposition is an expression of Cardinal Emmanuel Célestin Suhard's (1874–1949) challenge: "To be a witness does not consist in engaging in propaganda, nor even in stirring people up, but in being a living mystery. It means to live in such a way that one's life would not make sense if God did not exist."[17] Our groaning, weakness, and inability to pray are the precursors to the Trinity's *"communication about the welfare of God's children."*[18] These precursors and spirituality do not make sense if God did not exist.

Yet this is not a picture of the church retreating behind castle walls and raising the drawbridge. This is a picture of the church being honest about her need to groan in travail, acknowledging the pain of existence and in doing so embracing the vocation of being a living example of what it looks like to be the subject of the Spirit's prayer.[19] We presently experience pain in a world of pain and we are distinctive in that we have robust hope that the

---

16. Fee, *God's Empowering Presence*, 586. Fee makes the case that the groans of the Spirit's intercession are glossolalia (578–86). There are a range of views concerning the nature of the Spirit's groans, such as represented by Keener, *Romans*, 107–8: "Against some commentators, this is an experience different from tongues, which Paul values (1 Cor 12:10; 14:18) but regards as articulate. Some experiences were considered so sublime or sacred they were unutterable (2 Cor 12:4); Paul may transfer that sacredness to how God feels and responds to the sufferings of his children." It is my position that the "wordless groans" are not an expression of praying in tongues for the reasons that Keener offers.

17. L'Engle, *Walking on Water*, 22.

18. Gorman, *Romans*, 207; emphasis in original.

19. Wright, *Heart of Romans*, 133–34.

Spirit is in conversation with the Father about our plight in the here-and-now. In this, the will of God is fulfilled.

> The God of free grace will not abandon the church. This is the God the church must rely on even in seemingly unsurmountable difficulties—a God who makes our problems God's own problems. We can trust this God because we know who and what God is through the grace revealed in Jesus Christ.[20]

Again, this amounts to the necessary yet difficult realization that in those times when the church is groaning and does not know how to pray as they ought, the best thing is to do nothing. This is our paradoxical witness in being a living mystery and living is such a way that it wouldn't make sense if God didn't exist. In the agony of inactivity, or apparent fruitless activity, the Spirit is doing something humanly and divine. The words of Rom 8:18, 24–25 become the DNA of this spirituality:

> I consider that the sufferings of this present time are not worth comparing with the glory about to be revealed to us. . . . For in hope we were saved. Now hope that is seen is not hope. For who hopes for what is seen? But if we hope for what we do not see, we wait for it with patience. (NRSV)

This is one aspect of a manifold eschatological vision for the church. Suffering is for now and part of the church's identity, hope is the path, and glory is the destination. Groaning sustains us on the way and ushers us into the unexpected and incomprehensible experience of the Spirit facilitating the will of God. Groaning is an expression and exposition of Rom 8:18, 24–25, waiting patiently for what we hope for. Groaning is the living mystery and the ministry the church does when the only thing the church can do is *nothing*. Such a spirituality requires courageous leadership. The church needs leaders who know how to groan as they wait in hopeful patience, knowing that the Spirit groans with and for them by way of bringing their plight to the attention of the Trinity.

> The need for leadership is high. Yet leadership should not cajole the community to expend energy (the assumed model for leadership) but should beckon them to stay attentive in waiting, just as Jesus asks Peter and others in the garden of Gethsemane (Matt. 26:36). . . . Waiting is seeking . . . most church leadership see waiting as the enemy of survival because they have assumed, along with modernity, that the only human action that counts is the expenditure of energy. The goal is to do something, to

---

20. Mannen, "Proclamation of Free Grace."

expend some energy, to survive. But the only human action that can save us is to wait. Only waiting as a form of seeking readies us for an encounter with a God who is God. Waiting is the heart of faithful seeking.[21]

Groaning as we wait, together with all creation, is one way the church embodies and expresses her vocation in the name of Jesus.[22] To extrapolate the birth and first fruit imagery of Rom 8, the risk of acting instead of hoping and relying on the Spirit's intercession is to risk premature birth or worse, a miscarriage. So, at times, inactivity is the church's best practice.

THE SPIRIT'S INTERCESSION IS ANSWERED

I recall amid leading a Christian leadership planning exercise, the discussion became fraught, confused, and conflictual. We all left that day bewildered and maybe even wounded in some ways. After a broken sleep that night with the events of the day on my mind, I found myself eventually wide awake. I was at a loss to know what to do when we reconvened as a leadership forum in the morning. I then recognized the weakness in myself and in the situation and my heart and mind went to Rom 8 and the description of the Spirit's intercessory groans. This ministry was all that was left as an option. The experience in that moment, lying awake in the dead of night at a loss for words hoping that the Spirit would pick up on my sense of grief and groaning, was discombobulating. I *felt* I ought to be doing something ... anything. The perceived need to revert to activity was overwhelming. Yet I didn't know what I could do. So, I entrusted the situation into the silence that was full of the incomprehensible and unfathomable wordless groans of the Spirit. There was no peace in that moment but there was hope. The next morning when we reconvened, an authentic and courageous discussion began our day. We talked about the events of the previous day and we experienced redemption. It was only when one of the participants summed up the time as us "groaning" that it struck me that the Spirit's intercession had been lovingly answered. The Spirit had breathed life, love, and light into

---

21. Root, *Crisis of Decline*, 163–65.

22. "This isn't just about 'going through a rough time.' Nor is it simply 'something we occasionally have to put up with.' Paul is talking about our *vocation* not just to *get through difficult* times but to stand in prayer where the world is in pain so that God's own spirit may be present, and intercede, right there. This is one of the most revolutionary and innovative moments in the whole letter." Wright, *Heart of Romans*, 133–34; emphasis in original.

our gathering. If I had attempted to act in my weakness the previous day, the birth could have been premature and endangered life.

Anyone in Christian leadership, and anyone in a church let alone all creation, will resonate with times of weakness and helplessness that creates a chasm of uncertainty as we endeavor to seek the kingdom of God. Our passage from Rom 8 provides the hope we need so that we *can* hope. One of the definitive, if not one of the most harrowing, books to emerge from the Holocaust is *Night* by Nobel Peace Prize laureate Elie Wiesel (1928–2016). In a lecture describing the journey of writing and publishing *Night*, Wiesel locates that experience with the wider experience of the world over:

> *Night* is a foundation to say, "Look! This is what happened. Can we continue?" Even if the answer is "No," I would say we must continue. We must invoke a meaning even when there is no meaning. We must formulate a prayer for hope, even if there is no hope.[23]

Wiesel's question is our question: Can we continue? Wiesel's exhortation lands in our space: we must invoke a meaning . . . we must formulate a prayer for hope. That prayer for hope is generated by our ministry of groaning to which the Spirit responds by extrapolating our groaning in deep ways and in the hearing of the community of the Trinity. The experience of frustration and futility is resurrected by the fulfilment of all that is hoped for in Christ.

The Spirit's intercession invokes meaning for us when we groan that there is no meaning. The Spirit's intercession formulates a prayer for hope even when we groan that there is no hope. The Spirit's intercession enables us to continue when the temptation is to quit. The Spirit helps us because we have finally recognized that we need to be weak enough to offer such leadership to the people of God. We wait with patient hope, knowing that the Spirit is interceding beyond the register of human spiritual hearing. We realize that the apparent silence of God is not to be met with frenetic activity on the part of the church but with patient hope. We see that the majesty and mystery of Rom 8:18–27 continues the exodus story. The Spirit helps us because we have finally recognized that in our weakness, when we are at a loss for words, we need to do nothing . . . except groan and wait in patient hope.

---

23. Wiesel, "We May Use Words," 8:27–8:49.

BIBLIOGRAPHY

Buckley, Michael, SJ. "'Because Beset by Weakness...'" In *To Be a Priest: Perspectives on Vocation and Ordination*, edited by Robert E. Terwilliger and Urban T. Holmes III, 125–32. New York: Seabury, 1975.

Fee, Gordon D. *God's Empowering Presence: The Holy Spirit in Paul's Letters*. Peabody: Hendrikson, 1994.

Gorman, Michael J. *Romans: A Theological and Pastoral Commentary*. Grand Rapids: Eerdmans, 2022.

Han, Byung-Chul. *The Spirit of Hope*. Translated by Daniel Steuer. Cambridge: Polity, 2024.

Heschel, Abraham Joshua. *I Asked for Wonder: A Spiritual Anthology*. New York: Crossroad, 1983.

———. *The Prophets*. New York: HarperCollins, 2001.

Keener, Craig S. *Romans: A New Covenant Commentary*. Cambridge: Lutterworth, 2009.

L'Engle, Madeleine. *Walking on Water: Reflections on Faith and Art*. New York: Convergent, 2016.

MacCulloch, Diarmaid. *Silence: A Christian History*. New York: Viking, 2013.

Mannen, Sarah. "The Proclamation of Free Grace, Pt. 1." God Here & Now. Center for Barth Studies, June 11, 2024. https://barthcenter.substack.com/p/the-proclamation-of-gods-free-grace.

Moo, Douglas. *The Epistle to the Romans*. NICNT. Grand Rapids: Eerdmans, 1996.

Nicol, Charissa. "Flourishing in Frailty: The Efficacy of Weakness." Paper presented at the Flourish Conference, Carey Baptist College, Auckland, New Zealand, July 18–19, 2022.

Peterson, Eugene H. *Practice Resurrection: A Conversation on Growing up in Christ*. Grand Rapids: Eerdmans, 2010.

Root, Andrew. *Churches and the Crisis of Decline: A Hopeful, Practical Ecclesiology for a Secular Age*. Grand Rapids: Baker Academic, 2022.

Wiesel, Elie. *Night*. New York: Hill and Wang, 2006.

———. "We May Use Words to Break the Prison: Elie Wiesel on Writing Night." Facing History and Ourselves, Feb. 11, 2014. Video, 8:49. https://www.facinghistory.org/resource-library/we-may-use-words-break-prison-elie-wiesel-writing-night.

Wright, N. T. *Into the Heart of Romans: A Deep Dive into Paul's Greatest Letter*. Grand Rapids: Zondervan, 2023.

Chapter 10

A Means of Grace

A Pastor's Listening Within a Church Community as a Way of Sustaining the Body of Christ

SARAH PENWARDEN

INTRODUCTION

THIS CHAPTER PROCEEDS FROM two convictions about the local church and how it lives out its embodied, spiritual, and practical life. The first conviction is that the church is created through the work of the Spirit *and* made by the people of God, using their gifts to minister and serve. The second conviction is that while pastors shape the church, they also have a role to play in listening for the vision that is implicitly present in the local church and reflecting it back to the church. In this way, a leader is participating with the church as the people of God. In this chapter, I explore both these convictions and consider, not only why this is important but how a leader can help a church hear its own vision and contribute to its ongoing life. I then give an example of one practical means for this, through ethnographic research where a pastor studies their own church community. I describe how I conducted a small-scale ethnographic study in my church where I sought to listen to and highlight the church's own sense of its vision as a place where people can flourish. This data was captured through a survey and made into a quantitative pie chart and qualitative depiction of small stories of the congregants' experience of flourishing. Both were shared with the church itself. I thus show how ethnographic research within a leader's own church can spotlight the vision already existing in the church, and, in reflecting this back to the church, the leader can contribute to the local church's ongoing life.

FIRST CONVICTION: THE CHURCH IS MADE BY THE PEOPLE *AND* GOD AND ALREADY HAS ITS OWN VISION

We cannot make the church. Together as believers, we *all* make the church. These two statements seem irreconcilable, yet both are true. The church is the people of God made by God. In Catholic theology, the church is the "people of God," a "pilgrim people on the way to a heavenly city."[1] The church itself, though imperfect, is a sacrament, "the visible form of an invisible grace."[2] The church is both a sign of God's grace and an instrument of God's mission.[3] In this way, it is God who breathes life into the church. Indeed, Ruth Haley Barton highlights the God-breathed nature of the church: "The most important thing we need to understand deep in our souls is that Christian community—transforming community—is not something we create or bring about by human effort. . . . The community we are seeking already exists in Christ at the cosmic level, and all we can do is find ways to open up to that reality and live it . . . This community is breathed into life through the Holy Spirit of Christ, not by anything we ourselves can take credit for."[4] *And also*, as the people of God, we too make the church as a body, through each interaction we have with the church community and those in our neighborhood.

To "make" can mean to "bring into being by forming, shaping, or altering material."[5] It can also mean to "put into definite form, or to put parts together to make a whole."[6] *Making* the church does not mean laboring and building in a spirit of independence and self-reliance. Writing about *tov* churches,[7] McKnight and Barringer say, "We don't create *tov* churches

---

1. Kärkkäinen, *Introduction to Ecclesiology*, 23.
2. Macy, *Theologies of the Eucharist*, 40.
3. *Lumen Gentium*.
4. Haley Barton, *Life Together in Christ*, 26.
5. Merriam-Webster.com, "Make."
6. Collinsdictionary.com, "Make."

7. *Tov* is the Hebrew word for good. McKnight and Barringer advocate for ways of forming "a culture of *goodness* in our churches that will resist abuses of power, promote healing, and eradicate the toxic fallout that infects so many Christian organizations."

in our own strength, by grit and determination or by clever programming. *Tov* churches are the work of God's Spirit set free to create *tov*.[8] While we don't "make" a church through our own determination alone, as a church community every micro-action of relational, practical, and spiritual care creates the church, as it is through *our* God-breathed bodies that the Spirit does its work. In this sense, God uses us and our gifts; not just the leaders, but everyone.

While leaders have a significant role, it is crucial to see *all* believers as being called to minister and serve in some way. A participatory ecclesiology highlights the "rights and gifting of each believer for ministry as equal partners."[9] In this sense, "all members of a church depict and offer the manifold grace of God through their actions and words."[10] Furthermore, "the church comes into being and *comes to life* through the communication of salvation by mutual service with the pluriform gifts of the Spirit."[11] The people are the actual means through which the church comes to life. The people are not only recipients. They are not bystanders. They are the very form through which the Spirit makes the church.

While the metaphor of the church as a human body as used by Paul in 1 Cor 12 is very familiar, this metaphor can invite one to see leaders as the head of the church, when in fact Christ alone is the head of the church. Other ecclesial metaphors enable a more accurate understanding of the ministry of all believers. Interdisciplinary scholars Brown and Strawn suggest that a church is not a disparate group of individuals but a "dynamical system" that shapes individuals into a group with a higher cause.[12] They use the metaphor of an ant colony. In an ant colony, "because of the constant, ongoing interactions among all of the individual ants, the colony comes to function as a whole unified system."[13] This goes far beyond "the characteristics of individual ants."[14] Churches, like ant colonies, are dynamic systems that are primarily *self-organizing*. Thus, when there is "sufficient quantity and quality of communication and interaction among congregants" the church moves from being "a loose association of the independently spiritual" into

---

McKnight and Barringer, *Church Called Tov*, 22.

8. McKnight and Barringer, *Church Called Tov*, 22.
9. Kärkkäinen, *Introduction to Ecclesiology*. 65.
10. Kärkkäinen, *Introduction to Ecclesiology*, 140.
11. Kärkkäinen, *Introduction to Ecclesiology*, 140.
12. Brown and Strawn, *Physical Nature*, 125.
13. Brown and Strawn, *Physical Nature*, 74.
14. Brown and Strawn, *Physical Nature*, 74.

"an organized body—the Body of Christ."[15] Indeed, "once the community begins to organize, new properties and capacities emerge that go well beyond what one might predict."[16]

This *becoming* a body is both theological and highly material. While we are already the body of Christ, we can grow more fully into this expression as we take a part in making the church. As we are becoming a body, we become a "deeply interactive network of Christian persons . . . that constitute the present and manifest Body of Christ . . . [which] becomes a means of grace to its own members and to the world."[17] Thus we move from being individuals to being a community; "not God's person . . . but God's *people*,"[18] who together in their interactions with each other and their neighbors "reflect the divine nature."[19]

Indeed, as parts of the body, the ministry of the church is carried out by every believer because, in Anglican theology for example, "from baptism, their vocation is to witness to Christ in the world using the gifts the Spirit gives them."[20] Writing about Luther's strongly egalitarian theology of priesthood, Greggs argues that "the core theological insight . . . is that all Christians are priests as they speak the Word of God (which they have received) to each other (sharing in the Word's mediating of God to humanity) and engage in intercession for each other (holding the other before God)."[21] This does not mean we all have a public-facing ministry role, but we *all* minister and serve. A leader can help in growing the people's understanding of themselves as active parts of the body of Christ, by believing in the capacities, actions, and initiatives of the people; that in every micro-action of relational, practical, and spiritual care, believers build the church as the Spirit does its work.

---

15. Brown and Strawn, *Physical Nature*, 125.
16. Brown and Strawn, *Physical Nature*, 129.
17. Brown and Strawn, *Physical Nature*, 130.
18. Greggs, *Dogmatic Ecclesiology*, 102.
19. Grenz, *Theology for the Community*, 501.
20. *New Zealand Prayer Book*, 932.
21. Greggs, *Dogmatic Ecclesiology*, 102.

SECOND CONVICTION: PASTORS CAN LISTEN TO HEAR THE VISION THAT IS ALREADY EXISTING IN THE CHURCH

A second conviction is that *if* the body of Christ is a God- and self-organizing system, then while pastors can shape the church, they can also participate in the vision the church already has, because the "dynamical system" of a church *does* have its own vision.[22] This chapter thus highlights the role of the pastor as participating in the vision of the church that already exists, rather than necessarily or only imparting a fresh vision. Pastors can participate in this vision through deliberately listening for it.

Listening is at once a taken-for-granted, everyday ability and an attitude that requires careful practice. While hearing involves merely detecting sounds, listening involves attending to words, to "heed them, tune into them . . . or process them actively."[23] The "English word 'listen' comes from two Anglo-Saxon words. One of them means 'hearing', and the other means 'to wait in suspense.'"[24] To listen—to wait in suspense for what the other might say—requires both patience and vulnerability; and openness to being impacted by the other. Deep listening requires humility, and a "receptive posture [which] helps us listen to others and to God more deeply, with holy curiosity."[25] Listening also requires spaces in which it can occur. Hedahl describes "listening habitats," in which one can engage in "discerning listening . . . listening for patterns, themes, what is not said, the gaps and silences, sour notes and grace notes . . . for thresholds, for evidence of change, for God and others simultaneously."[26]

If a pastor does seek to listen to a church, there are three particular things one can hear. One can listen vertically to what God is saying. Ruth Haley Barton describes a Christian community as "men and women gathered around the presence of Christ for the purpose of being transformed in Christ's presence so they can discern and do the will of God";[27] to grow in the "ability to recognize where God is at work so that we can join God in it."[28] There is also a kind of horizontal listening we can do in listening to each other. This can be challenging at times to hear people's frustrations,

---

22. Brown and Strawn, *Physical Nature*, 125.
23. Baab, *Power of Listening*, 5.
24. Baab, *Power of Listening*, 5.
25. Baab, *Power of Listening*, 12.
26. Hedahl, *Listening Ministry*, 98, 100.
27. Haley Barton, *Life Together in Christ*, 23.
28. Haley Barton, *Life Together in Christ*, 124.

disappointments, or difficulties in regard to church life or leadership, yet this is part of the bumpy journey of sanctification. Another kind of horizontal listening is listening to a church community for something particular, to hear the vision of the church.

If a pastor can hear the implicit vision of the church, they can then reflect it back to the people so they can be more aware of their active calling as believers who make the church through their actions and interactions. In considering "listening habitats" for listening to an implicit vision, this may be during a whole church prayer meeting, during prayer in home groups, intercessory prayer in a service, or even at an annual general meeting![29] Creating a space for intra-community listening like this can allow the leader *and* the whole church to hear what the "passion and priorities" are of this particular local church.[30] Lynne Baab gives an example of intra-community listening when, during a prayer time where a church was considering a mission focus, a lay leader encouraged the church "to ask themselves three questions as they pondered what they heard in conversations: What's your passion? What burns on your heart? Why are you here?"[31]

HOW MIGHT A PASTOR HELP A CHURCH HEAR ITS OWN VISION?

One means through which a pastor can listen to the local church body is through ethnographic research. Ethnographic research is research where a person, either within or outside a particular community, spends time listening to it, learning, and watching how a community lives, in order to understand its culture.[32] Ethnographic researchers seek to learn directly from the community and understand it on its own terms.

Thinking about a church's theology, Moschella says that ethnographic research can be a form of pastoral practice, where a pastor inquires of their own church, "What is going on here among us theologically?"[33] This inquiring may allow the discovery of *lived* theology—to see how particular theologies are embedded in the lives of ordinary believers. Ethnographic research can be a way of "opening your eyes and ears to understand the ways in which people practice their faith."[34] Rather than only introducing new the-

29. Hedahl, *Listening Ministry*, 100.
30. Baab, *Power of Listening*, 12.
31. Baab, *Power of Listening*, 3.
32. Ericksson and Kovalainen, *Qualitative Methods*.
33. Hedahl, *Listening Ministry*, 74.
34. Moschella, *Ethnography*, 4, 40.

ologies, "the pastor as ethnographer becomes an interpreter of the theology that the people are already expressing through their lives."[35] Moschella thus advocates for a pastor doing ethnographic research as a way to listen deeply within the congregation and as a way to reflect back to the people their own vision.[36] She suggests that as well as helping a leader listen, it can "allow the people to articulate their stories and reflect on the composite themes and subplots that come to light. The congregation can then begin to reevaluate and intentionally revise its corporate story, entertaining new ideas."[37] She suggests that ethnography can thus be a "form of pastoral listening that can analogously help a congregation or a community to find its collective voice. Ethnography can be used as a means for listening to a group, helping to call forth both individual and collective stories."[38]

Moschella also suggests that by sharing the results of such storytelling research with the community itself, this can be a way of weaving together the personal faith stories into overarching narratives the church community has about itself.[39] Through the congregation hearing the key stories that shape their common life—both human and divine stories—this can go on to amplify the effect of the community's vision.

CONDUCTING ETHNOGRAPHIC RESEARCH AS A WAY OF HIGHLIGHTING AN IMPLICIT VISION

Considering intra-community listening, I was curious about the vision my own church[40] holds about itself. As a priest, counsellor, and qualitative researcher, I love to hear people tell stories. I am often curious about the effects of such stories, and how they impact the person telling them. I was curious about my church's vision. In particular, given this volume's focus on hope and flourishing, I was curious about how this church—a very small, close-knit Anglican church that I will call St. Bede's—understands how it creates conditions in which people can flourish. In order to understand this, I conducted a small-scale survey, approved by both an ethics committee and the church's governing council.[41] I detail below both the survey, the

35. Moschella, *Ethnography*, 40.
36. Moschella, *Ethnography*.
37. Moschella, *Ethnography*, 6.
38. Moschella, *Ethnography*, 13.
39. Moschella, *Ethnography*, 145.
40. By describing it as "my own church," I mean the church I attend and also where I minister as one of a team of priests.
41. Ethical permission was gained to conduct the research from Laidlaw College's

findings, and the responses from the church when I shared it with them. The research was a form of ethnographic research, studying some of the theology of my own church community, and it featured in particular an Appreciative Inquiry focus.

Appreciative Inquiry is a philosophy and practice used primarily within business that seeks to inspire people "to produce effective, positive change."[42] Appreciative Inquiry's distinctive focus deliberately moves away from problem identification and towards only focusing on "the positive experiences of the people and the gifts of God," giving "a priority on the flourishing of humans and creation."[43] Its four-step cycle of inquiry begins with a Discovery phase, appreciating "the best of what is" and "what gives life," before moving to a Dream phase ("What might be?"), a Design phase ("How can it be?"), and finally Destiny ("What will be?").[44] This particular project strongly resembles the Discovery phase, a phase which seeks to find "bright spots";[45] to look for "what gives 'life' to a living system when it is most effective, alive, and constructively capable,"[46] and then to focus on growing/expanding this aliveness. In this survey, I sought to discover "what gives life" to a system; to find what it is within the life of this particular church that promotes flourishing and greenness for church members.

One key contribution of Appreciative Inquiry is its belief that groups and organizations have their own momentum, their own spirit which propels them forward. Indeed, "Appreciative Inquiry assumes that all organizations have significant life forces, and these forces are available in stories and imaginations."[47] Branson goes on to argue that "organizations are heliotropic . . . plants lean toward the sun. Similarly, organizations lean toward the source of energy, especially if there is a hopeful, imagined future."[48] He suggests that within churches we help them grow if they hear "life-giving stories"; perhaps stories from within the church itself, of their own life.[49] In this way, "the church gains clarity about itself and the Holy Spirit's life around and among them."[50]

Research Ethics Committee, and also from St. Bede's church council.
    42. Cooperrider et al., *Appreciative Inquiry Handbook*, xv.
    43. Branson, *Memories, Hopes, and Conversations*, 25.
    44. Cooperrider et al., *Appreciative Inquiry Handbook*, 5.
    45. Heath and Heath, *Switch*.
    46. Cooperrider et al., *Appreciative Inquiry Handbook*, 3.
    47. Branson, *Memories, Hopes, and Conversations*, 24.
    48. Branson, *Memories, Hopes, and Conversations*, 35.
    49. Branson, *Memories, Hopes, and Conversations*, 65.
    50. Branson, *Memories, Hopes, and Conversations*, 67.

THE "CHURCH AS A PLACE OF RESTORATION" SURVEY

I designed an Appreciative Inquiry survey within my own church, which invited participants to consider the elements of our church life that enable them to flourish. The survey acted as a means of intra-community listening to the people's vision and also a means through which to grow this vision by sharing the findings with them once they had been gathered.

The key question the survey sought to answer was: What are the elements within church life of St. Bede's that facilitate hope and flourishing in one's faith? In this Appreciative Inquiry focus, I sought to find what it is within our church life that helps people flourish "like a tree planted by streams of water, which yields its fruit in season and whose leaf does not wither" (Ps 1:3 NIV). In the information about the survey, I described how "flourishing" might be understood as leaving a service feeling that one's faith had been reinvigorated, or feeling more hopeful, or knowing one is a valued part of a community. It might mean feeling encouraged that God is present on one's spiritual journey. The survey contained both quantitative and qualitative aspects. In the first part, participants were invited to choose six elements of church life from a list of nineteen elements that in their opinion helps them flourish.

The nineteen elements were:

- Being welcomed at the door
- The service leaders or church leaders
- The worship and music
- The sermon
- Hearing Scripture being read
- Communion
- Knowing a sense of God's presence through the Spirit in the service
- Healing prayer or intercessory prayer
- Morning tea
- Hearing about missions work or contributing to it
- Being actively involved in this church and using my gifts
- The values, culture, or way of being of this church, such as hospitality
- Being cared for in this church and feeling like I belong
- Outreach groups to the surrounding community

- The church building and decorations
- Bible study/home group/life group
- Receiving prayer during the week or praying for others
- Doing social activities together or being part of other church groups
- Something else (please name it)

Participants were asked to rate the six elements according to the importance to flourishing, from one as most important to six being less important but still significant. In the second part of the survey, participants were invited to choose two particular elements that significantly contributed to their flourishing and then tell a small story in only a few words about this element. I invited participants to reflect on this question: What is it about each element that means I often leave church feeling refreshed or reinvigorated in my faith?

While conducting an online survey is very feasible, given the demographics of the congregation, I chose to conduct the survey using hard copy forms to be completed anonymously and returned to me.[51] Ethically, I was mindful of the potential conflict of interest with me being one of the priests in the church. In sharing the rationale and details of the survey one Sunday, I emphasized the importance of informed consent. While dual relationships are often problematic, my church role might potentially facilitate more engagement from congregants. Indeed, participants might be *more* honest in their responses given that the researcher was one of their own priests with a real investment in the church community.

Once I had the completed surveys, I turned the data into a quantitative representation with a pie chart displaying as percentages the most significant elements of church life that contribute to flourishing. I also created a qualitative representation by clustering together participants' small stories of the key elements into poem-like compositions.

---

51. Information about the research was shared at a Sunday service, and the next Sunday the survey forms were left at the back of church to be completed and deposited in a box. This was in order to keep the surveys anonymous. From a small church with an average of thirty attendees on a Sunday (but with fifty people on the roll) I gained eighteen completed surveys.

SEEING THE VISION THROUGH NUMBERS: A PIE CHART OF FINDINGS

After receiving the completed survey forms, I tallied the numbers of the most highly scoring elements out of the nineteen and converted these into a pie chart.

The Top Three Most Meaningful Elements of Church Life at St. Bede's which Contribute to Flourishing

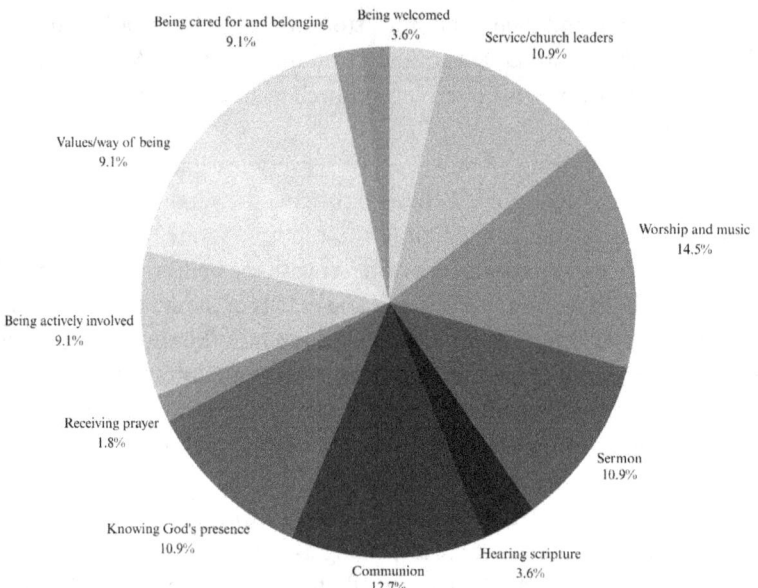

In this chart, one can see the most highly scoring elements of church life at St. Bede's church in this present era are: the service/church leaders, worship and music, the sermon, communion, knowing God's presence, being actively involved in church, the values/way of being of the church, and being cared for. In making sense of the findings, I briefly discuss here my responses, and how these findings tally with another recent church survey. I then display the qualitative data of participants' small stories about two particular elements, and discuss how I shared the findings with St. Bede's and their response.

As a priest at St. Bede's, I was very pleased to hear that these elements were "working" for those who responded to the survey, in relation to their own flourishing. I was particularly pleased to hear that congregants rated highly the sense of being cared for and the values/way of being of the church. What surprised me was how highly congregants valued being actively involved in church. I had previously felt a caution that as leaders we should not weigh people down with expectations of involvement, given that some people burnout through church volunteering. However, the findings here ran counter to that assumption. Being actively involved was something participants valued. This made me reconsider how I saw this church as one in which there were multiple ways a person could contribute and be part of the branches of it. Service was not limited to the few. I could see afresh the significance of people participating in the making and doing of church.

Considering these findings in the light of other surveys, a comparable survey is the Church Life Survey of New Zealand (CLSNZ). Conducted every five years since the 1990s, this survey aims to gauge the "perspective, character and values of church attendees across Aotearoa New Zealand."[52] The last survey in 2023 garnered more than twenty thousand respondents from Christians across denominations including Catholic, Anglican, Presbyterian, Methodist, Salvation Army, and Open Brethren churches. Like my survey, this survey asked participants to identify the most valued aspect of local church life. Participants could select three options from a list of seven elements, which were wider community care, traditional worship, contemporary worship, communion, sermons, practical care, and social activities.

Focusing on Anglican results for comparison with my survey, the CLSNZ found that out of all seven elements, Anglicans valued communion as the most important element to them. Indeed, there had even been an increase in valuing communion among Anglicans since the last survey in 2001. Anglicans valued communion more than any other denomination, including Catholics. There may be a number of reasons for this, some of which are described by my participants below. Within Anglican theology, communion is highly symbolic and significant. While eschewing the notion of transubstantiation, one major strand of Anglican theology sees communion as *anamnesis*: a living remembrance of Christ's sacrifice which continues to give us grace in the present.[53] Thus, "the signs of the eucharist are much more than mere reminders of the past and completed event of Christ's presence and sacrifice . . . [these] material things are the means by which that presence is known in the eucharist here and now, and by which that sacrifice is renewed and made available as a gift to all who receive it."[54] Thus,

---

52. Church Life Survey New Zealand, "Insights," 133.
53. Douglas, "Philosophical Assumptions," 133.
54. Douglas, "Philosophical Assumptions," 134.

communion is one key way Anglicans receive the grace of God. Participants' words below echo this.

From the CLSNZ, it is also possible to see that Anglicans value sermons, and that the value of sermons rose between the last survey in 2021 and this one. In the CLSNZ one could see that Anglicans preferred traditional worship. While unsurprisingly, wider community care was the highest rated element of church life for Salvation Army congregants, yet Anglicans also rated this element strongly, to the same extent as Methodists and Presbyterians. Each one of the elements in the CLSNZ and my survey at St. Bede's carry with them an embedded theology of who Jesus is, what the church is, and how we are to be the body of Christ together and in the world.

SEEING THE VISION THROUGH WORDS: SMALL STORIES OF LIFE-GIVING FORCES IN THE CHURCH

In the second part of the survey, participants told small stories about two particular elements of church that help them flourish. I collated together participants' utterances under the element name itself, choosing to display three or four utterances per element. I arranged the participant utterances as a "cluster," a poem-like composition which includes only the participants' actual words.[55] This kind of representation of participants' words is a form of data analysis known as "poetic representation."[56] It was pioneered by sociologist Laurel Richardson as a way to capture the richness of the speaking and recreate this richness textually.[57] While Richardson's poetic re-presentation mainly involved representing the speaking of one participant, in this approach below, I utilized Butler-Kisber's use of a "cluster" poem, showing different speakers' utterances gathered under one theme.[58] In Butler-Kisber's understanding, this can create a "prism-like rendition of the subtle variations of a phenomenon."[59]

---

55. Butler-Kisber, "Inquiry Through Poetry," 95.

56. Richardson, "Poetic Representation of Interviews."

57. Poetic re-presentation has been used for multiple purposes: as a way of capturing the vibrancy of speaking. See Galvin and Prendergast, eds., *Poetic Inquiry II*. Poetic inquiry has also been used to honor participants' speaking or to distil or condense data. See Richardson, "Poetic Representation of Interviews," and Furman, "Poetic Forms and Structures."

58. Butler-Kisber, "Inquiry Through Poetry," 95.

59. Butler-Kisber, "Inquiry Through Poetry," 95.

The Stories

Knowing God's Presence Through the Spirit

God's presence through the Spirit in the service
leaves me with a sense of
God's love in action.
The space, the worship, the camaraderie,
the communion
all bring God's Spirit alive
and I feel blessed for
whatever may happen in the week ahead.

Communion

I love how natural, inclusive, and accessible communion is.
It's meaningful for me to kneel at the rail
in openness to God.
As one of the sacraments, Holy Communion is
a core part of my week.
It's when I feel closest to God.
It reconnects me to Christ and our community.
It's grounding and hopeful.
Taking communion is very strengthening and healing.
I leave church feeling stronger and, in many ways, healed.

The Values and Culture of Way of Being of This Church

I appreciate spending time with like-minded people
in a peaceful, beautiful environment.
Our church observes the sacraments and has a community culture.
For many, the church is a rock, as life has its ups and downs.
It's real people with real faith expressed in a way that is relevant.
The values of this church leave me with confidence that
"all's right with the world."
This is a community without factions—
we all share the one bread.

Being Cared for and Feeling Like I Belong

The sense of being cared for shows in
numerous ways, from the simple acts
of kindness and support
to the pastoral care offered by the leaders.
This care makes me feel valued and seen,
not just as a church member
but as an individual with unique experiences.
Every time I leave church feeling refreshed,
it's because I have known this profound sense of care and
belonging.
It revitalizes my spirit, reassures me of my worth, and reinforces
my faith.
In this church, we really care for each other and know
God has a sense of humor!

Church Leaders

The leaders of the church encourage me to
extend the same care and
sense of belonging to others,
creating a ripple effect that strengthens the entire community.
The commitment of the church leaders makes me feel I am part
of a caring and dedicated church.

Being Actively Involved in the Church and Using My Gifts

Being actively involved gives me a sense of purpose
and is an important expression of shared life.

In reading/hearing these small stories from congregants, what struck me was the consistent picture of a community that had a culture of caring. One participant described the "ripple effect" of receiving care from the leaders and then sharing this care with others in the church. This was a picture of bonds of relationship, through which care was given and received: an image of a shared life. This was a church where communion, worship, and faith is taken seriously and meaningfully, one where everyone had a part to play. This was the vision of St. Bede's.

THE HEALTHY CHURCH MODEL

I shared the findings of the survey at St. Bede's one Sunday, and invited people to talk to the person next to them and reflect on what they were appreciating about St. Bede's in hearing this. I then shared my own reflection on the findings. I did not approach the survey with a deductive lens but found that when I was looking at the pie chart, I remembered the Healthy Church Model (Auckland Anglican Diocese).[60] This model describes healthy church life in four dimensions that circle a central core of "loving God and loving God's world." These dimensions, in no particular order, are, "Knowing God" through "inspiring worship, maturing faith, and prayerful life." "Shaping community" features creating "authentic loving community, stewardship, governance, and intergenerational participation." "Growing in Christ" contains elements of being "formed for mission, empowering leadership, ministry and gifts for all." "Living beyond ourselves" is the remaining dimension, featuring "proclaiming the gospel, relevant outreach, and pursuing justice."[61]

Viewing the quantitative findings through the overlay of this model, the elements that were valued by St. Bede's fit in three dimensions in particular: "Knowing God," "Shaping community," and "Growing in Christ." Indeed, the congregants rated all these elements highly. However, the dimension of "Living beyond ourselves" was not represented in the participants' assessing of elements of church life that helped them to flourish. During the presentation of the findings, I displayed the Healthy Church Model and showed, in the spirit of Appreciative Inquiry, where there were "bright spots" in our local church life; all the ways we were creating a church where people could grow in knowing God and living together. This focus fit with the first step of Appreciative Inquiry, where one can *discover* what is working well.

The next step of Appreciative Inquiry is *dream*, where we can consider what *might* yet be. Identifying a potential area for focus in our vision as St. Bede's, I invited congregants to consider four questions:

- Is anything missing from our life and ministry at St. Bede's?
- Where might we go from here?
- What can we dream for the future?
- What is the community beyond our fringes asking for?

---

60. Anglican Diocese of Auckland, "Healthy Church Model."
61. Anglican Diocese of Auckland, "Healthy Church Model."

In hearing people discuss the findings after church, some people talked about how encouraged they were from the pie chart (particularly the musicians, who scored highly!). Others were curious about why some elements, such as prayer ministry, had a relatively low score. Talking about living beyond ourselves, one person said outreach is our Achilles' heel because of the age of the congregation members. Yet another person had some ideas of how we could find out from the community what they might want from us via social media. The survey created fresh considerations at St. Bede's about who we are, what we are doing well, and also areas we are yet to make traction in. The Appreciative Inquiry focus enabled a renewed valuing of who we are and what we do as a local expression of the body of Christ. For me, this gave extra confidence in the health-producing quality of soil of this church for the congregants.

PRACTICING LISTENING TOGETHER: FINAL THOUGHTS

Every believer is called to participate in making the body of Christ; ministering both within the church and outside it. Every believer, as filled with the Holy Spirit, makes the church, which is ultimately "breathed into life through the Holy Spirit of Christ."[62] The local church is a participatory network in which we all have a role to play. While leaders minister to form/shape the local church, the highly dynamic nature of church life means leaders are always only *part* of the self-organizing system that is the church. Leaders can help congregants grow in their ministry as believers by making space to hear what the church members are saying. Leaders can do this by creating a "listening habitat" so congregants can hear the vision implicitly present in their own church;[63] to "become more conscious and intentional about their theology-in-action."[64] While having a vision means being able to imagine how a group might develop into the future, having vision means being able to see. In creating a listening habitat through ethnographic research, the congregants of St. Bede's were able to see some significant aspects of their vision as a church. They could also see elements to continue to grow in. This kind of intra-community listening can help both leaders and people be mindful of the communal journey we walk on together as a community of faith. It can encourage us to all take our part in allowing God

---

62. Haley Barton, *Life Together in Christ*, 26.
63. Hedahl, *Listening Ministry*, 98.
64. Moschella, *Ethnography*, 254.

to breathe the life of his Spirit into us as a people; a community of faith in which "we all share the one bread" (1 Cor 10:17 NET).

BIBLIOGRAPHY

Anglican Diocese of Auckland. "Healthy Church Model." https://aucklandanglican.org.nz/healthy-church-model/.

Baab, Lynne. *The Power of Listening: Building Skills for Mission and Ministry*. Lanham, MD: Rowman & Littlefield, 2014.

Branson, Mark Lau. *Memories, Hopes, and Conversations: Appreciative Inquiry, Missional Engagement, and Congregational Change*. Lanham, MD: Rowman & Littlefield, 2016.

Brown, Warren, and Brad Strawn. *The Physical Nature of Christian Life: Neuroscience, Psychology, and the Church*. New York: Cambridge University Press, 2012.

Butler-Kisber, Lynn. "Inquiry Through Poetry: The Genesis of Self-Study." In *Just Who Do We Think We Are? Methodologies for Autobiography and Self-Study in Teaching*, edited by Claudia Mitchell et al., 95–110. New York: RoutledgeFalmer, 2005.

Church Life Survey New Zealand. "Insights from the 2023 Church Life Survey New Zealand." Auckland, New Zealand, 2023.

Cooperrider, David, et al. *Appreciative Inquiry Handbook: The First in a Series of Ai Workbooks for Leaders of Change*. Bedford Heights, OH: Lakeshore, 2003.

Douglas, Brian. "Philosophical Assumptions Underlying Anglican Eucharistic Theology: A Study in Multiformity." *Studia Liturgica* 47 (2017) 124–37.

Eriksson, Paivi, and Anne Kovalainen. *Qualitative Methods in Business Research: A Practical Guide for Social Research*. 2nd ed. Thousand Oaks, CA: Sage, 2015.

Furman, Rich. "Poetic Forms and Structures in Qualitative Health Research." *Qualitative Health Research* 16 (2006) 560–66.

Galvin, Kathleen, and Monica Prendergast, eds. *Poetic Inquiry II—Seeing, Caring, Understanding: Using Poetry as and for Inquiry*. Rotterdam: Sense, 2016.

Greggs, Tom. *Dogmatic Ecclesiology: The Priestly Catholicity of the Church*. Grand Rapids: Baker Academic, 2019.

Grenz, Stanley. *Theology for the Community of God*. Grand Rapids: Eerdmans, 2000.

Haley Barton, Ruth. *Life Together in Christ: Experiencing Transformation in Community*. Downers Grove, IL: IVP, 2014.

Heath, Chip, and Dan Heath. *Switch: How to Change Things When Change Is Hard*. New York: Random House, 2011.

Hedahl, Susan. *Listening Ministry: Rethinking Pastoral Leadership*. Minneapolis: Fortress, 2001.

Kärkkäinen, Veli-Matti. *An Introduction to Ecclesiology: Historical, Global, and Inter-Religious Perspectives*. Downers Grove, IL: InterVarsity, 2021.

Macy, Gary. *The Theologies of the Eucharist in the Early Scholastic Period*. Oxford: Clarendon, 1984.

McKnight, Scot, and Laura Barringer. *A Church Called Tov: Forming a Culture of Goodness That Resists Abuses of Power and Promotes Healing*. Carol Stream, IL: Tyndale House, 2020.

Moschella, Mary Clark. *Ethnography as a Pastoral Practice: An Introduction*. Cleveland, OH: Pilgrim, 2008.

A New Zealand Prayer Book / He Karakia Mihinare o Aotearoa. Auckland: Anglican Church in Aotearoa, New Zealand, and Polynesia, 2024.

Richardson, Laurel. "Poetic Representation of Interviews." In *Handbook of Interview Research*, edited by Jaber Gubrium and James Holstein, 877–91. Thousand Oaks, CA: Sage, 2002.

Vatican II. "Dogmatic Constitution of the Church, *Lumen Gentium*." Vatican website. Nov. 21, 1964. https://www.vatican.va/archive/hist_councils/ii_vatican_council/documents/vat-ii_const_19641121_lumen-gentium_en.html.

Chapter 11

Tūmanako Me Whakahounga
Forms of Hope and Renewal in the Context of Contemporary Aotearoa

Lyndon Drake

INTRODUCTION

After years in ministry in Aotearoa/New Zealand, my family and I have moved back to Oxford, where we had lived previously. There is a great deal I miss about my homeland and the church in Aotearoa. There are also joys in renewing life in Oxford, and one of those joys is the chapel at Oriel College, where the forms of communal prayer have remained constant for hundreds of years and are still central to the life of the college community. Most days as part of morning prayer, the Benedictus is said. It opens with these words, based on Zechariah's prayer in Luke 1:68–79:[1]

English	Māori
Blessed be the Lord the God of Israel, who has come to his people and set them free.	Kia whakapaingia te Ariki, te Atua o Īharaira: kua titiro mai hoki ia, kua hoko i tāna iwi,

[1]. This version is from the Church of England's *Common Worship* for the English text, and *A New Zealand Prayer Book / He Karakia Mihinare o Aotearoa* for the Māori text.

English	Māori
He has raised up for us a mighty Savior, born of the house of his servant David.	Ā kua whakaarahia ake e ia he haona whakaora mō tātou: i roto i te whare o Rāwiri, o tāna pononga;
Through his holy prophets God promised of old to save us from our enemies, from the hands of all that hate us,	Ko tāna hoki ia, i kōrerotia e te māngai o āna poropiti tapu: nō te tīmatanga iho anō o te ao: Hei whakaora i a tātou i ō tātou hoa-whawhai: i te ringaringa anō hoki o te hunga katoa e kino ana ki a tātou;
To show mercy to our ancestors, and to remember his holy covenant.	Hei whakaputa mō te mahi tohu ki ō tātou tūpuna: hei whakamahara ki tāna kawenata tapu;
This was the oath God swore to our father Abraham: to set us free from the hands of our enemies,	Ki te oati i oati ai ia ki a Āperahama: ki tō tātou tūpuna. Kia tukua mai e ia ki a tātou he oranga i te ringaringa ō tātou hoa-whawhai:
Free to worship him without fear, holy and righteous in his sight all the days of our life.	ā, kia mahi wehi kore atu ki a ia, i runga i te tapu, i te tika, ki tōna aroaro: i ngā rā katoa e ora ai tātou.
And you, child, shall be called the prophet of the Most High, for you will go before the Lord to prepare his way,	Ā ko koe, e tama, ka kīia ko te poropiti a te Runga rawa: e haere hoki koe i te aroaro o te Ariki, hei whakapai i ōna ara:
To give his people knowledge of salvation by the forgiveness of all their sins.	Hei whakamātau i tāna iwi ki te whakaoranga: i ō rātou hara e murua ana;
In the tender compassion of our God the dawn from on high shall break upon us,	He mea hoki nā te aroha, nā te mahi tohu a tō tātou Atua: nā reira hoki i puta mai ai te pūaotanga o runga ki a tātou,
To shine on those who dwell in darkness and the shadow of death, and to guide our feet into the way of peace.	Hei whakamārama i te hunga e noho ana i te pōuri, i te ātārangi hoki o te mate: hei whakatika i ō tātou waewae ki te huarahi o te rangimārie.

The image of God's compassion dawning from on high is especially evocative, as is the contrast between the darkness of the world around and the light of God's saving action coming into the world. The picture painted by Zechariah's words is of a God who has made commitments and is keeping them. It is a hopeful picture—a picture of hope embodied in the person of Zechariah's son, John the Baptist, and a picture of hope's expectation of

God keeping his promises. All of us, like Zechariah, live with the embodied signs of God's action, and in the expectation of seeing God keep his promises. These twin hopes ought to inform our commitment to the renewal of the church in Aotearoa/New Zealand.

While I now say the Benedictus in English, its words have also formed part of the pattern of Christian worship in Aotearoa since the earliest days of Te Haahi Mihingare, the missionary church.[2] Conversions to Christianity began to take place after the translation of the Morning and Evening Prayer services into Māori enabled a pattern of daily prayer. In Te Tai Tokerau and other parts of the country, He Karakia Ata and He Karakia Ahiahi are still well-known and well-used parts of Māori life.

This pattern of prayer, including the use of the Benedictus in Māori, was pragmatically fruitful—that is, it worked as a programmatic evangelistic approach. But the fruitful outcome was the result of a theological understanding of mission activity. That understanding is centered on hope in God's promises and in a commitment to telling a certain type of theologically-informed story. Renewal, I suggest, is indeed possible, and the way in which the gospel was first embodied here in Aotearoa can inform our hopeful expectation for the flourishing of the gospel in the years that lie ahead of us.

In what follows, I first want to acknowledge that talk of renewal, or to use an even more loaded term, "revival," has sometimes led to cynicism. Romanticism about an imagined past, or which justifies current patterns as the way forward, or towards theological revisionism, all create implausible hope, so I first want to distinguish what I see as an essential theological foundation for plausibility and some examples of implausible directions. Then, I suggest that hope should be centered in God's promises to the church, both in general and in the specifics of God's story in Aotearoa/New Zealand. And lastly, I propose that renewal—if it comes—will arise from a retelling of the broken story by attending to the factors that produced such an extraordinary work of God in the mid-nineteenth century, while thoughtfully repenting of the actions that damaged that work so severely since then.

PLAUSIBLE HOPE FOR RENEWAL

While in a general sense, we expect the gospel to progress and God's kingdom to grow, there is no certainty that this will be the case in any particular place and time. The church does sometimes vanish from countries,

2. Te Haahi Mihingare is the Māori Anglican church.

through opposition or obsolescence. The general trend in Aotearoa is well-established and stable, and will, if some sort of radical change does not take place, lead in the relatively near future to the church vanishing entirely from Aotearoa—perhaps within the lifetime of the children in the church.

As we look back over the last few decades, ever since the decline in Christian allegiance in Aotearoa/New Zealand began, we can observe that the church has tried a number of different strategies to halt or reverse the decline. In my view, the church in Aotearoa should seek to identify strategies that are first of all theologically-informed and then which attend to the practical situation we find ourselves in.

A lack of explicit theological work in attempts to focus on church renewal is hardly new. As an example, I went to the library and picked two books at random off the shelves to compare the degree to which their prescriptions were informed by theology. The first, entitled *Church Renewal: A Handbook for Church Leaders*,[3] seems to contain sensible practical advice but fails to make clear what the author thinks the church actually *is* and what part God might play—but it is clear that the author believes success in renewal depends on a clear strategy and good execution. In other words, the hope is to my mind implausible, because it depends on an idea of church which has no theological warrant. By contrast, another book published the same year is *On Being Church: Essays on the Christian Community*.[4] This book has much more to offer in terms of theological depth, but is of a type which I hear discussed much less in church renewal conversations. While I do not know of scholarly accounts of implausible hope, when I reflect on my experience of Christian ministry in Aotearoa, a number of commonly occuring factors in church life and mission seem to me to damage the plausibility of hope for renewal.

Failing to Address Past Injustice

First of all, it seems astonishing to me that we expect God to bless our efforts when we are still living as a collective church on the fruits of past injustice. Many of our churches are built on land that has a checkered history at best, and in some cases there is a clear and direct connection between unjust taking of land and a current church community.[5] This particularly affects the early missionary denominations: Anglicans, Roman Catholics,

---

3. Kornfield, *Church Renewal*.
4. Gunton and Hardy, *On Being the Church*.
5. An example is Taranaki, for which see Waitangi Tribunal, "Taranaki Report"; Scott, *Ask That Mountain*; and Keenan, *Te Whiti o Rongomai*.

and Methodists arrived early and had largely Māori constituencies, and later settler churches formed almost as parallel structures under those wider denominational umbrellas.[6] Later on, other settler arrivals formed denominations which had no prior missionary presence among Māori, such as the Baptist and Brethren movements.[7] Among those early settler denominations, and then among the more recent church movements such as the Assemblies of God and other Pentecostal churches and movements, the issues of justice tend to be somewhat different. What strikes me as implausible, though, is for the church to collectively fail to address these complex problems while expecting God to bless their more explicitly spiritual work.

Trusting Programs

Secondly, while I have given considerable support to programs such as the Alpha Course, and indeed to programs which help organize church life and activity, a problem can arise when programs are invested with hope and energy beyond their ability to deliver. Programs need to serve a theological vision and be selected or developed in the light of that theological vision, rather than used as a strategy in themselves. In practice, of course, we will always be dependent in Aotearoa/New Zealand on tools which originated from overseas. We lack sufficient theologically-informed leadership to develop tools ourselves that can match those from overseas in terms of quality, and the cultural tides upon which overseas tools sail are not dissimilar to those found here. It is well worth developing home-grown tools for church mission and life—I have helped to develop some myself—as long as we recognize that they are likely to remain somewhat niche. We may be an island nation geographically, but we are not an island sociologically. But the issue I want to identify is not so much the origins of the programs we use, but the degree to which we place hope in programs. All too often churches either implicitly or explicitly define themselves in terms of programmatic

---

6. Chambers, "New Zealand Anglican Church," 29–45; Simmons, *Brief History*; Lange, *Māori and the Missionaries*; Davidson, *Christianity in Aotearoa*, 2004; Falloon, "Māori Conversion"; Williams, *Self-Governing Church*; Davidson et al., eds., *Te Rongopai 1814*; Davidson, *Christianity in Aotearoa*, 1991; Wall, "Methodism in New Zealand," 3–18; Lineham, "Methodist Church," 153–71; William Morley, *History of Methodism*. See also Carpenter, "Reshaping of Political Communities."

7. Woodfield, *Story of the Baptists*; Troughton, "Open Brethren," 105–26; Lineham, *There We Found Brethren*; Lineham, "Bible and Society," 19–25; Hilliard, "Unorthodox Christianity," 85–104; Davidson, "Baptists and Evangelicalism," 243–60; Blair, *Presbyterians*.

activities, instead of in a theologically-informed vision of being, mission, and ministry.

Leadership

I was recently at a conference where Rowan Williams, the former archbishop of Canterbury, was invited to participate in an interview session. He was asked for his view on leadership, and immediately and incisively pointed out that leadership is a term which cannot be found in the New Testament.[8] While perhaps an obvious point, it is one which constantly needs to be made. The lack of focus on effective leadership in the New Testament stands in stark contrast to the obsession with leadership in popular Christian culture. Attempts to address Christian leadership abound, including many excellent examples, including the Laidlaw Centre for Church Leadership and Arrow Leadership, both of which are located within my own theological and church tribe.[9] Both of these are excellent in themselves, and similarly to programs, the issue is not the attempts themselves but the degree of investment of hope and resources that attention to leadership attracts.

Authority

The other side of the leadership coin is an often radical rejection of authority within the church, especially the authority of ministers. The modern West generally struggles to develop a positive and constructive view of authority, and the church is not immune to this wider problem. The church in Aotearoa/New Zealand is exposed to a particularly strong secular challenge to a Christian view of authority, at least within churches which are dominated by Pākehā cultural norms, because of the uniquely New Zealand internalization of a strong egalitarianism.

---

8. I realize that the term "leadership" is an English word, and so of course did Archbishop Rowan. The point is that no Greek term for leadership features prominently in the New Testament, and neither is the concept given the attention that other matters in the church are.

9. An example of a name that reflects a different emphasis is what used to be called the Auckland Church Leaders' Network, which renamed itself to the Auckland Church Network.

Structure

Lastly, it is still common for me to hear criticism and optimism around particular church structures in ways closely tied to approaches which place a high value on leadership development. Especially common at the moment is a focus on governance and creating structures that create accountability and oversight groups for church ministers. Most of these efforts lack a theological account of the structures being proposed and often fail to interact with the forms of church structure that the majority of the world's Christians function within (that is, ordained ministry with some form of episcopacy), or with a theologically-rich understanding of Christian ministry. Once again, my criticism is not of attending to structure but is a criticism of the hope invested in structural reform and the lack of theologically-informed views on structure.

HOPE IN GOD'S PROMISES AND PATTERN

Recognizing these factors which have, I believe, damaged the church and which ought to be attended to if we are to see renewal, I now turn to the first of two major factors that I argue create plausibility for our hope to see renewal. The first of these is hope that is theologically-informed by attending to God's promises. A theologically-informed vision of the church centers its expectations in God's promises to act, in contrast to locating hope primarily in human obedience or ability to execute. God has made promises that are both general, telling us how he will write the story of the world through time and for the whole of humanity. God has also given us indications of the way he is writing the specifics of that story in Aotearoa, by how he has acted specifically here in the past, and by setting a pattern for us to recall and retell.

God's General Promises

Turning first to God's general promises, central to any theologically-motivated approach to church renewal needs to be an attention to what the church *is*. Historically, accounts of the church's being have been Christological, drawing from texts such as these:

> God has put all things under the authority of Christ and has made him head over all things for the benefit of the church. And the church is his body; it is made full and complete by Christ, who fills all things everywhere with himself. (Eph 1:22–23 NLT)

As Augustine argued, the church is united with Christ, its head, and the church has a role in which God chooses to bring salvation to the world by giving grace through the church.[10] The church then acts especially through the ministries of word and sacrament, as especially clearly articulated by both Luther[11] and Calvin[12] among the Reformers. Because the church's being, participation in God's saving work, and activities in word and sacrament are ordained by God, we can expect them to be effectual.

Recent theological work has taken these themes and developed them. For example, Karl Barth similarly makes a key identification of the church as the body of Christ.[13] Dietrich Bonhoeffer goes so far as to say that the church is "Christ existing as community."[14] Others connect the ministries of word and sacrament to the church's identity,[15] participation in Christ,[16] and in Christ's mediation.[17] To internalize this theological vision of the church requires a reliance on God, and has substantial implications for approaches to church renewal. For example, a confidence that the church is God's ordained means of saving the world ought to guard us from attempting to deconstruct the church or move away from it, despite the flaws that the New Testament so openly critiques. The Reformers understood this, seeking not to destroy the church but to reform it.

Alongside this confidence, we also ought to invest our hope and energy into those practices that are central to the church's activity. Reading the Scriptures and preaching from them, and the administration of baptism and holy communion, are activities that Christians who seek the renewal of the church ought to place their hope in, not because those activities are understood to be pragmatically effective but because God has chosen to act through the church and through these means of grace. It also ought to give

---

10. See Augustine, *Expositions on the Psalms*, particularly Pss 26:2 and 50:2, where he reflects on the church as the body of Christ. Additionally, his views are articulated in Augustine, *City of God*, bk. 19, where he contrasts the heavenly city (the true church) with the earthly city. See also Ratzinger, *Theology of History*; Markus, *Saeculum*.

11. "Where the Word of God is, there is the church" (Luther, "On the Councils"). For Luther, the preaching of the word and the administration of the sacraments were the marks of the true church (see Luther, "Babylonian Captivity").

12. The church is recognized by "the preaching of the Word and the lawful administration of the Sacraments." Calvin, *Institutes*, bk. 4, ch. 1.

13. Barth, *Doctrine of Reconciliation*, particularly §§62–64; see especially pp. 650–65 for his detailed treatment of the church's Christological foundation.

14. Bonhoeffer, *Sanctorum Communio*, 119–35.

15. Williams, *On Christian Theology*, 215–28, 231–37;

16. Congar, *Mystery of the Church*, 152–73; Tanner, *Christ the Key*, 102–15.

17. Torrance, *Mediation of Christ*, 76–92.

us the confidence to inhabit the forms of church that the Scriptures encourage, even if those seem odd or impractical to us.

None of this, by the way, ought to be seen as in any way rejecting the work of the Spirit. Some church fathers, drawing on the creed's affirmation of the Spirit as "the giver of life," explicitly identified the Spirit as the one by whom the community of the church participates in the divine life[18] and the Spirit as the one by whom the church gains unity.[19] I am skeptical of approaches that draw too strong a comparison between the Trinity and the community of the church.[20] While I see the attraction, I think the Trinity is a different kind of community from the church and has a unity of being that the church does not possess. I see more worth in approaches such as Wolfhart Pannenberg's, in which he argues that the Spirit sustains the church in its mission and sanctification, grounding its renewal in eschatological hope.[21]

God's Pattern in Aotearoa

Often the way God has worked in the past can inform us about how God is likely to continue working in a place or among people. Reflecting on the extraordinary past of the church in Aotearoa can act as an encouragement to us about God's intent and will, giving us hope that is centered on his saving works in the past. In actively remembering God's work in Aotearoa in the past, we echo the practices of God's people over the centuries in which a recollection of the past is central to hope for the future. For example, the preamble to Deuteronomy contains this liturgy for Israel to recount:

> We were Pharaoh's slaves in Egypt, but the LORD brought us out of Egypt with a mighty hand. (Deut 6:21 NRSV)

Other similar texts include the Song of Moses and Miriam (Exod 15:1–21), the "Wandering Aramean" confession (Deut 26:5–9), the setting up of memorial stones when Israel entered the land (Josh 4:1–7), several psalms (e.g., Pss 78, 105, and 136), and Nehemiah's prayer (Neh 9:6–37). Scripture models this practice of recounting God's work in the past in order to inspire hope for the future and to encourage participation in God's action

---

18. Gregory of Nyssa, *On the Holy Spirit* PG 46.695.

19. Basil the Great, *On the Holy Spirit*, 16.38.

20. See, for example, Moltmann, *Church in the Power*, 64–85; Volf, *After Our Likeness*, 191–215; and Zizioulas, *Being as Communion*, 102–19.

21. Pannenberg, *Systematic Theology*, 3:14–27. See also Chan, *Pentecostal Ecclesiology*, 56–78.

in the present. This has also long been part of liturgical practice among many Christians, for example in the recitation of the *Te Deum Laudamus* ("The Song of the Church") in morning prayer:

> You, Christ, are the King of glory, the eternal Son of the Father. When you took our flesh to set us free you humbly chose the Virgin's womb. You overcame the sting of death and opened the kingdom of heaven to all believers.[22]

The point of reciting this canticle in the morning is to orient oneself towards hopeful action and participation in God's saving work during the day which lies ahead. The reminder of the past inspires hope and conditions our activity.

Similarly, we might consider the fact that in Aotearoa, Māori such as Te Pahi and Ruatara invited Christian missionaries to come and share the good news of Jesus Christ here.[23] Many of those early missionaries were flawed in their characters and unable to entirely escape the constraints of their cultural conditioning. Still, early converts such as Taiwhanga saw a power in the message of Christianity that they brought, and over time many others—whose names live on in memory such as Rota Waitoa, Wiremu Te Tauri, Kereopa, Manihera, Piripi Taumataakura, and so on—did too.[24] In their individual stories and the collective conversion of Māori to Christian faith and worship, we can discern God's activity as he inspired the carrying of the message to these shores and inspired the agency of Māori in embodying and conveying the message to their own people.[25]

The practice of thankful memorialization of this story has the potential to inspire us with hope for a future which resembles that past, a future in which the church in Aotearoa is renewed and fills this land with the worship of Jesus Christ. It also has the potential to inspire a pattern for our own participation in God's work in the present, trusting that the same God who wrote that story in our recent past still possesses the same will to see people saved from judgment and is still active. My view is that attending to the ways the story of Christian witness in Aotearoa New Zealand has

---

22. "Song of the Church," 802.

23. See Pikaahu, "Te hari a Ngāpuhi."

24. Many of these stories are recalled in the canticle "Poi" by Tā Kingi Ihaka, which recounts the story of Te Rongopai in Aotearoa through the medium of a poi chant (that is, a chant which can be accompanied by rhythmically swung tethered weights). The canticle itself can be found in *New Zealand Prayer Book*, 154–56. For my own discussion of the canticle, see Drake, "Theological Facets."

25. For general accounts of the church in Aotearoa/New Zealand, see Davidson, *Christianity in Aotearoa*, 1991; Newman, *Bible and Treaty*. For the formation of the indigenous Māori church, see Kaa, *Te Hāhi Mihinare*.

flourished and floundered in the past is of great significance to the ways the story of Christian witness can have a renewed telling in the present and lead to future flourishing. This is why I have titled this chapter with two Māori words—as a reminder that renewal (whakahoutanga) and hope (tūmanako) are connected, I believe, to a retelling of the broken story of Christianity in the past.

HOPE IN RETELLING THE BROKEN STORY

So, having given attention to God's promises and pattern I will give three examples of how I believe the church can enact theologically-informed practice for Aotearoa that offers a plausible pathway to renewal. These proposals are a product of my own reflection and ministry experience. They are drawn from the whakapapa of the church in Aotearoa, which as Royal has argued is an important aspect of a kaupapa Māori approach to scholarly work.[26] In some instances I have provided specific citations, but in general these proposals reflect knowledge passed on in oral form in the church[27] or which is available in general accounts of the church and its history in Aotearoa.[28]

Restore Missionary Activity

Firstly, we should consider the ways in which Māori agency was central to the proclamation of the gospel in the past and seek to center and support Māori agency in gospel proclamation in the present. While it is well-known that Māori evangelists were central to the proclamation of the gospel in Aotearoa in the 1800s, recent research has emphasized how significant the fruitfulness and agency of Māori evangelists was. Malcolm Falloon's recent thesis shows that perhaps as much as 90 percent of the Māori population was in weekly Christian worship in the 1850s.[29]

This is a story that needs to be celebrated and replicated. The church in Aotearoa has tried many other strategies but has never repeated the strategy which has been most effective in the past, namely empowering Māori evangelists to share the gospel widely. Hope for renewal should begin by raising

---

26. Royal, "Mātauranga Māori."

27. Smith, "Indigenous Knowledge."

28. For more general accounts and surveys of the literature, see Williams, *"Te Kooti Tango Whenua"*; Ward, *An Unsettled History*; Simmons, *Brief History*; Owens, "Christianity and the Maoris," 18–40; O'Malley, *Great War*; Lange, *Māori and the Missionaries*; Davidson, *Christianity in Aotearoa*, 2004; Belich, *New Zealand Wars*.

29. Falloon, "Māori Conversion."

up and supporting a new generation of many Māori evangelists to share the good news of Jesus Christ throughout Aotearoa. I am certain that the Lord would bless this work now, as he did in the past.

Do Better at Ordering of the Church

While the Church Missionary Society (CMS) missionaries did an excellent job of empowering Māori to share the gospel, the church did a poor job of ordering the church that resulted, especially in terms of ordaining Māori ministers. Anglicans ordained late and in low numbers, as did the Methodists, while the Roman Catholic church went through decades with no Māori ministers at all.[30] More recent church movements and denominations are often decentralized, and so the structural injustice of limited Māori representation is difficult to address because individual local congregations make choices around leadership based on their own constituencies. In a largely Pākehā congregation, it does not necessarily make sense to appoint a Māori senior pastor. When that local decision is repeated across every congregation in a denomination, though, it results in an aggregate lack of Māori leadership that does not represent the population as a whole.

While in an Anglican context much of the blame for this has rightly been placed on the first bishop of New Zealand, George Augustus Selwyn, the blame ought to be shared more widely. Selwyn's high church instincts led him to a paternalistic lack of willingness to ordain Māori, but Henry Venn's ideal of a self-governing church also embodied a different form of paternalism that envisaged parallel indigenous and settler churches, each with their own bishops. This theologically malnourished idea, a product of Victorian colonialism, lacked the theological imagination necessary to conceive of a Māori bishop presiding over Pākehā settlers. Without being aware of this idea's whakapapa, much of the Māori Anglican church now sees this as an ideal to maintain, but a better ordering of the church would see indigenous leaders as a symbol of visible unity for the whole church.[31] Working this out will require theological attention to the definition of the church and the right ordering of the church, in particular around the episcopacy and its canonical status.[32]

Another aspect of the church's whakapapa in Aotearoa is Pākehā egalitarianist aversion to the right exercise of authority and power. This seems to me to be one instance of a wider Pākehā egalitarianism, often characterized

30. Lange, "Ordained Ministry," 47–66.
31. Williams, *Ideal of the Self-Governing*.
32. Drake, "Episcopal Fragmentation."

as the "tall poppy syndrome," which derives from planned patterns of selection and settlement in the process of nineteenth-century colonization.[33] This aversion to authority is one reason why leadership so often struggles in culturally-Pākehā church settings, and the many efforts to attend to leadership typically fail to attend to the sociological issues that intersect with theology. But Scripture is clear:

> Obey your leaders and submit to them, for they are keeping watch over your souls and will give an account. Let them do this with joy and not with sighing—for that would be harmful to you. (Heb 13:17 NRSV)

These words sit uneasily with most Pākehā Christians in Aotearoa. I can more or less guarantee that if I read that verse, instead of wholehearted acceptance, I will be given caveats that the author of the Letter to the Hebrews somehow neglected to include. This is one important area where the Pākehā church can learn a great deal from the Māori church. In Māori contexts it was obvious that people generally saw their relationship with me as one in which I had care of their souls as their minister, where they sought my involvement in their spiritual lives more than they sought to rate my conduct in office, and saw their obedience to me as spiritually significant. In Māori terms, this has to do with mana and tapu, with spiritual power and with spiritual accountability, both central concepts to Māori life. Within the church, mana and tapu are (rightly in my view) associated with the ministers of the church.

So, rightly ordering the church is about more than just structural changes, important though those are. It is also about cultivating a right attitude, even when that is culturally challenging, and there is a great deal that the Pākehā church can learn from the Māori church in these matters.

Restore Land

While "effective leadership" is never presented in Scripture as a solution to the church's many problems, moral behavior certainly is seen as central to the flourishing of God's people throughout Scripture. This cannot be separated from doctrinal correctness, but neither can doctrinal accuracy substitute for the character of the church. All the letters to the churches in the New Testament, the Gospels and Acts, and Revelation contain sharp criticisms of churches who diverge from passing on the teaching that has been handed down to them—that is, of unorthodoxy of belief or instruction

---

33. Fischer, *Fairness and Freedom*.

to their congregations—or who diverge from acting to obey the commands of God. Critically, in the case of Aotearoa, there will be a sense of obligation to participate in the redemption and restoration of Māori as an action of justice. This must include restoration of land.

Doing so will not be easy. Church property is often consolidated into trusts, some of which are established by statute, and the beneficial purposes of those trusts are often tied to the church, making distributions to hapū or iwi legally restricted. Many of the old denominations are also shrinking in size and influence, leading to enormous pressure within the denominations to retain and use their historic assets to financially support the existing denominational staff and buildings. Newer denominations and movements are composed of churches that have typically *purchased* the land their buildings stand upon. This means that the injustice of land loss has no direct connection with the past actions of the church, and it is not at all obvious how a local congregation that owns a single building could materially contribute to mitigating the injustices of the past without simply collapsing themselves.

Still, the fact that obeying God is difficult would be a poor excuse. The church needs to recognize that land loss was a substantial issue for Māori hapū and iwi in the decades after 1840, and the sense of the church having been complicit in these unjust processes contributed significantly to Māori leaving the church. It is also a theological issue. God is known in Scripture for his resolute opposition to injustice, especially around land, and committed to calling the people of God to just action. "Woe to you who add house to house and join field to field till no space is left and you live alone in the land," said the prophet Isaiah (5:8 NIV). Woe to us, perhaps we need to say, who have retained land and buildings and investment funds, while hapū and iwi have nothing.

But as Christians we believe in repentance and the mercy and blessing of God in response. I believe that we should see land restoration as an opportunity to tell out in action the sacrificial behavior of Jesus which the gospel narrates. It should call Christians with wealth and property to lay down their rights, just as Jesus laid his down, in order to create the potential for Māori who have inherited injustice to experience restitution in the generous behavior of the church.

One of my real concerns with contemporary political engagement by the church in Aotearoa is the tendency to rebuke the nation while acting unrepentantly. I have in the past called on the Anglican Church in Aotearoa, New Zealand, and Polynesia to give assets back to iwi and hapū Māori, at our General Synod / Te Hīnota Whānui (the overall governing body). I dare say that the Anglican Church has perhaps done this more than other churches, but I do not believe that we could argue that the Anglican Church in particular, or the churches in Aotearoa/New Zealand generally, could plausibly claim that we have been the leaders in restitution and repentance.

I am convinced that a genuinely repentant approach to historic injustices, even if it requires us to divest ourselves of our church buildings and the land they rest on, would do more for the plausibility and effectiveness of gospel proclamation in Aotearoa than any program of activity or leadership strategy. I also believe it would be an act of hope in God's promises and power.[34]

Restore Orality and Liturgy

It is now recognized in scholarship that the significant turning point in the conversion of Māori to the Christian faith was the translation of the Anglican Book of Common Prayer into the Māori language, and the publication of such huge numbers of the "Rawiri" ("David," as it is still known today) that at one point there was one copy for every two Māori.[35] And, because many Māori could not read, and because Māori culture values orality, this was a primarily oral transmission of the Christian faith.

Māori culture remains a setting where orality is prized and where liturgy fits well, especially for karakia. Without wanting to labor this point, I believe that we could learn from the success of the use of liturgy and its oral transmission to reach both Māori and, through the medium of the beauty of the liturgy in the Māori language, a much wider section of contemporary Aotearoa society.

Restore a Focus on Word and Sacrament in Worship

Finally, of all the activities I undertook in ministry, the most fruitful came as a complete surprise to me. Even now, years later, the online services I led during the COVID-19 lockdowns for Karakia Ata (Morning Prayer), along with the Karakia Ahiahi (Evening Prayer) services that my bishop, Te Kitohi Pikaahu, led, had more effect in seeing people come to a new or renewed faith in Christ. These simple liturgical services with a short sermon connected with people, it turned out, all over the world. To me, this stands as a reminder that it is possible to overcomplicate Christian ministry. The basic tasks of a minister (to lead and care for a flock entrusted to their care by offering Christ in word and sacrament) are achievable tasks. And in God's

---

34. Fischer, *Fairness and Freedom*.
35. Carpenter, "Reshaping of Political Communities," 129.

providence, because he has promised to act through these simple tasks, he does indeed act.

This should give us hope. Renewal is possible, not because we are brilliant but because God has not set us too hard a task. It is possible because what God calls us to do is doable, and because God has promised to act. We should restore a focus on word and sacrament, being willing to sacrifice the endless multiplication of programs and strategies for a renewed church that expresses its trust in God by a commitment to God's call to a particular way of communal life. And I have a confident hope that if we do so, God will act in renewal.

SOME CONCLUSIONS

The central argument I have made in this chapter is that hope for renewal needs to be theologically-informed. This means identifying the church as the body of Christ and having confidence that giving priority to the ministries of word and sacrament are the means God has ordained to renew the church and give hope to the world. This is preferable to investing confidence in programs or structures as a means of renewal, and instead draws from a recognition that God acts through his Spirit to renew the church when we share in the life of the community in the ways God has ordained for us.

I want to conclude by sharing an experience I had some years ago. I was cycling out near Ihumatao,[36] close to sunrise, and had been wondering whether ministry in the Aotearoa church was wasted effort. In that contested place, which had been the focus of so much possibility and so much injustice, I had a deep sense that God still loves Aotearoa and is still writing his story—as I would put it, retelling his story once again. I still have hope for the renewal of the church in Aotearoa.

GLOSSARY

This glossary presents only the main contextual English gloss. For a more general and comprehensive definition of any of these words, please consult a Māori-language dictionary.

Aotearoa	the lands also known as New Zealand
hapū	subtribe

---

36. Fernandes, "Ihumātao Land Battle." See also Te Tari Whakatau, "Deed of Settlement"; New Zealand Government, "Deed of Settlement."

iwi	tribe
kaupapa Māori	a Māori methodology
mana	spiritual authority
Māori	the indigenous people of Aotearoa
Pākehā	people of European descent
tapu	restricted, set apart
te rongopai	the gospel
Te Tai Tokerau	the northern part of Te Ika a Māui/the North Island
whakapapa	lineage

BIBLIOGRAPHY

Augustine. *Expositions on the Psalms.* https://www.newadvent.org/fathers/1801.htm.

———. *City of God.* https://www.newadvent.org/fathers/1201.htm.

Barth, Karl. *The Doctrine of Reconciliation.* Vol. IV.1 of *Church Dogmatics.* Edinburgh: T&T Clark, 1956.

Basil the Great. *On the Holy Spirit.* https://www.newadvent.org/fathers/3203.htm.

Belich, James. *The New Zealand Wars and the Victorian Interpretation of Racial Conflict.* Auckland: Auckland University Press, 1986.

Blair, David. *Presbyterians and the New Zealand Missionary Movement: 1860–1940.* Philadelphia: Presbyterian Historical Society, 1985.

Bonhoeffer, Dietrich, *Sanctorum Communio: A Theological Study of the Sociology of the Church.* Dietrich Bonhoeffer Works 1. Minneapolis: Fortress, 1998.

Calvin, John, *Institutes of the Christian Religion.* Translated by John Allen. Westminster John Knox, 1960.

Carpenter, Sam. "The Reshaping of Political Communities in New Zealand: A Study of Intellectual and Imperial Texts in Context, c. 1814–1863." PhD thesis, Massey University, 2020.

Chambers, Douglas A. "The New Zealand Anglican Church and Its Mission to the Māori." In *The Future of the Anglican Church in Aotearoa New Zealand*, edited by John Stenhouse and Brett Knowles, 29–45. Christchurch: Theology House, 2002.

Chan. Simon. *Pentecostal Ecclesiology: An Essay on the Development of Doctrine.* Dorset: Deo, 2011.

Common Worship: Services and Prayers for the Church of England. London: Church House, 2000.

Congar, Yves. *The Mystery of the Church.* Translated by A. V. Littledale. London: Chapman, 1960.

Davidson, Allan K. "Baptists and Evangelicalism in New Zealand." In *Southern Baptists and the World of the Nineteenth Century*, edited by Keith Harper, 243–60. Macon, GA: Mercer University Press, 2008.

———. *Christianity in Aotearoa: A History of Church and Society in New Zealand.* 3rd ed. Auckland: Education for Ministry, 2004.

———. *Christianity in Aotearoa: A History of Church and Society in New Zealand* Auckland: Education for Ministry, 1991.

Davidson, Allan, et al., eds. *Te Rogopai 1814, "Takoto Te Pai!" Bicentenary Reflections on Christian Beginnings and Developments in Aotearoa New Zealand*. Auckland: The Anglican Church in Aotearoa New Zealand, and Polynesia, 2015.

Drake, Lyndon. "Episcopal Fragmentation in Te Pouhere." In *Te Korowai o te Rangimārie*, edited by Donald Moffat and K. D. Taylor, 57–71. Auckland: St. John's Theological College, 2022.

———. Forthcoming. "Theological Facets of He Poi, an Indigenous Chant." In Reclaiming Our Tribal Voice, edited by Anne Pattel-Gray. Melbourne: ATF.

Falloon, Malcolm. "The Māori Conversion and Four Early Converts." PhD thesis, University of Otago, 2020.

Fernandes, Kimberlee. "Ihumātao Land Battle: A Timeline." Radio New Zealand, July 26, 2019. https://www.rnz.co.nz/news/national/395281/ihumatao-land-battle-a-timeline.

Fischer, David Hackett. *Fairness and Freedom: A History of Two Open Societies: New Zealand and the United States*. Oxford: Oxford University Press, 2012.

Gunton, Colin E. and Daniel W. Hardy. *On Being the Church: Essays on the Christian Community*. Edinburgh: T&T Clark, 1989.

Hilliard, David. "Unorthodox Christianity in New Zealand: The Brethren and Other Sects." In *Religion and Society in New Zealand*, edited by Brian Colless and Peter Donovan, 85–104. Auckland: Tertiary Christian Studies Programme, 1980.

Kaa, Hirini. *Te Hāhi Mihinare: The Māri Anglican Church*. Wellington: Bridget Williams, 2020.

Keenan, Danny. *Te Whiti o Rongomai and the Resistance of Parihaka*. Wellington: Huia, 2015.

Kornfield, David. *Church Renewal: A Handbook for Christian Leaders*. Paternoster, 1989.

Lange, Raeburn. "Ordained Ministry in Maori Christianity, 1853–1900." *Journal of Religious History* 27 (2003) 47–66.

———. *Māori and the Missionaries: Early Christian Missions in the North Island of New Zealand*. Auckland: Auckland University Press, 1991.

Lineham, Peter. "Bible and Society: A Nineteenth Century Story." *Stimulus* 1 (1993) 19–25.

———. "The Methodist Church and the Working Class in New Zealand Society." In *Southern World: Social History in New Zealand*, edited by Tom Brooking and Judith Smart, 153–71. Dunedin: Otago University Press, 1994.

———. *There We Found Brethren: A History of Assemblies of Brethren in New Zealand*. Palmerston North: GPH Society, 2013.

Luther, Martin. "The Babylonian Captivity of the Church, 1520." Pages 3–126 in *Word and Sacrament II*. Translated by A. T W Steinhäuser. Revised by Frederick C. Ahrens and Abdel Ross Wentz. Edited by Abdel Ross Wentz. Vol. 36 of *Luther's Works*. Edited by Helmut T. Lehmann. Philadelphia: Fortress, 1959.

———. "On the Councils and the Church, 1539." Pages 3–178 in *Church and Ministry III*. Translated by Charles M. Jacobs. Revised and edited by Eric W. Gritsch. Vol. 41 of *Luther's Works*. Edited by Helmut T. Lehmann. Philadelphia: Fortress, 1966.

Markus, R. A. *Saeculum: History and Society in the Theology of St. Augustine*. Cambridge: Cambridge University Press, 1970.

Moltmann, Jürgen. *The Church in the Power of the Spirit: A Contribution of Messianic Ecclesiology*. London: SCM, 1977.

Morley, William. *The History of Methodism in New Zealand*. Wellington: McKee and Co., 1900.

Newman, Keith. *Bible and Treaty: Missionaries Among the Māori: A New Perspective*. New York: Penguin, 2010.

New Zealand Government. "Deed of Settlement Between the Crown and Te Ākitai Waiohua." Dec., 23, 2020. https://www.govt.nz/assets/Documents/OTS/Te-Akitai-Waiohua/20201222-taw-settlement-summary-final.pdf.

A New Zealand Prayer Book / He Karakia Mihinare o Aotearoa. Auckland: Anglican Church in Aotearoa, New Zealand, and Polynesia, 2024.

O'Malley, Vincent. *The Great War for New Zealand: Waikato 1800–2000*. Wellington: Bridget Williams, 2016.

Owens, J. M R. "Christianity and the Maoris to 1840." *New Zealand Journal of History* 2 (1968) 18–40

Pannenberg, Wolfhart. *Systematic Theology*. Vol. 3. Translated by Geoffrey W. Bromiley. Grand Rapids: Eerdmans, 1998.

Pikaahu, Te Kitohi. "Te hari a Ngāpuhi—the Dance (of Joy) of Ngāpuhi." In *Te Rongopai 1814, "Takoto Te Pai!" Bicentenary Reflections on Christian Beginnings and Developments in Aotearoa New Zealand*, edited by Allan Davidson et al., 22–30. Auckland: The Anglican Church in Aotearoa New Zealand, and Polynesia, 2015.

Ratzinger, Joseph. *The Theology of History in St. Augustine*. Translated by Michael Waldstein. Chicago: Henry Regnery, 1968.

Royal, Te Ahukaramū Charles. "Mātauranga Māori: Paradigms and Politics." Paper presented to the Ministry for Research, Science, and Technology, Auckland, New Zealand, Jan. 13, 1998.

Simmons, David R. *A Brief History of the Catholic Church in New Zealand*. Auckland: Catholic Publications Centre, 1978.

Scott, Dick. *Ask That Mountain: The Story of Parihaka*. Auckland: Heinemann, 1975.

Smith, Linda Tuhiwai. "Indigenous Knowledge, Methodology, and Mayhem: What Is the Role of Methodology in Producing Indigenous Insights? A Discussion." *Knowledge Cultures* 3 (2019) 131–56.

"The Song of the Church." In *Common Worship*. London: Church House, 2000.

Te Tari Whakatau. "Deed of Settlement of Historical Claims: Te Ākitai Waiohua and Te Ākitai Waiohua Settlement Trust and The Crown." https://whakatau.govt.nz/assets/Treaty-Settlements/FIND_Treaty_Settlements/Te-Akitai-Waiohua/DOS_documents/Te-Akitai-Waiohua-deed-of-settlement-historical-claims-12-Nov-2021.pdf.

Torrance, Thomas F. *The Mediation of Christ*. Exeter: Paternoster, 1983.

Troughton, Geoffrey. "Open Brethren and Evangelicalism in New Zealand." *Brethren Historical Review* 4 (2008) 105–26.

Volf, Miroslav. *After Our Likeness: The Church as the Image of the Trinity*. Grand Rapids: Eerdmans, 1998.

Waitangi Tribunal. "The Taranaki Report: Kaupapa Tuatahi." https://forms.justice.govt.nz/search/Documents/WT/wt_DOC_68453721/Taranaki%201996.compressed.pdf.

Wall, Terry. "Methodism in New Zealand: Continuity and Change." *Proceedings of the Wesley Historical Society (New Zealand)* 57 (2011) 3–18.

Ward, Alan. *An Unsettled History: Treaty Claims in New Zealand Today*. Wellington: Bridget Williams, 1999

Williams, David V. *"Te Kooti Tango Whenua": The Native Land Court 1864–1909*. Wellington: Huia, 1999.

Williams, C. Peter. *The Ideal of the Self-Governing Church: A Study in Victorian Missionary Strategy*. Studies in Christian Mission 1. Leiden: Brill, 1990.

Williams, Rowan. *On Christian Theology*. Oxford: Blackwell, 2000.

Woodfield, Elaine. *The Story of the Baptists in New Zealand*. Auckland: New Zealand Baptist Research and Historical Society, 1996.

Zizioulas, John D. *Being as Communion: Studies in Personhood and the Church*. London: Darton, Longman, and Todd, 1985.

Section IV

Missional Hope
Nourishing the Wider Community

Chapter 12

Different with Distinction
Revitalizing the Church's Mission Through Applying Newbigin's Insights

GREGORY J. LISTON

INTRODUCTION

BEFORE I WAS A senior pastor, I worked as a management consultant.[1] I loved pastoring a church, but (in truth) a lot of my pastoral work did not seem that different from my previous role. In both jobs I was concerned with strategy, competitive advantage, vision casting, personnel management, logistics, and balance sheets. All these are necessary and important activities, but what became increasingly obvious during my first stretch as a church leader is that the way I was feeling and what I was doing each day was not significantly different from my previous and entirely secular occupation. When I left pastoring to study and research, one of my main objectives was to determine how leading a church can be fundamentally different, both in terms of my being (who I am) and my doing (how I lead). I have found a lot of the answers for what it means to *be* a church leader in the notion of Christ's vicarious humanity.[2] This important theological truth has

---

1. My first pastoral role was as the senior pastor of a five-hundred-person Baptist church in suburban Auckland. Prior to this I worked for a large American-based management consulting firm.

2. A helpful introduction to this theme can be found in Purves, *Crucifixion of*

become a simple and often repeated refrain through which I can constantly remind myself to live day by day in the profound reality that Christ has already done everything for us, and that through the Spirit we get to join in with his ongoing worship of the Father and mission to the world. Living in this truth has released a lot of the angst I used to feel as a pastor and has transformed being a church leader from a role where stress levels were high and expectations virtually unachievable into one where I can relax and genuinely enjoy my calling.

But such a change in attitude still leaves open the question of what we are called to *do* as church leaders. If a pastoral role is about more than just keeping the machinery of the institutional church running, then what kind of communities are we called to fashion, and how can we go about crafting churches that reflect that calling? At an overarching level, I am finding an equally helpful answer about what church leaders *do* in the writings of British theologian Lesslie Newbigin.[3] In particular, Newbigin's constant insistence that it is only by leaning into the differences we have with the narrative of the surrounding culture that our church communities can have a meaningful missiological engagement with society has been insightful, clarifying, and liberating for me. I have great hope for the church. It is God's church, and it always will be. We can trust him to do with us and in us what he intends, independent of who we are and what we do. But I want to be one of those people that genuinely partners with God in bringing about his purposes for our church. Newbigin provides a welcome guide on how to do this.[4] Consequently, this chapter addresses three key questions. First, what are Newbigin's pertinent missiological insights? Second, why are his insights applicable? And third, how can we implement his missiological insights?

Ministry.

3. Lesslie Newbigin is justifiably famous. After serving as a missionary in India for thirty-five years, he returned to his home in England in 1974 to discover that Britain had largely abandoned Christianity for secularism. For a brief and compelling introduction to Newbigin's life and journey see Stafford, "God's Missionary to Us," 24–33.

4. The content of this article has emerged primarily out of a theological course on Christian confidence that I have taught at Laidlaw College with Paul Windsor over the last several years. I gratefully acknowledge Paul Windsor's substantial input into many of the ideas in the following article, as well as some of the more helpful and memorable phrases utilized, such as the title: Different with Distinction." I also appreciate the input of several student groups who have helped shape the material in this chapter into its present form.

WHAT ARE NEWBIGIN'S PERTINENT MISSIOLOGICAL INSIGHTS?

People sometimes find Newbigin's writings too esoteric to be accessible. This section aims to concretely convey Newbigin's thoughts in a way that is immediately applicable to the contemporary New Zealand church. Consequently, the key question addressed in this section is: What are Newbigin's pertinent missiological insights (for the church in Aotearoa)? The following analysis arranges Newbigin's missiological thinking into five key points.[5]

First, Newbigin sees the church as the primary, and to a great extent, the only missionary body that exists. He writes, "The New Testament knows of only one missionary society—the Church."[6] Newbigin's point is not that the church does mission in the sense that the church needs to work out what will be missiologically effective and then do that. Nor is he saying that the church is a missiological recruitment and training agency, in that its job is to inspire and equip its people to go out and be missionaries in their day to day lives. Both points are true (in a secondary sense), but Newbigin's point here is more pivotal. Newbigin is saying that the church does mission by being the church, and by being the church it is missional. Missiology and ecclesiology for Newbigin are consequently mutually intertwined concepts that cannot be understood separately from each other.[7] This leads to the understanding that the church's primary missional role in this world is simply to be the church, and to be it surrounded by a non-Christian culture.[8] The twin-pronged implication arising is that the church in and through its very existence can and must demonstrate gospel truth, but also that it should do this in a way that can be seen, heard, and understood. The church can neither accommodate so much to the surrounding culture that it ceases to proclaim and live genuine gospel truth, nor can it so doggedly cling to previous articulations of gospel truth that the surrounding culture fails to understand what it is saying.[9] Fulfilling this identity, says Newbigin, will

---

5. This essay, and this section in particular, makes no attempt to convey the entirety of Newbigin's thought. Rather it focuses on those aspects of his line of thinking that, in the opinion of the author, are particularly applicable for the church in New Zealand at the current time. For a broader and extremely helpful analysis of Newbigin's missiological insights see Goheen, *Church and Its Vocation*. Chapters 5 and 6 of this book are particularly valuable.

6. Newbigin, *Reunion of the Church*, 11.

7. See for example the discussion on this point in Liston, "Spirit, Church and Mission," 22–28.

8. Note the echoes here with Hauerwas's assertion that "the first social ethical task of the church is to be the church." Hauerwas, *Peaceable Kingdom*, 99.

9. See for example Newbigin, *Foolishness to the Greeks*, 5–6. See also Goheen,

require significant and simultaneous insight into both the gospel and the surrounding culture.

Newbigin's second point is that all cultures indwell an underlying story that is incompatible with the gospel. It has become commonplace over recent years in both theological colleges and churches to talk about how being Christian means intentionally living lives that participate in the overarching narrative of God's interaction with humanity. Newbigin would agree with this understanding. He would insist, however, that all people everywhere live lives that are consistent with the overarching narrative through which they interpret and understand the world. Every culture has a story, he argues, and virtually all the inhabitants of that culture live in accordance with that story. The incredibly important, although obvious, insight that Newbigin alerts us to is that stories underlying other cultures are vastly different from the gospel story, and at those points where they do differ, the two belief systems are incompatible.[10] This incompatibility emphatically and definitively includes the narrative underlying Western culture.[11] Newbigin thoroughly rejects the idea that Western culture provides an even playing field in which all ideologies and religious systems can exist. In contrast he asserts that Western culture has an underlying story that can be either accepted or rejected. He writes, "The idea that we ought to be able to expect some kind of neutral secular political order, which presupposes no religious or ideological beliefs, and which holds the ring impartially for a plurality of religions to compete with one another, has no adequate foundation."[12] The story underlying Western culture and the gospel story are to a great degree completely incompatible.[13]

Any attempt to faithfully indwell the gospel narrative, while surrounded by a culture that is indwelling an entirely different narrative, invariably leads to the ongoing experience of painful tension.[14] This is Newbigin's third point, and when understood, it is extremely confronting. One important way that we can measure whether we are effectively and faithfully fulfilling our missional identity and living according to gospel truth, he argues, is to gauge the extent to which we experience our lives as Christians and as the church as one of uncomfortable tension. It is impossible to exist in genuine relationship with a culture that inhabits a different narrative from the gospel

---

Church and Its Vocation, 138–40.

10. Goheen, *Church and Its Vocation*, 142–45.
11. See for example Smith, *Desiring the Kingdom*.
12. Newbigin, *Trinitarian Doctrine*, 46.
13. See for example Newbigin, *Pluralist Society*, 172–73.
14. Goheen, *Church and Its Vocation*, 145–48.

and not feel and act out of place.[15] As Christians living according to the gospel narrative, we will question what no one else chooses to question, but (hopefully) do it in a way that people understand what we are questioning. Our lives and our message will be familiar but appear absurd. Not that we are absurd, but that appearance arises because the story to which we align ourselves is fundamentally incompatible with the narrative underlying the surrounding culture. We can only avoid such a painful existence either by withdrawing from the culture surrounding us, which leads to irrelevance, or by accommodating our Christian witness to the surrounding culture, which leads to syncretism.[16] Both options, however, are incompatible with a genuine missiological encounter between church and culture. Regarding the first error of irrelevance, churches can withdraw from their culture either literally, through intentional separation, or essentially, through becoming so consumed with the church's internal life that there is little or no interaction with the surrounding society. Regarding the second error of syncretism, churches can uncritically and often unwittingly adopt the idols of their culture.[17] While Newbigin critiques both irrelevance and syncretism and even notes that the church at times has made both errors simultaneously, he most strongly critiques the contemporary Western church for its syncretism. The Western church has an "advanced case of syncretism," he claims. "Instead of confronting our culture with the gospel, we are perpetually trying to fit the gospel into our culture."[18]

Newbigin's fourth point is that the primary way churches can avoid falling into the twin errors of irrelevance or syncretism is by deliberately viewing and crafting themselves as plausibility structures for the gospel.[19] With this language of plausibility structures, Newbigin means that people

---

15. See for example Newbigin, *Pluralist Society*, 220–21.

16. Syncretism is the (often unintentional) mixing of belief systems, where we pick and choose which aspects of varying belief systems to accept and which to neglect. Newbigin sees syncretism occurring when we attempt to assert a belief in gospel truths while simultaneously living according to intrinsically contradictory elements of Western culture.

17. The use of terminology such as idols or idolatry within this essay is referring specifically to something taking the place of God. When Western culture takes something that is intrinsically good, such as the individual, or consumption, or reason, and makes it the ultimate thing (taking the place of God) that is idolatry by this definition. So, if the needs of the individual become primary, in that what I want and need becomes more important than what God's desires for me are, then the valuing of the individual has morphed into individualism, and this is idolatry. See for example the discussion in Kierkegaard, *Sickness Unto Death*.

18. Newbigin, *Word in Season*, 67.

19. See for example Goheen, *Church and Its Vocation*, 156–58.

both outside and inside the church should be able to look at the churches in their midst and say, "I can see that the God you serve is real and the narrative you indwell is true because your church could not exist and act like it does if those things were not real and true." In other words, local churches, even when viewed from the outside, should make gospel truth plausible. We are called to be growing into counter cultural communities that live lives that are too attractive (and too unusual) to be ignored. Deliberately living out a gospel-derived plausibility structure while also being intentionally embedded in a culture that is an alternative plausibility structure for an entirely different narrative is (almost by definition) a painful existence, but it is only through embracing such tension that a genuine missiological encounter with the culture surrounding us can be maintained. Some aspects of our surrounding culture and its underlying narrative will be affirmed and embraced; many will be rejected.[20]

While Newbigin's assertions to this point are perhaps unsurprising, it is at his fifth and final point that his ecclesial vision most clearly diverges from the approach taken by certain sectors of the church in Aotearoa. For Newbigin argues that rather than intentionally leaning into the *similarities* between the gospel truth and that underlying the surrounding culture, we should in contrast lean into the *distinctions* that exist between these two narratives.[21] Constructing churches as alternative plausibility structures requires deliberately emphasizing the differences that exist between the gospel narrative and the story underlying the surrounding culture.

It is worthwhile pausing to emphasize at this point just how contrary and counterintuitive this idea of deliberately leaning into differences is to the way churches in Aotearoa have operated for the last several decades. Consider two of the key trends that have dominated our church landscape over the last few decades. The first is our adoption of seeker services. Imported from American megachurches such as Willow Creek and Saddleback Community Church, the central idea of seeker services is to craft gatherings that intentionally minimize the differences between the surrounding culture and the local church.[22] The purpose of doing this is so that people will feel as comfortable and welcome as possible. Most Kiwi churches, rather than adopting the practice in total and running two distinct types of services each week—one for seekers and one for believers—opted to redesign their existing services to be intentionally more welcoming and accessible

---

20. See for example Goheen, *Church and Its Vocation*, 152–54.

21. See for example Goheen, *Church and Its Vocation*, 191–95.

22. For the rationale behind seeker services, see for example Pritchard, *Willow Creek Seeker Service*; and Warren, *Purpose Driven Church*.

for people who weren't used to church experiences. There is no suggestion here that in moving in the direction of seeker services there was any intent to water down core aspects of our faith, nor even that such accommodation occurred. The simple point being made is that this approach is the exact opposite of Newbigin's suggestion that we should deliberately lean into the differences between the gospel narrative and the story that underlines our culture.

The second trend illustrating this distinction is the commonly used mantra of belong, believe, behave (often contrasted with the opposing logic of believe, behave, belong).[23] The idea of the altered order of this trio of words is that in contrast to a previous era, where a conversion experience often came first, followed by a subsequent change of behavior, and only then genuine acceptance into the Christian community, it makes more evangelistic sense in this postmodern setting to create communities where unbelievers can immediately feel welcome and included in church settings. As Dixon comments, "The highest priority must be to help them [i.e., unbelievers] find a place within the community, to allow them to feel at home and accepted."[24] This belonging will hopefully lead to a conversion experience (believe) and eventually to a radically altered lifestyle (behave). Such intentional hospitality to strangers joining our church communities is both understandable and welcome. Placing such high priority on making the unbeliever feel at home among us, however, inevitably leads to us emphasizing those aspects of our communal life we have in common with unbelievers and downplaying or delaying those aspects where the difference between their underlying story and ours is most stark. The mantra of belong, believe, behave encourages the church in a direction that is almost exactly opposite to Newbigin's recommendation, which in contrast says that we should deliberately lean into those features of the gospel narrative that are the most different from surrounding society.[25]

This section has argued that Newbigin's most pertinent missiological insight is that the church should be a plausibility structure for the gospel, which has a clear implication that the church should lean into its differences from wider society, rather than leaning into its similarities, and consequently minimizing, downplaying, or delaying the distinctives of the narrative through which it is defined. Newbigin argues that adopting such

---

23. See for example Dixon, *Villages without Walls*, 72–73.

24. Dixon, *Villages without Walls*, 73.

25. For a thoughtful reflection on this trio of words and its helpfulness and challenges, see Windsor, " Gospel of Community?"

an approach will enable the church to fulfill its primary missional role of demonstrating gospel truth to the surrounding culture.

WHY ARE NEWBIGIN'S INSIGHTS IMPORTANT AND APPLICABLE?

Why are Newbigin's missiological insights particularly important and applicable to the contemporary church in Aotearoa? Why should churches in this place and time intentionally and specifically lean into the differences between the gospel narrative and the surrounding culture's narrative? There are numerous indicators pointing in this direction, which in the following analysis have been divided into four categories: negative external, negative internal, positive internal, and positive external.[26]

First, consider the negative consequences that can arise (and indeed have arisen) from churches not leaning into the differences between the gospel narrative and the surrounding culture's underlying narrative but instead leaning into the similarities and overlaps that exist. From an external perspective, it is statistically and sociologically clear that the latter strategy of pursuing contextual relevance that churches in Aotearoa have increasingly adopted over the last sixty years has not been missionally effective or numerically successful, either in growing the numbers of people attending our churches or in producing a positive perception of the Christian church. Indeed, by whatever metric we use to measure missional effectiveness, a strategy of pursuing contextual relevance has not been fruitful in New Zealand.[27] For example, over the last sixty years, the percentage of the population claiming to be Christian has dropped from 90.4 percent (in 1961) to 34 percent (in 2023). Over the same period, the percentage claiming to have no religion has grown from 1.4 percent to 53 percent.[28] From the 1960s to the 1980s, this loss was primarily experienced in the traditional mainline churches who assumed "people would be born into them and baptized as infants, when the figures showed they had very few baptisms from the mid-1970's and very few children in their Sunday schools by the 1980's."[29] This exodus from mainline churches led to some numerical growth in

---

26. This section demonstrates its claim primarily through leveraging off recent research undertaken by postgraduate students within Laidlaw College.

27. Given that this point is reasonably well accepted, it is not proved in detail or with great statistical rigor. For more detail, see for example Ward, *Post-Sixties New Zealand*; and Ward, *Losing Our Religion*.

28. See www.stats.govt.nz/. See also Wilberforce Foundation, "Faith and Belief," 7.

29. Ward, "Religion in New Zealand," 194.

evangelical, Pentecostal, and charismatic churches for a time, but primarily it was transfer rather than conversion growth. For example, sampled studies suggest that less than 4 percent of growing churches at this time had a non-churched background,[30] and after the 1990s, having exhausted the transfer growth coming from mainline denominations, many evangelical, Pentecostal, and charismatic churches have ceased numerically growing as well.[31]

The New Zealand church's missional strategy of pursuing relevance has not been statistically effective. One could add to this statistical failure the marginalization of the church's voice and influence in both public spaces and policy that has occurred over the last sixty years. In terms of the church's place within the public sphere, the decreasing prevalence of Bible in schools, the introduction of sport, shopping, and recreation opportunities on Sundays, and more recently, the removal of references to Jesus Christ, or "true religion" in public prayers, all provide data pointing to the sidelining of the church within Aotearoa. Regarding the church's influence on public policy, independent of one's particular positions on these significant issues, the recent debates about marriage equality and euthanasia make it abundantly clear that much of New Zealand society has little interest in the church's viewpoint. The data and examples given here about the church's decline in both size and significance are only offered in broad strokes. Moreover, correlation is not causation, so one cannot conclude that it is precisely and exactly the church leaning into its similarities with the wider culture that has directly led to the church's decline. But what can be concluded is that there is no evidence that a strategy of pursuing contextual relevance has had a positive statistical or sociological impact for the Christian church.

Second, and from an internal perspective, this subsection explores the negative results that have occurred within the New Zealand church from us leaning into the similarities we have with the surrounding culture's underlying narrative. These consequences are perhaps even more severe. For through minimizing the differences we have with the outside culture, the church in New Zealand has, perhaps unwittingly, embraced the idols of secularism, consumerism, and individualism. Newbigin's analysis seems eerily prophetic for the contemporary situation in New Zealand when he writes, "If the biblical story is not the one that really controls our thinking then inevitably we shall be swept into the story that the world tells about itself. We shall become increasingly indistinguishable from the pagan world of which we are a part."[32] When we lean into the similarities we have with

---

30. Ward, *Losing Our Religion*, 51.
31. Ward, *Losing Our Religion*, 52. See also Ward, *Post-Sixties New Zealand* 194–97.
32. Newbigin, "Biblical Authority," 2, as quoted in Goheen, *Church and Its Vocation*,

the world, we inevitably open ourselves and our churches to mingling the worship of the true and living God with the worship of other gods. This creates, in the words of the apostle Paul, "a form of godliness, but denying its power" (2 Tim 3:5 NIV). We increasingly adopt a secular mindset, where our Christianity becomes a thin veneer of the gospel overlaying a much more solid and fundamental core where most of our lives are lived without reference to God. In this way, we also adopt a consumer mindset, "which wants and can only cope with Christianity and the Scriptures delivered in a no-bother, pre-cooked, easily digestible servings."[33] And we adopt an individualistic mindset, where our Christian walk affects us vertically, but impacts only minimally on our relationship with the surrounding world.

One does not have to look hard to uncover illustrations of this phenomenon. Two recent studies provide compelling examples. First, a recently-completed thesis entitled "A Practical Ecclesiological Response to Depression-Promoting Values" explored a potential link between the prevalence of depression within those attending churches in New Zealand and the church's adoption of prominent Western cultural values such as individualism, consumerism, and narcissism.[34] Even more significantly, this research analyzed how the church adopting values and liturgical practices that intrinsically display these Western understandings has deprived it from acting as a kind of institutional antidepressant, combatting the depression promoting values of the surrounding Western culture.[35] A second research example explores the increasing prevalence of diet culture within the church in New Zealand.[36] This research demonstrates that the biblical narrative, contemporary science, and Western culture each have a position on appropriate dietary practices and acceptable body image, particularly among women. The positions of the biblical narrative and contemporary science are remarkably similar, and both are decidedly inconsistent with that pursued by contemporary Western culture. Remarkably, the New Zealand church's commonly-accepted position on appropriate dietary practices aligns much more closely with that of Western culture and contrasts significantly with the understanding promoted by both the biblical narrative and contemporary science.[37] In this instance, similarly to so many other

---

155.

33. Marshall, "Re-Engaging with the Bible," 17.
34. Van Ingen-Kal, "Practical Ecclesiological Response."
35. See in particular Van Ingen-Kal, "Practical Ecclesiological Response," 10–21.
36. See Bowden and Habets, "Fat Bodies, Diet Culture," 1–8; and Bowden, "Idolizing Thinness," 43–59.
37. See Bowden and Habets, "Fat Bodies, Diet Culture," 1–2.

situations, the church has chosen to embrace an idolatrous understanding that does not match the biblical narrative. Both externally and internally, pursuing contextual relevance has not had a positive impact on the church in New Zealand.

Having considered the negative consequences of leaning into the commonalities that exist between the gospel narrative and the surrounding culture, consider now the positive impacts of intentionally leaning in the other direction, and what results from emphasizing the points of distinction the gospel narrative has with Western culture. Again, we divide these into internal and external consequences.

Research into the effectiveness of adopting a posture that leans away from contextual relevance is starting to emerge.[38] For example, the study of depression mentioned above explored how to facilitate a minimally syncretistic ecclesiological response to depression and as a result cultivate what the researcher termed "antidepressant kingdom values" within our church liturgies. This would occur, the researcher noted, through the interplay of engaging our kingdom imaginations, leaning into God's presence, and demonstrating consistent practice, enabling the church to deliberately and intentionally participate with the Spirit's healing and transformational work.[39] The research explored some very specific examples of how this might occur and noted how an appropriately non-syncretistic approach to the Eucharist can foster communal living, purposefulness, and joy. The researcher concluded that "several studies showed that creating church environments that embody these values could indeed mitigate depression and improve overall mental well-being."[40] The research also explored daily practices outside of church gatherings and noted how within everyday life New Zealand Christians can cultivate simple yet formative practices that promote joyful, purposeful, communal, and other-focused living and counter the Western values of narcissism, individualism and consumerism. The research noted how making habits of these kingdom values through regular practice can complement and enhance the institutional response, forming a holistic and ultimately effective response to depression-promoting values common in Western culture.[41]

---

38. This exploration is to some degree merely initial, as leaning away from contemporary culture is not the posture adopted by the majority of the New Zealand church. Some specific examples of churches pursuing this approach will be considered in the next section.

39. Van Ingen-Kal, "Practical Ecclesiological Response," 29–39.

40. Van Ingen-Kal, "Practical Ecclesiological Response," 39.

41. Van Ingen-Kal, "Practical Ecclesiological Response," 40–49.

The second research project about the prevalence of diet culture within the New Zealand church is more extensive and currently ongoing, but even at this early stage similar conclusions are emerging. "The time is overdue for the church to recognize that faith-based diets do not align with theological anthropology,"[42] the researcher argues. The strong suggestion emerging from this research points to the possibility of the church in New Zealand adopting an approach to health and wellness known as HAES (health at any size). In this alternative approach, instead of focusing on dieting as the means to both health and holiness, the church can help its members grow a healthy relationship with food, one that honors the "social aspects of fellowship over food for the embodied unitary being,"[43] recognizing the way "Jesus used hospitality and shared meals to bring people together."[44] The church can also help its members realize that their "value and self-worth lie in God's eyes, not their dress size."[45] By adopting this kind of approach, "the church will ultimately benefit the entirety of the embodied spiritual being, the ongoing spiritual formation of the church community, and thus by supporting [those] in the community to flourish, the entire community will produce more fruit."[46] All in all, initial research provides several concrete examples of how leaning away from the narrative underlying Western culture could have a significant, sustained, and ultimately positive effect on the church community in New Zealand as well as on the individuals of which it is comprised.

Having considered the negative external and internal consequences of leaning into the similarities we have with the narrative of the outside culture, and the potential positive consequences that emerge within the church of deliberately doing the opposite, the final subsection of this exploration of the appropriateness of applying Newbigin's missional insights to the church in New Zealand is to explore the externally focused positive implications of leaning into our distinctives. Emerging research from within the New Zealand church provides strong indications that increasingly missionally focused communities can be directly linked to the adoption of a posture that deliberately leans away from pursuing contextual relevance. For example, a remarkably wide-ranging and insightful piece of research completed recently explored the journeys of six church communities that have deliberately, intentionally, and effectively fashioned or refashioned themselves

---

42. Bowden and Habets, "Fat Bodies, Diet Culture," 6.
43. Bowden and Habets, "Fat Bodies, Diet Culture," 5.
44. Bowden and Habets, "Fat Bodies, Diet Culture," 5.
45. Bowden and Habets, "Fat Bodies, Diet Culture," 5.
46. Bowden and Habets, "Fat Bodies, Diet Culture," 6.

so that mission is central.⁴⁷ The research outlined three key themes that enabled churches to adopt and prioritize a missional focus, namely leadership, relationships, and discipleship. In terms of leadership, every one of the leaders of these communities went through a distinct phase where they explicitly rejected the influence of the surrounding culture both individually and within the church communities they fashioned and led. The research notes, "All six new communities centered on relationships and discipleship to counteract cultural influences and equip Christians to pursue their vocation."⁴⁸ Leaning into relationships deliberately countered the Western ideology of individualism, which meant removing previously adopted styles, programs, and structures that reinforced these ideologies, and recentering relationships around a common missional purpose. The researcher concluded, "The starting point for a new community with a relational focus was the re-discovery of the *missio Dei*. . . . Their ideas flowed from an understanding that the Triune God sends the church into the world to participate in His mission, the reconciliation of all things to Himself (2 Cor 5:11–21). This makes God's mission the central purpose of the church."⁴⁹

Leaning into discipleship deliberately countered the Western value of consumerism, through abandoning the pursuit of numerical over spiritual growth, and of the desire and demand for professionalism that makes church and Christianity a product that you can sell. The practices that enabled this discipleship growth were remarkably traditional, including prayer, Bible reading, teaching, and hospitality. The research noted the distinction that enabled genuine growth in discipleship, however, arguing that it "is the intentionality, accountability and authenticity behind them [the traditional practices] to seek intimacy with God and others that is key."⁵⁰ Specific, clear, and accountable processes that do not enable people to remain as strangers, and has strong expectations of character growth led inevitably to a clear missional focus and outcomes. In short, deliberately crafting communities that lean away from Western ideologies has been a necessary and sufficient condition for mission to become central in the life of the churches researched in this project.

The argument of this section has been that intentionally leaning into the differences between the gospel narrative and the surrounding culture's narrative is both a timely and appropriate missional approach for the church in New Zealand. It has explored the negative consequences of leaning into

47. Wood, "New Forms of Community."
48. Wood, "New Forms of Community," ii.
49. Wood, "New Forms of Community," 49.
50. Wood, "New Forms of Community," 65.

similarities, both externally (noting the loss of size and status the church has encountered during the decades it has adopted a strategy of contextual relevance) and internally (noting how the pursuit of similarities has unwittingly opened the church's doors to syncretism and idol worship). And it has explored the positive implications of leaning into differences, recognizing both internal consequences (utilizing the examples of depression and diet culture to explore how the church deliberately distinguishing itself from the community outside could have positive impact for both the overall church community and the individuals within it) and external implications (noting how a rejection of cultural norms within the church appears to be a necessary and sufficient condition leading to a renewal of the church's missional focus). While the positive examples are predominantly anecdotal, there is, even at this early stage, more than enough evidence to suggest that a change in posture is both helpful and welcome within the New Zealand church.

HOW CAN WE IMPLEMENT NEWBIGIN'S MISSIONAL INSIGHTS?

How can Newbigin's missional strategy of leaning into the differences we have with the culture around us, rather than leaning into the similarities, get proactively actioned? This final substantive section explores two communities that (either explicitly or implicitly) have adopted this approach.

The first example is a church planted in 2016 in the Pt. Chevalier area of Auckland: Church@126. While it is not accurate to say that the leaders of this community have intentionally applied Newbigin's insights to their church plant, exploring their carefully considered distinctives reveals quite clearly, both how the core values undergirding their church plant align with gospel truth but also, and more pertinently for this discussion, how each one deliberately leans into the distinctions that exist between the biblical narrative and the narrative underlying the surrounding culture. The four key aspects undergirding the forming of this church plant are that they aspired to be (and have become) a family, in a place, on a mission, together.[51] The following paragraphs explore how the outworking of each of these features represents, not just a crucial aspect of gospel truth but also explicitly distinguishes the church community from the surrounding culture.

First, the community's leaning into the core idea of the church as a family derives not just from their belief that this is a non-negotiable aspect of gospel truth but also from the recognition that modern Western culture

---

51. Webb, *Redemptive Family*, 170–74. In the analysis below, the latter two distinctives will be addressed together.

does not place a high priority on family. Just like a family, Church@126 is not a community where you can attend and be invisible. Everyone is known and everyone is welcome, but, unlike many other church communities, it is not a place where anyone can hide. Such an approach pushes back against the shallow level of acquaintance that is both common and even sought after within Western culture. The church leaders recognize how the number of close friends the average person relates to has halved in the last twenty years, leading to an epidemic of loneliness.[52] One of the leaders, Howard Webb, writes, "Churches often fret about their relevance to the culture or how much they have to offer. But it is not our accommodation to the culture that makes us relevant. It is the unconditional love for those we invite to the family table and our constancy in living out the values of the Kingdom together that make us a 'city on a hill.'"[53]

The second core aspect is that Church@126 see themselves as strongly rooted in a particular place. In this case, they are called to the community of Pt. Chevalier. Clearly, this affirmation pushes back against contemporary trends of dislocation, enabled, not just by increasing ease of travel but also by online access to relationships, goods, and services. The leaders of this church, however, recognize that leaning into this value also strongly pushes back against Western consumerism. Webb writes, "Church for consumers can also be anywhere, needing only a suitable venue that brings together church people and the resources needed to provide the spiritual services on offer. The question of where this [consumer-driven] church is located is driven by economics and ease of access, rather than a desire to be grounded in a place."[54] Church@126 recognizes that the emphasis on being called to a specific locality enables the church community to replace transactional relationships (which are transitory and occasional, primarily about meeting immediate needs and providing services) with truly functional family relationships (which are regular and habitual, and where each person, independent of what they bring or do not bring to the community, is needed and plays an indispensable part).[55]

The third and fourth aspects are that this church see themselves as called to join God in his mission together.[56] In a sentiment that almost exactly matches Newbigin's point above that the church is the primary, and to

52. Webb, *Redemptive Family*, 49.
53. Webb, *Redemptive Family*, 50.
54. Webb, *Redemptive Family*, 57.
55. Webb, *Redemptive Family*, 57.
56. In his book, Webb deals with the calling to mission and the togetherness in two separate chapters. The intrinsically communal nature of the missional calling is his primary point in both these chapters.

a great extent, the only missionary body that exists, Church@126 maintains that the church is not just called to equip people to go out and do mission as individuals, but that everything the church is and does should be missional. They write, "Our mission is to invite those we befriend to join our church family so that, in the power of the Holy Spirit, we can bring restoration and healing to our place and God's world together."[57] Further, and by its very nature, this communal approach to mission, which brings evangelism and discipleship right into the core of not just the purpose of the church family but of their communal gathering itself, leans in a distinctly different direction from the functional and individualistic tendencies favored in modern Western culture and by many modern Western churches. Moreover, because of this communal approach, evangelism and discipleship—transformation—are not optional but expected and accountable. As Webb writes, "In the West it seems that, whatever is preached or taught, changing behavior as a consequence is entirely optional—even for good churchgoers."[58]

There is a great deal that is attractive about Church@126, and their experience speaks significant hope into the realities the church is currently facing in Aotearoa. Primarily, their example shows that leaning into the differences we have with the society surrounding us does not have to be complicated. The central idea that church is family is worked out among them in a simple but profound manner, and my personal experience of having attended there as an intentional and introverted stranger (even though I am known by some of the leadership team) is that it would be virtually impossible to visit and not conclude that the God this community is serving is real, because Church@126 simply could not exist as it does, surrounded by a Western culture that is so extraordinarily different from it, if God was not real. Church@126 is different from the surrounding culture, but they are different with distinction, in a way that is too attractive to ignore.

The second church community chosen as an example differs from Church@126 in three ways. First, it is not a recent church plant but has been in existence for well over three decades. Second, it is not New Zealand based but exists overseas, namely in Manhattan, New York.[59] Finally, and most crucially, rather than implicitly utilizing Newbigin's missional understanding, its leaders have explicitly and intentionally determined how they should act as a church community based on their reading and application of Newbigin's work. The example is Redeemer Presbyterian Church, which

---

57. Webb, *Redemptive Family*, 117.

58. Webb, *Redemptive Family*, 139.

59. The author is not aware of any New Zealand based church that has explicitly incorporated Newbigin's missional insights.

Tim Keller founded in downtown Manhattan in 1989. Nearly thirty years later, in the 2017 Kuyper Lecture at Princeton Theological Seminary, Keller spoke about the influence of Newbigin's writings on how he chose to form and fashion that community and how it has continued to develop. After noting that he is not a Newbigin scholar, Keller addressed the question of why he should be talking about Newbigin's missiological insights. He said,

> I'm a practitioner. Here's what I have to offer.... In the 1980s, I was reading... [Newbigin's work], and 1989 when *The Gospel in Pluralistic Society* came out, I went to New York City, I went to Manhattan, and I started a church from scratch, in an environment quite resistant to orthodox Christianity. And I remember reading his stuff and [realizing] ... there's nobody else that is even describing what I'm trying to do, let alone prescribing. And the reason I call this [lecture] "Answering Lesslie Newbigin" ... is I wanted to [answer Newbigin's questions] ... Can the West be converted?... Can the church have a missionary encounter with Western culture? ... [Newbigin] actually suggested [a missionary encounter with the West] would happen along certain lines ... and I'm here to tell you that on the basis of my almost thirty years of experience in New York, Lesslie Newbigin is basically right.... I think we need to answer Lesslie Newbigin, "Yes, it is possible ... to have a missionary encounter" and it is largely, I think, along the lines ... that he sketches.[60]

In the lecture, Keller outlines seven key facets he has gleaned from Newbigin's writings that have been crucial for Redeemer Presbyterian Church to have a genuine missiological encounter with the surrounding culture.[61] While all these facets, obviously, fit within Newbigin's overarching missiological strategy as explained in this essay, two are particularly pertinent.[62]

First, Keller talks about how Redeemer has adopted, and churches in the West need to adopt a *strategy of subversive fulfillment* in order to have a genuine missiological encounter with Western culture. By this Keller means

60. Keller, "Answering Lesslie Newbigin," 6:09–7:50.

61. Note that Keller bases his seven key ideas on Newbigin's final chapter in *Foolishness to the Greeks*, which also has seven key ideas. Keller refashions the ideas and revises them based on his experience with Redeemer. For Newbigin's seven key points, see Newbigin, *Foolishness to the Greeks*, 134–50.

62. Note that all of Keller's insights from Newbigin as outlined in this lecture can be related to the core idea of leaning into the differences between the gospel narrative and that of the surrounding culture. However, due to space restrictions, this essay focuses only on those that have the most immediate and obvious application to the themes outworked in this chapter.

first that churches need to identify the baseline narratives that characterize the surrounding culture and intentionally subvert those narratives. Indeed, Keller argues that local churches should confront these alternative narratives as idols and intentionally craft communities that lean in an alternative direction. But he even goes one step further and argues that it is precisely through this subverting of cultural expectations that the deep desires that undergird those alternative narratives and idols can actually be fulfilled. To illustrate this principle, Keller notes how in 1 Cor 1 Paul uses the cross to subvert the wisdom-seeking cultural norms of the Greeks and the power-seeking cultural norms of the Jews. Both are disestablished in the cross as powerless idols, for the cross (at least initially and superficially) is neither wise nor powerful. But then Paul reveals that in the cross true wisdom and true power can be found (1 Cor 1:18–31). So what Greeks are seeking (in wisdom) and what Jews desire (in power) is truly found only in and through Christ. In the same kind of way, says Keller, churches should demonstrate to a Western culture that is highly individualistic or consumeristic, "what you're after is good, it's extremely important, but you're looking for it in the wrong place. . . . It [individualism and consumerism] can never deliver what you think it will give you."[63] Keller argues that subversive fulfillment should be true of our churches on a micro and a macro level. By this (I presume) he means that all our individual communication should be modelled on this approach (micro level), where we understand someone's cultural frame by entering into it, and then intentionally subvert it, only to show how the deep desire undergirding that cultural frame will be ultimately fulfilled in Jesus, upon whom all plotlines and desires converge. But also, subversive fulfillment should also characterize each of our church communities as a whole (macro level). In other words, our church communities should be intentionally designed and continually fashioned by first understanding the idols that undergird our Western society; second, by intentionally subverting them; and third, and most importantly, Keller argues that the very nature of our communities should demonstrate how the deep desires undergirding Western culture are actually fulfilled in a gospel community centered on the life of Jesus Christ and his empowering Spirit. Keller says, "Christianity offers a meaning that suffering can't take away, a satisfaction not based on circumstances, a freedom that doesn't destroy love because it's not the absence of constraints but the liberating ones, an identity that doesn't crush you or exclude others because it's not an achieved identity, it's received, a justice that doesn't create new oppressors, and a hope that's not mere optimism."[64]

---

63. Keller, "Answering Lesslie Newbigin," 43:21–43:31.
64. Keller, "Answering Lesslie Newbigin," 45:37–46:04.

Our communities should be demonstrations of these truths, and they can only do that if they lean away from cultural norms and expectations in a way that is both intriguingly different and undeniably attractive.

Another of Newbigin's insights that Keller has deliberately enacted within the Redeemer community is that churches should be *unique category disrupting social projects*. Keller notes how the center of Newbigin's understanding is that the life of the church community demonstrates and unpacks the truth of the gospel. He says, "You embody the gospel in your community and in a sense that proclaims the gospel more powerfully than your words. . . . Your words will not in any way hit home unless it's backed up by a community that embodies the words."[65] Keller then asks what such a community would look like and argues it will always contradict cultural and political expectations, whatever side of the political or cultural divide with which you are aligned. He notes, for example, Hurtado's analysis in *Destroyer of the Gods* that the early church was characterized by five features: multi-ethnic community, generosity to the poor, non-retaliation and forgiveness, positive action combatting abortion and infant exposure, and strict sexual ethics.[66] Keller argues the first two features align with the political left, the latter two features with the political right, and the middle feature (non-retaliation) does not align with any political movement. Keller continues, "Do you not see that one of the greatest ways to explain that the gospel is not the product of a particular culture but actually comes from God is that the community that it creates would actually break through the categories?"[67]

On a recent trip to America, I attended a church gathering at Redeemer Presbyterian Church. Actually, I went several times. My first visit was motivated by curiosity, but I returned again and again because the church demonstrated in so many ways, some subtle and some incredibly obvious, that they had fashioned themselves both around gospel truth and on being distinctive from the surrounding culture. Church@126 and Redeemer are not similar communities. What they have in common, however, is that they are both intentionally crafting themselves to be different from the society around them. For Church@126, the call to be a family, in a place, on a mission together, means that they are deeply called to a particular location, while deliberately leaning away from many of the features that characterize society in that location. Redeemer is more explicitly following Newbigin's guidelines for having a missiological engagement with the surrounding culture. But both are deliberately and intentionally constructing themselves

---

65. Keller, "Answering Lesslie Newbigin," 46:55–47:08.
66. Hurtado, *Destroyer of the Gods*.
67. Keller, "Answering Lesslie Newbigin," 50:30–50:43.

as plausibility structures for the gospel. People engaging with both communities can tell that God is real and Jesus is Lord because it is immediately obvious that church communities like Redeemer Presbyterian Church and Church@126 simply could not and would not exist if God was not real and Jesus was not Lord.

CONCLUSION

Newbigin's analysis suggests that many expressions of the church in New Zealand, like in much of the Western world, have "an advanced case of syncretism."[68] Syncretism is almost always unacknowledged; no one ever labels themselves as a syncretist. Moreover, Newbigin suggests that it is precisely this syncretism, rather than any lack of contextual relevance, that is the root cause of the church's missional ineffectiveness.

Over previous decades, many churches in New Zealand have eagerly embraced program changes in the hope that it will lead to a genuine missional encounter with the surrounding culture. Most of these have been ineffective; very few have been sustained. This chapter has suggested, in contrast, that genuine hope for missional effectiveness lies not in the adoption of any new program but rather in embracing a new posture. This posture is one where the church in New Zealand deliberately and intentionally leans into the differences the gospel narrative has with the outside culture, rather than leaning into the similarities that exist. It is important to recognize nuance in the wording used here. Abandoning all similarity with the surrounding culture would result in a scenario where we fall into an unwelcome isolationism that would remove even the possibility of interaction and deny any genuine missional encounter. But gently leaning into the differences that exist could enable us to be distinctive in a way that is both attractive and intriguing.

The adoption of such a posture will not lead to a single big change in the church's activities, but it could encourage a thousand small decisions where we increasingly adjust what we prioritize and where we choose to invest our time. Based on some initial research projects, and a couple of case studies as noted above, there are grounds for cautious hopefulness that such a change in posture would lead to a renewed prioritization of mission and a welcome rejection of idolizing worldliness. Perhaps by leaning into our distinctive differences with society, and recognizing our need to continually be empowered by the Holy Spirit, the church in New Zealand can increasingly

---

68. Newbigin, *Word in Season*, 67.

become a dynamic agent of God's love and reconciliation in the nation, offering hope and healing in a complex and changing world.

BIBLIOGRAPHY

Bowden, Jennifer. "Idolizing Thinness: Critiquing the False Claims of Diet Culture." In *Pursuing Perfection: Faith and the Female Body*, edited by Maja Whitaker, 43–59. London: SCM, 2025.

Bowden, Jennifer, and Myk Habets. "Fat Bodies, Diet Culture, and Human Flourishing: How Did We Get It So Wrong?" *Dialog* (2024) 1–8.

Dixon, Nigel. *Villages Without Walls: An Exploration of the Necessity of Building Christian Community in a Post-Christian World*. Palmerston North: Vox Humana, 2010.

Goheen, M. W. *The Church and Its Vocation: Lesslie Newbigin's Missionary Ecclesiology*. Grand Rapids: Baker, 2018.

Hauerwas, Stanley. *The Peaceable Kingdom*. Notre Dame: SCM, 1983.

Hurtado, Larry W. *Destroyer of the Gods: Early Christian Distinctives in the Roman World*. Waco, TX: Baylor, 2017.

Keller, Tim. "Answering Lesslie Newbigin." Kuyper Lecture, Princeton Theological Seminary, Apr. 6, 2017. https://www.youtube.com/watch?v=V0LG26k6ngs&t=855s.

Kierkegaard, Søren. *Sickness Unto Death*. New York: Start, 2013.

Liston, Gregory J. "Spirit, Church, and Mission: Toward a Third Article Theology of Ecclesial Mission." *Evangelical Quarterly* 92 (2021) 21–38.

Marshall, Chris. "Re-Engaging with the Bible in a Postmodern World: A Discussion." *Stimulus: The New Zealand Journal of Christian Thought and Practice* 15 (2007) 17–20.

Newbigin, Lesslie. "Biblical Authority." Unpublished manuscript, 1997. University of Birmingham Newbigin Archives, Birmingham, England.

———. *Foolishness to the Greeks: The Gospel and Western Culture*. Grand Rapids: Eerdmans, 1986.

———. *The Gospel in a Pluralist Society*. Grand Rapids: Eerdmans, 1989.

———. *The Reunion of the Church: A Defence of the South India Scheme*. London: SCM, 1960.

———. *Trinitarian Doctrine for Today's Mission*. Carlisle: Paternoster, 1998.

———. *A Word in Season: Perspectives on Christian World Missions*. Grand Rapids: Eerdmans, 1994.

Pritchard, G. A. *Willow Creek Seeker Services: Evaluating a New Way of Doing Church*. Grand Rapids: Baker, 1996.

Purves, Andrew. *The Crucifixion of Ministry*. Downers Grove: IVP Books, 2007.

Smith, James K. A. *Desiring the Kingdom: Worship, Worldview, and Cultural Formation*. Grand Rapids: Baker Academic, 2009.

Stafford, Tim. "God's Missionary to Us." *Christianity Today* 40 (1996) 24–33.

Van Ingen-Kal, Tyran. "A Practical Ecclesiological Response to Depression-Promoting Values." BTh diss., Laidlaw College, 2024.

Ward, Kevin. *The Church in Post-Sixties New Zealand: Decline, Growth, and Change*. Auckland: Archer, 2013.

———. *Losing Our Religion: Changing Patterns of Believing and Belonging in Western Societies*. Eugene: Wipf & Stock, 2013.

———. "Religion in New Zealand Since the 1960s: Some Sociological Perspectives." *New Zealand Sociology* 31 (2016) 186–206.

Warren, Rick. *The Purpose Driven Church*. Grand Rapids: Zondervan, 1995.

Webb, Howard. *Redemptive Family*. Wellington: Torn Curtain, 2020.

Wilberforce Foundation, "Faith and Belief." Nov. 2023. https://faithandbeliefstudynz.org/wp-content/uploads/2023/11/willberforce-report-2023-digital-2.pdf.

Windsor, Paul. "The Gospel of Community?" The Art of Unpacking, Sept. 6, 2006. https://paulwindsorblog.com/2006/09/the-gospel-of-community/.

Wood, Kevin. "New Forms of Community: The Habits, Shape, and Posture of Mission-Focussed Churches in Aotearoa." MTh thesis, Laidlaw College, 2024.

Chapter 13

Sharing Faith, Imaging God, Nourishing Hope
Faith and Hope That Is Relational, Mysterious, and Transformational

LYNNE TAYLOR

INTRODUCTION

As Christians and as churches, we're invited and called to be people and places who support transformation and healing. We're invited to share hope with those we encounter—people both inside and outside the church. This chapter explores how we might do that, today.

Our contemporary context has changed and is changing. In the latest census, over half of New Zealand's population indicated that they have no religious affiliation: Christians now comprise just under a third of the population. Church attendance is also generally declining, and Christianity has considerably less influence in the public square. Further, Christians and churches (and related agencies) have been complicit in and responsible for various abuses and misdemeanors, and that has (rightly) harmed our reputation.[1]

---

1. For example, the Royal Commission on Abuse in Care's final report was released in 2024. It noted that "the authority of religious institutions and of clergy and church leaders created conditions for abuse and neglect in care to occur in faith-based care

And yet! Christians and churches seek to share hope. As they do, people, including some who were previously unchurched, continue to embrace and grow in their faith. In my research on contemporary faith formation, I love hearing stories of why people choose to embrace Christianity today. I hear diverse stories from and about unique people, but the stories hold common themes that give me hope. These stories can build our confidence in a gospel that remains true, and hope filled. They can inspire us to share about our own faith in ways that are connective and meaningful today. They might challenge us to live out genuine hospitality. They can also encourage us that we don't need to have all the answers.

This chapter begins by briefly describing our current context before introducing my recent research on faith formation. It briefly outlines the process by which people adopt faith today, the affects they were experiencing, and the role that other Christians played in their journeys to faith.[2] It then homes in on one interesting finding: the connection between people's aspirations towards an ideal self and the attributes of God that they appreciate. The main part of the chapter offers a range of suggestions about what churches and Christians might learn from these insights and how we might emphasize a faith that is relational, mysterious, and transformational.

CONTEXT

The Anglican church I was baptized in popped up on my Facebook page recently. "For sale: price by negotiation." When I was born, my family lived a couple of kilometers away in the Ōhoka schoolhouse in North Canterbury. I don't remember much about church in those early days, but I do remember the community, including people who remained my parents' life-long friends. Being reminded of St. Albans Anglican Church got me thinking about the fourteen churches I've been part of over my fifty-something years. I realized there are three things I look back on with particular appreciation: spiritual growth, community, and an emphasis beyond the church. Not all churches have been good at all three of these, but I reckon that together,

---

settings." Royal Commission of Inquiry, "Whaneketia," 602. In 2022, an independent review was released, "commissioned by the board of Arise Church . . . in light of the stories which were shared in the public domain about hurts and harm some people had experienced during their involvement with Arise Church." See Cummings et al., "Independent Review," 2. Both received extensive media coverage and include disturbing stories of harm caused by church leaders and churches.

2. My use of the word "affects" follows psychologists who use the term to describe a range of positive and negative emotional states. American Psychological Association, "Affect."

they are what church is about. In "spiritual growth," I am including worshiping God, along with teaching and discipleship more broadly. But that is not all: church is about more than Sunday worship and spiritual growth. It is also about being caring communities—people caring deeply for one another. We're made for relationship with others, and worshiping together, learning together, serving together, celebrating joys, and supporting one another in difficulties are expressions of that relationality. Further, many of the churches I've been part of also lived out their understanding that church wasn't just for them. They recognized that as churches and as Christians, we're also called beyond the church to help support transformation and healing, for those outside (as well as those inside) the church. That's what church is about. Worship, discipleship, community, and helping make our world a better place.

Of course, churches do not always live up to this calling: some have been better at one or two of these areas than the others. For example, churches might be great at celebrating and supporting existing members but not good at appropriately welcoming newer people. They might run meaningful worship services for those who are part of the church but never consider the wellbeing of the wider community. But there's a bigger problem as well. Many churches and church-based organizations have been complicit in (or, worse, responsible for) various forms of abuse. Some have created cultures that (even while perhaps well-meaning) have caused deep and abiding harm.[3] At times, we've doubled down and refused to take responsibility for this harm. We need to recognize the damage that has been done (and that continues to be done) in the name of Christ and the church. Patriarchy, racism, misogyny—these are all criticisms we need to take seriously. People have been harmed because of such teachings and actions. The Scriptures, the gospels, and Jesus call us to a different way of living, where every person is recognized as equally beloved, precious, and made in the image of God.

There is fallout from such unchristian attitudes and actions, fallout that has undoubtedly resulted in less people joining and more people leaving the church.[4] But it's not just what's been happening inside the church and associated agencies that has led to declining religious affiliation and declining church attendance in Aotearoa and other Western countries. Changing populations are an obvious additional factor, but my first church in Ōhoka hasn't closed because of population decline—the small rural community has been growing as farms are replaced by lifestyle blocks, and the school

---

3. See footnote 1. These harms are not unique to New Zealand. See, for instance, Bogen et al., "It Happens at #ChurchToo," Poyner-Smith and Loebs, "'You Are Not.'"

4. For instance, see Furborough, "Pākehā Young Adults Changing."

roll is now triple what it was when Dad started teaching there. Something else is going on.

Secularization processes are complex. As noted, in New Zealand there has been a decline in religious affiliation (people of no religion now make up 52 percent of the population, Christians just 32 percent) and in church attendance (amplified by the COVID-19 pandemic).[5] There is also a decline in the influence of Christianity beyond the church: while Christian values are deeply embedded in society and laws, a so-called "Christian perspective" on contemporary issues is unlikely to be sought or valued. Sometimes, we struggle with that, and how we respond is noticed: our responses to cultural changes matter. In understanding our current moment in time, more helpful than just counting bums on seats or census affiliates, is a recognition that the "conditions of belief" have changed.[6] Religious belief is contestable and contested. Many people believe they can experience flourishing without drawing on anything beyond the self. For those who are interested in faith and spirituality, Christianity is just one among a myriad of options.

Despite these declines and attitudes, spirituality is valued by many in Aotearoa. For instance, it is recognized in te whāre tapa whā and in other indigenous health models as a necessary dimension of health and wellbeing.[7] The recent Faith and Belief Study revealed that most people remain open to spirituality and to exploring faith.[8] Some people choose to adopt the Christian faith despite not having been brought up in it. I'm curious about this and have dedicated several years to investigating why they do so.

CONTEMPORARY FAITH FORMATION

My 2017 PhD explored why previously unchurched Australians become Christians today.[9] I interviewed people who had come to faith in the previous two years, none of whom had grown up in the church. I discovered that there's a common process people follow towards embracing faith, and that what's happening in their gut is as (or perhaps more) important than what they were thinking about or discussing cognitively. They told me how other Christians had helped their journeys to faith and how they understood God to have been at work. They also told me what it was about God

---

5. Taylor, "2023 Religious Affiliation"; Taylor, "Attendance of Baptist Churches."
6. Taylor, *Secular Age*, 3.
7. Durie, "Maori Perspective on Health."
8. McCrindle, *Faith and Belief (Short Report)*, 8; McCrindle, *Faith and Belief (Long Report)*.
9. Taylor, "Redeeming Authenticity."

they appreciated—and often there were fascinating connections between what they appreciated about God and the attributes and characteristics they wanted to be like themselves. More recently, I've been exploring in more depth this connection between appreciated attributes of God and people's aspirations towards living better lives.

Early Stages

I asked those I interviewed for my PhD to tell me how and why they embraced Christianity. While each story I heard was unique, there were common themes and a common process. Hamish[10] was in his thirties, a young dad who had come to faith eighteen months before I interviewed him. You might have met someone a bit like Hamish: he told me he had been a "militant evangelical atheist" who loved to argue with Christians and to tell and show them how "silly" their religion was. He was pretty good at it too. He'd read widely and regularly watched videos of all the atheist greats, and he was convinced by them—until he wasn't. Hamish's grandparents were Christians, and he'd occasionally gone to Sunday school with them. He had also had some Christian friends at his school, who he remained in contact with (and argued with). One day, Hamish noticed a flash of gold leaf in his bookcase and wondered what it was. Pulling out a Bible, he started to read it. The King James Version he had found was difficult to understand, but "for some reason [he] thought, 'I'll just Google Bible translations and see what else is there.'" He found the New International Version "a bit easier to read," and when reading John's Gospel, he realized, "This is really powerful stuff." God spoke to him through what he was reading. He told me,

> And then one day [six months after he had noticed and started reading his Bible], I had to let my little dog out to go to the toilet, [at] three o'clock in the morning. [I] looked up at the stars. And in my head, I heard, it sounds strange, but I will say it, I heard "the heavens will declare his majesty" when I was looking up at the stars. And I sort of just went . . . I didn't fall to my knees, I didn't burst out crying, I just went, "Uh. I'm a Christian now," and walked back inside.

Hamish's story illustrates very well the process that was common to everyone I interviewed (see Figure 1). They had some initial exposure to the Christian faith. Something happened that functioned as a catalyst or trigger, and they began engaging in spiritual practices—usually following an

---

10. All participant names are pseudonyms.

invitation to do so (although Hamish skipped that step). They kept saying "yes" to the journey they were on towards Christianity and eventually realized and named (generally in understated ways) that they were Christians.

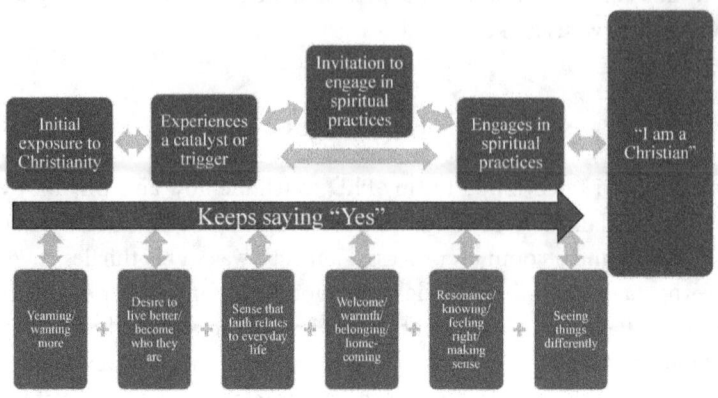

Figure 1: Conversion Process and Affects

But the process is only part of the story. Beyond cognitive understanding and deeper than emotions, other things were happening within each of those I interviewed. I called these "affects," and they are shown in the bottom part of the diagram. For Hamish, a sense of dryness fed his yearning. He "felt that [he] had got to the end of . . . atheism and [he] was just staring into the abyss. There was just nothing left there." The dryness encouraged Hamish to begin (and then continue) exploring Christianity, including by reading the Bible. This sense of yearning or wanting more was, for him (as for the others I interviewed), an important part of his journey to faith. Hamish also "didn't like who he had become" and was actively seeking ways to remedy that. His desire to be a better person was also common to the others I interviewed.

Those I interviewed had become aware that faith relates to everyday life—usually because of their interactions with Christian friends, as they shared deeply in each other's lives. Often, this was coupled with a deep and genuine hospitality that led to a feeling of belonging. For some, like Olivia, this belonging was vital, as it "helped [her] keep coming back [to small group] to learn more." Many also described experiencing a sense of homecoming, which they generally attributed to God, perhaps as they attended church or were baptized.

Two further affects were also commonly experienced: a resonance, knowing, feeling right, or making sense; and seeing things differently. Grace described her newfound faith as "one of those things that you just know" and had been prepared to suspend her previous "closed-minded[ness]" as she opened herself to faith in God. Hamish's story again illustrates the final affect: seeing things differently. He noticed his Bible (which had been on his bookcase for some time) and chose to read it and then to seriously explore Christianity. As a result, he began to see things differently, including as he started to "see God in everybody." Hamish summarizes as follows: "I think [God] gave me the lens to be able to see that all creation is his and that everything coming out of it is working for good and there is beauty in all of it. Even when it is not explicitly . . . proclaiming him. He is still there."

Of course, Hamish and the others I interviewed weren't alone in their journey to faith. They had Christian friends who (mostly) helped the process. An exposure to Christianity is generally resourced through, or at least enhanced by, engagement with other Christians. Christians might invite their friends to engage in spiritual practices and then resource such engagement. Other Christians also contributed to the affects experienced—especially the sense that faith makes sense to everyday life and the sense of welcome and belonging.

Six more things were also important. Those I interviewed told me that other Christians were helped by their faith; they were different because of their faith; they were open and honest; they were hospitable; they had room for doubt, questions, and complexity in their faith; and they helped their friends in various ways. These ways of acting and being were noticed and appreciated.

Essentially, these Christian friends talked about and lived out their faith authentically. They were open about what was happening in their lives and, in doing so, witnessed to God's goodness and activity, healing, comforting, and strengthening them. They didn't pretend to have all the answers or that their lives were all wonderful. They contributed to the good of others. Crucially, they also allowed themselves to be helped and supported by others, including those I interviewed. Their relationships were frequently characterized by mutuality and reciprocity. We'll return to explore the implications of this.

Ideal Selves, in the Image of God

One of the unexpected findings from my PhD was the way that people's personal aspirations towards being a better person matched with the attributes that they appreciated in God. Those I interviewed told me that God was loving, patient, accepting, forgiving and powerful—and they also told me that they wanted to be more loving, patient, accepting and forgiving. Young mum

Jean recalled song lyrics drawn from Ps 145:8 in which God is "slow to anger and rich in love" (NIV) that helped her parent her toddler. As she prays "every day [for] patience," the song makes her "think nearly every day . . . we're here to love and not be angry."

Lately, I've been looking at this a bit closer, including by surveying recently baptized adults and seeing if a similar match exists for them. It does![11] We asked the New Zealand Baptist participants to write a couple of sentences, and then five words, to describe attributes of God (and Jesus) that they appreciated, and (later in the questionnaire) five words to describe what they wanted to be more (and less) like themselves. For all of them, there was at least one matching attribute set—sometimes several. For instance, one person named a desire to be more generous and noted that God is generous. Another wanted to be more faithful and obedient and less self-centered and weak: they described Jesus as faithful, obedient, and strong.

Insights from theology and psychology help us understand what is happening here. It seems people are naming their desire to live into their status as people made in the image of God to reflect God's character and image. A theology of *imago Dei* recognizes the significance of such desires—the image of God both defines who we inherently are and impacts how we live and aspire to live. Participants were naming desires to be more like God. The psychological concept of the "ideal self" recognizes the motivational significance of what one wants to be like: one's "desires, hopes and wishes."[12] The recently baptized participants have ideal selves that match attributes of God, and it seems that this helps motivate them towards ongoing faith development. Importantly, the greatest number of matches related to being self-giving, and many other matches related to contributing positively to the good of others.

Today, we're invited to be attentive to our contemporary context, to people's journeys to faith, and to their motivations and aspirations in how we communicate the good news of the Christian faith to those inside and outside the church. I'll explore how we might do so next.

---

11. I am grateful for Jessica Bent's research assistance on this project, and for funding and insights from the Birmingham University Cross Training Theologians in Psychology Fellowship (John Templeton Foundation), including mentoring from Daryl van Tongeren.

12. Ganesan, "Ideal Self," 2126.

HOW MIGHT CHURCHES AND CHRISTIANS RESPOND?

What might churches and Christians offer that is both faithful to the gospel and connective for those beyond the church? Crucial to our contemporary witness is communicating a faith and hope that is relational, mysterious, and transformational.

A Loneliness Epidemic

Relational connections are vital, and in Aotearoa, New Zealand, as elsewhere, we're experiencing what many describe as a loneliness epidemic. Recognizing the magnitude of the problem, the UK appointed (in 2018) a minister of loneliness.[13] Social isolation and loneliness is also one of the focus areas in the UN's current "Decade of Healthy Ageing" initiative.[14] According to the latest data, in 2021, 17.6 percent of New Zealanders aged fifteen years and over reported feeling lonely at least some of the time in the last four weeks. This loneliness was not evenly experienced across the life cycle: young people are most likely to report feeling lonely, with over a quarter of those aged between fifteen and twenty-four saying that they were lonely at least sometimes.[15] In an increasingly individualized and atomized world, this is unsurprising. Within this epidemic, churches are uniquely able to be places of genuine connection and reciprocal care.

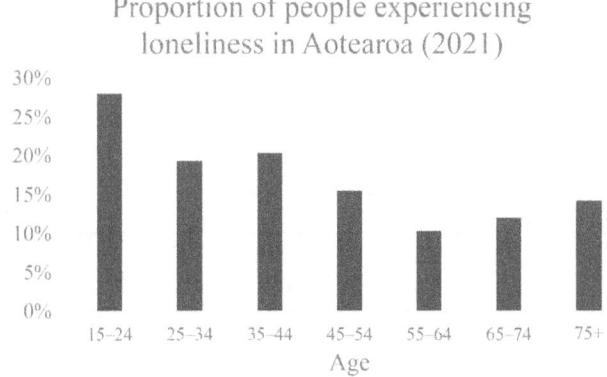

Figure 2: Loneliness in Aotearoa New Zealand (2021)[16]

13. Pimlott, " Ministry of Loneliness," 166.
14. World Health Organization, "Social Isolation and Loneliness."
15. Stats NZ, "Loneliness." Women, Māori, and disabled people are also more likely to experience loneliness.
16. Stats NZ, "Loneliness."

Created in the image of the triune God (Father, Jesus, Spirit, in relationship) human beings are, like God, inherently relational. We're made to be in relationship with one another (as well as with God). The loneliness that so many people feel is not how life is supposed to be. Amid this loneliness epidemic, churches can be places where genuine connection and reciprocal care can occur. While preschool activities, youth groups, craft groups, and the like won't solve the loneliness problem, they can all provide places for people to connect on a regular basis. Also, as people with similar interests or needs come together, relationships that exist beyond the activity might form. While these relationships might be with church people, any healthy connections can be encouraged.

Reciprocal Relationships

As well as emphasizing the importance of connections, I use the word "reciprocal" intentionally. While churches can be great at providing activities for people to participate in, we can sometimes hinder others from getting the full benefit from such initiatives by not providing opportunities for them to contribute. Sure, it is better to give than to receive. But that is true for all, not just churchgoers. Everyone benefits from helping others, and contributing to a group can be an important part of belonging.

I remember when one young woman began attending our church plant. She was seriously exploring faith and would have loved to come to our church camp, but she had other commitments. "Can I send cookie dough for you to bake into cookies?" she asked. I swallowed my "There's no need to do that" and thanked her. She wanted to contribute to our weekend together and did so.

When I interviewed Luke for my PhD, he recounted how he had been welcomed into a group of Christian friends who invited him to join them, not just for church but for fun, meals, chats and whatever they were doing. His friends "were pretty interested in [him] as a person and [wanted] to know a bit more about [him] and invite [him] to a lot of different events." He was doing life with them.

Olivia described getting to know her university friend, who was a Christian, when that friend suffered a personal tragedy, and Olivia offered her condolences. In the conversation that followed, Olivia provided care and support. She told me, "That was kind of how I got to know her. . . . We talked a lot about [the tragedy] and how [my friend] saw God's role in her life and in [the tragedy]. . . . And you know, obviously it wasn't so much at that stage like she was trying to evangelize or anything, like she was just literally telling me like how it was for her and how she viewed her relationship with God. . . . So, I felt like it was really like made a big impact on me. To be able to talk to her and just, I dunno, I guess see where her head was at. And I was just really listening, mostly." It was this same friend who, years later, invited Olivia to her church and helped Olivia find and flourish in her Christian faith.

Jean's Christian friend, whose father was unwell, would often say to Jean, "Please just . . . come and pray with me." Jean saw the comfort that prayer brought her friend and the measure of healing that the father had received. This experience "just kind of got [Jean] thinking as to maybe this prayer stuff is real."

There was a reciprocity in these relationships that doesn't usually make it into the evangelism books! Of course, it is not an evangelism technique: reciprocity flowed out of genuine relationships. Hearing these accounts helped me realize the importance of what I call "relational authenticity," which I define as "the project of becoming the person you are, imaging the relational God."[17] One way that Christians support faith formation is by embracing and exhibiting relational authenticity in their personal, social, and spiritual lives. This includes receiving as well as offering support.

There's Room for Doubts and Complexity

Such openness requires honesty about the difficult parts of life, including spiritual challenges and doubts. Doubts are not to be feared. In fact, theologian Frederick Buechner describes doubts as "the ants in the pants of faith. They keep it awake and moving."[18] This playful and wise understanding resonates with contemporary faith formation. Those I interviewed didn't expect that all areas of faith would make complete cognitive sense. Olivia, for example, was reassured by people sharing that "everyone has doubts and you don't ever feel like you know everything." She realized that she could commit to God before she knew all about God: you don't need to be "good enough" or know enough to become a Christian.

Rather than telling him that "believing in Jesus is going to solve all your problems," Luke's friends told him about the challenges they were experiencing. This helped Luke see there is room for faith amid struggle, which resonated with the difficulties he was experiencing. Those I interviewed also recognized that Christianity is complex, and that different Christians can have different opinions, embrace different beliefs, and take

17. Taylor, "Redeeming Authenticity," 277.
18. Buechner, *Beyond Words*, 85.

different approaches to their faith. Again, this was not seen as inherently negative.

Recent research on young people's faith development reached similar conclusions. The book *Growing Young* reported that when young people "have opportunities to express and explore doubts . . . doubt is actually correlated with greater faith maturity."[19] We do not need to fear doubts, complexity, and messiness: these should be explored openly rather than hidden away.

The careful arguments for the Christian faith that Christians have honed over many decades were made in response to our cultural age. Writing in 1996, theologian Stanley Grenz said, "Enlightenment realists . . . assert at least in theory that the human mind can grasp reality as a whole and hence that we can devise a true and complete description of the way the world actually is. . . . They maintain that we can attain sure knowledge in all realms of human inquiry."[20] Such an understanding seems to require a Christian faith that can be neatly and completely explained rationally, and this has certainly been attempted by generations of apologists. But even having seen the risen Jesus, "some doubted."[21] As James Smith says, "We don't believe instead of doubting; we believe *while* doubting. We're all Thomas now."[22] Philosopher Charles Taylor wisely says that "those who believe in the God of Abraham should normally be reminded of how little they know him, how partial is their grasp of him."[23] To pretend otherwise is problematic. It is actually good that we cannot fully understand God. While we have partial knowledge, "our doubt is part of our faith."[24] In fact, it is as we acknowledge our own limitations and inability to fully understand that "God's glory may appear larger and more mysterious."[25]

It was important that the Christian friends of the men and women I interviewed had room in their faith for doubts and uncertainties, and this is good news for us all. We don't need to have all the answers. In fact, we are invited to resist modernist tendencies to attempt to rationally explain every element of the Christian faith and to instead embrace mystery and wonder and to be honest about complexities—even uncertainties and doubts.

---

19. Powell et al., *Growing Young*, 157.
20. Grenz, *Primer on Postmodernism*, 41.
21. Matt 28:17.
22. Smith, *(Not) to Be Secular*, 4.
23. Taylor, *Secular Age*, 769.
24. Adeney, *Graceful Evangelism*, 19.
25. Adeney, *Graceful Evangelism*, 62.

Christianity Is Much More Than Rational

We might expect Hamish, the former "militant evangelical atheist" to have needed to be convinced by rational argument, and he certainly thought deeply about his faith. But even for him, it was not merely an intellectual exercise; it was deeply spiritual and affective as well. Hamish found the Progressive Christian Channel[26] and Home Brewed Christianity[27] to be helpful as he "wrestled with [faith] intellectually and spiritually." It was a relief to him that he did not need to "throw out [his] intellect" to become a Christian. While he had previously thought Christianity was at odds with his "understanding of science and biology," he discovered online that "so many people, millions of people, didn't [understand Christianity in that way]." His awareness that others, "even going way back to the third or fourth century, didn't necessarily hold [the] Genesis [creation story] as a literal account; more like a poem that holds the truth of what God was doing in the world," points to the importance of sharing such insights in public places. However, his talk of poetry, attention to spirituality, and the affects he was experiencing remind us that it's not merely about being convinced by careful argument. Hamish was feeling deeply, and that was driving his explorations. He knew that his "love for [his] wife and children were more than just a biological urge to reproduce or care for [his] offspring," and as he read the Gospel of John, he saw the love he had for his family reflected in the Bible's descriptions of God's love for the world. These affective experiences were crucial in his faith journey.[28]

With Room for Mystery, Wonder, and Awe

Hamish's experiences are not unique. Our world has changed and the modernist idea that everything can be known seems no longer tenable.[29] Of course, this doesn't mean we shouldn't draw on insights from the sciences as we seek to understand and describe the human experience, including religious and spiritual experiences. Rather, it means humility is needed as we acknowledge that we do not and cannot know everything. As noted above,

---

26. Patheos.com/progressive-christian.com.

27. Homebrewedchristianity.com.

28. Also, see Brierley, *Surprising Rebirth of Belief*, 189–91. While Brierley notes the importance of the intellect in Robbie's and Jen Fulwiler's quests, both named affective experiences (a sunset and a symphony, and having a child) as crucial in their journeys to faith.

29. Grenz, *Primer on Postmodernism*, 41.

rather than diminishing Christianity, this recognizes that God and the work of God is more than we can ever know or imagine (Eph 3:20).

Recent National Church Life Survey (NCLS) research shows that nearly six of every ten Australians (58 percent) believe in a higher power: 26 percent say "there is a personal God," and 32 percent say "there is some sort of spirit or life force."[30] Around a fifth (21 percent) say they don't know, while another fifth (21 percent) say that they do not believe. While religious affiliation is higher in Australia (44 percent Christian; 39% no religion in 2021), this shows that four points more people believe in a higher power than state an affiliation with any religion (54 percent).[31] I'd love to hear their stories of what and why they believe. I suspect one of the things that drives or feeds belief in "some sort of spirit or life force" are things that make them go "wow." Mystery, wonder, and awe call us beyond our finite selves. They invite us to a "wow" that doesn't always need explanation.

Cole Arthur Riley describes awe as "an exercise, both a doing and a being. . . . A spiritual muscle."[32] She names the importance of moments of wonder when she pays attention to both the marvellous and the mundane, and she recognizes the significance of wonder for her own faith. Mental health researchers also note the importance of awe and wonder, including "Take Notice" among the Five Ways to Wellbeing.[33] When we gaze at a sunset or are transfixed by a fern frond in the process of unfurling or delight in the feel of warm sand under our feet, what is important is the experience of awe and wonder. While some of us might be inspired to Google an explanation for the color of the clouds or to discover the way that sunlight causes protective young fiddleheads or koru to unfurl, we don't need to understand to experience the "wow."

In part, this is about self-transcendence: recognizing human limits. Awe directs attention beyond the self, to things that are vaster than us. To try to fully understand them or explain them can work to diminish or domesticate them, which is surely counterproductive. There is much about God we do not and cannot understand, and that is OK.

Recognizing the Desire for Personal and Societal Transformation

I started this section by talking about relationality—a loneliness epidemic—and in some ways, we've come full circle, back to an emphasis on

30. NCLS Research, "Is There a God?"
31. Australian Bureau of Statistics, "Snapshot of Australia."
32. Riley, *This Here Flesh*, 61.
33. Aked et al., *Five Ways*.

humans-in-relationship: looking beyond the self. As well as helping us recognize our own smallness in a vast and wonderful universe, awe can also lead to heightened communal concern, diminishing the significance placed on personal goals and individual concerns.[34] Striving towards growth is one of our primary human motivations.[35] That growth is towards a unified sense of self as well as integration into social structures.[36] My research demonstrates that this growth (and the motivation behind it) can be towards godliness: people want to image God, to display attributes of God, in their own lives.[37]

This was evident in the stories of those new to Christianity who had been motivated in their journeys to faith by wanting to be better people and who reported appreciating attributes of God that matched those aspirations. When describing why they had become Christians, several participants named aspirations towards an ideal self that they believed were further realized because of their newfound faith. For example, after attending a church-run conference, Luke realized "the sort of ideas that are being talked about . . . could really . . . make [him] a better person." Tallulah was aware that her lifestyle might be harmful for her young child and explored Christianity as a means of making her a better person.

As I noted earlier, these aspirations frequently matched the attributes of God that the participants particularly appreciated or admired. They described God as loving, patient, accepting, forgiving, and powerful and named their own desire to be more loving, patient, accepting, and forgiving. For instance, Sarah (who had a difficult relationship with an adult child) described how particular song lyrics about God "just sort of bring you back to [acting with] non-judgmental and unconditional love." They wanted to display attributes of God in their own lives.

We confirmed this finding with research on recently-baptized, New Zealand Baptists who all reported that "reflecting on what God is like makes me . . . want to be more like God." In their descriptions of what they appreciated about God and Jesus and what they wanted to be more (and less) like, all participants reported at least one matching pair of appreciated attributes

---

34. Piff et al., "Awe, the Small Self," 884.
35. Rusbult et al., "Michelangelo Phenomenon," 9.
36. Deci and Ryan, "'What' and 'Why.'"

37. Greg Liston (chapter 12 of this volume) alerted us to Tim Keller's use of the phrase "subversive fulfillment" to describe how churches are invited to "identify" and "subvert" the "baseline narratives that characterize the surrounding culture." My research (and Brian Harris's reflections in chapter 14) remind us that baseline narratives are not necessarily inherently bad. They can be towards healthy (and Christlike) growth and flourishing.

and aspirations.[38] For example, one person wanted to be more humble and less prideful and noted that Jesus is humble. Another desired to be less complacent and noted that God is intentional. While some were explicit about a desire to be "Christlike" or "Christ-centered," others made implicit matches as they described their own aspirations and appreciated characteristics of Jesus. One wanted to be more faithful (noting Jesus is faithful), more obedient and less self-centered (Jesus was obedient), and less weak (Jesus is strong).

The desire to be like God was common to everyone who responded to those questions. However, the attributes that they aspired to be like differed. Intriguingly, for these Baptist respondents, the most frequent attribute-aspiration matches related to being self-giving (e.g., self-control, humility, selflessness, obedience, and sacrifice). Being active (powerful, helping, generous), Christ-like, and loving were the next most frequent matches. These desires were oriented, not just to their own personal growth but towards the good of others.

Quantitative analysis of data from a general Christian population (n=123) further supported these findings. The correlation between respondents' ranking of the attributes of God they deemed most important and the attributes they most aspired to display were highly statistically significant.[39] Qualitative analysis of the same data showed at least one set of matches between attributes of God and personal aspirations for over 80 percent of respondents. Additionally, the vast majority (87.5 percent) of respondents reported that "reflecting on what God is like makes me . . . want to be more like God."

The findings from these three studies suggest that the desire for personal and societal transformation can function as a motivation for faith formation, as people see in God attributes that they aspire to reflect. While they were certainly seeking personal growth and development, the desire was not selfish but for the good of others.

This invites a deeper call in both evangelism and discipleship to Christlikeness and, more generally, to imaging God. Jesus is "the authoritative exemplar of what it means to be truly human"[40] and Jesus-as-exemplar

---

38. Respondents answered these open-ended questions by writing sentences or words. The two sets of questions (about attributes of God and Jesus; and about what they desired to be more and less like) were separated by other questions, so they did not have their responses to one set in mind when answering the others.

39. Significance was <.001 for Faithful, Forgiving, Holy, Loving, Patient, Active (doing good in the world), Relational, and Wise; and <.004 for Self-giving. Only Powerful was not statistically significant (.382).

40. Zimmermann, "Being Human," 58.

was certainly important in these faith journeys. But that was not all. Those interviewed and surveyed also named other attributes of the triune God as being desirable to live out. As Joel Green says, the human vocation is "to bear the divine image."[41] It seems that desire motivates faith formation.

The diversity of appreciated attributes and relative importance of attributes that are other-focused invites us to pay careful attention to what attributes of God are being talked (or sung) about in church (for example, in sermons and worship), in small groups and other settings, including in community ministries. A diverse range of attributes of God were appreciated by research participants. It is important that different attributes of God are emphasized in church.

Considering diverse attributes of God can help people connect their existing aspirations (towards what psychologists might call an ideal self) to the character of God. Because humans have an inherent desire to image God, naming these attributes can also serve as a way of defining what that ideal self might be like. Surely that is a healthy source of one's personal aspirations.

CONCLUSION: THIS IS GOOD NEWS FOR US ALL!

Emphasizing a faith that is relational, mysterious, and transformational can increase our confidence in the gospel and bear good and lasting fruit. We don't need to pretend to be what we're not to share our faith and hope with others. We're invited to live out relational authenticity in our personal, social, and spiritual lives and point to God as the source of all we are and all we can be.

Humans are inherently relational, and we all need genuine, reciprocal relationships. Let them bake the cookies! Invite new friends into your friends' group and your lives. Form and deepen relationships, not for the sake of evangelism but because you like them. Value what they have to say. Be appropriately vulnerable. Enjoy. Further, we don't need to have all the answers. Owning up to our doubts and acknowledging the complexities of faith, including its deeper mysteries, is seen positively by people who have recently embraced faith. Be humble and honest. Relatedly, there is room for mystery. While we can work to understand and make sense of ourselves, our world, and God, there is more about each than we will ever know; particularly, there is more about God. This is not to be used as a cop-out but rather an awareness of our own limits—our smallness in a vast and wonderful world and universe and our finitude in the face of an infinite God.

---

41. Green, *Why Salvation?*, 12.

Finally, while Christianity doesn't offer easy lives where everything goes perfectly, it does offer meaning and purpose. Many people are striving towards ideal selves that are oriented towards the good of others. They want to make the world a better place and can find in Christianity, in God, and in Jesus Christ ways to live that help them become more authentically themselves. We are all made in the image of God and will find fulfilment and purpose as we reflect the attributes of God in all our lives.

This is good news for all of us. We're called and invited to share ourselves with others, to be relational, acknowledging mystery and wonder (as well as doubts and complexity), to say "wow!" Knowing that not everything can be explained, we're called to be transformed into Christ's likeness—and to point to God in whose image we are made.

BIBLIOGRAPHY

Adeney, Frances S. *Graceful Evangelism: Christian Witness in a Complex World.* Grand Rapids: Baker Academic, 2010.

Aked, Jody, et al. *Five Ways to Well-Being: A Report Presented to the Foresight Project on Communicating the Evidence Base for Improving People's Well-Being.* London: New Economics Foundation, 2008.

American Psychological Association. "Affect." APA Dictionary of Psychology, Apr. 19, 2018. https://dictionary.apa.org/affect.

Australian Bureau of Statistics. "Snapshot of Australia." June 28, 2022. https://www.abs.gov.au/statistics/people/people-and-communities/snapshot-australia/2021.

Bogen, Katherine W., et al. "It Happens in #ChurchToo: Twitter Discourse Regarding Sexual Victimization Within Religious Communities." *Journal of Interpersonal Violence* 37 (2020) 1338–66. https://journals.sagepub.com/doi/10.1177/0886260520922365.

Brierley, Justin. *The Surprising Rebirth of Belief in God: Why New Atheism Grew Old and Secular Thinkers Are Considering Christianity Again.* Carol Stream, IL: Tyndale Elevate, 2023.

Buechner, Frederick. *Beyond Words: Daily Readings in the ABC's of Faith.* San Francisco: Harper, 2004.

Cummings, Charlotte, et al. "Independent Review—Arise Church." New Zealand: Pathfinding, 2022. https://arisechurch-website.s3.ap-southeast-2.amazonaws.com/production/pathfinding/pathfinding-report-for-release.pdf.

Deci, Edward L., and Richard M. Ryan. "The 'What' and 'Why' of Goal Pursuits: Human Needs and the Self-Determination of Behavior." *Psychological Inquiry* 11 (2000) 227–68.

Durie, M. H. "A Maori Perspective on Health." *Social Science and Medicine* 20 (1985) 483–86.

Furborough, Luke Paul. "An Examination of White/Pākehā Young Adults Changing Their Religious Identity in New Zealand." MSocSc thesis, University of Waikato, 2021.

Ganesan, Asha. "Ideal Self." In *Encyclopedia of Personality and Individual Differences*, edited by Virgil Zeigler-Hill and Todd K. Shackelford, 2126–28. Berlin: Springer, 2020. https://doi.org/10.1007/978-3-319-28099-8_1485-1.

Green, Joel B. *Why Salvation? Reframing New Testament Theology*. Nashville: Abingdon, 2013.

Grenz, Stanley J. *A Primer on Postmodernism*. Grand Rapids: Eerdmans, 1996.

McCrindle. *Faith and Belief Te Patapātai Whakapono: Exploring the Spiritual Landscape in Aotearoa New Zealand (Long Report)*. Auckland: Wilberforce Foundation, 2023.

———. *Faith and Belief Te Patapātai Whakapono: Exploring the Spiritual Landscape in Aotearoa New Zealand (Short Report)*. Auckland: Wilberforce Foundation, 2023.

NCLS Research. "Is There a God or Higher Power?" Oct. 2024. https://www.ncls.org.au/articles/is-there-a-god-or-higher-power/.

Piff, Paul K., et al. "Awe, the Small Self, and Prosocial Behavior." *Journal of Personality and Social Psychology* 108 (2015) 883–99.

Pimlott, Nicholas. "The Ministry of Loneliness." *Canadian Family Physician / Le Médecin de famille canadien* 64 (2018) 166–66.

Powell, Kara, et al. *Growing Young: Six Essential Strategies to Help Young People Discover and Love Your Church*. Grand Rapids: Baker, 2016.

Poyner-Smith, Karly, and Pat Loebs. "'You Are Not the Victim Here': Conspirituality and the Framing of Evangelical Patriarchy as a Victim of #Churchtoo Disruption." *Communication Studies* 76 (2025) 109–24.

Riley, Cole Arthur. *This Here Flesh: Spirituality, Liberation, and the Stories That Make Us*. New York: Convergent, 2023.

Royal Commission of Inquiry. "Whaneketia: Through Pain and Trauma, from Darkness to Light. Whakairihia Ki Te Tihi O Maungārongo." Abuse in Care. https://www.abuseincare.org.nz/reports/whanaketia.

Rusbult, Caryl E., et al. "The Michelangelo Phenomenon in Close Relationships." In *On Building, Defending, and Regulating the Self: A Psychological Perspective*, edited by Abraham Tesser et al., 1–29. Milton Park: Routledge, 2005.

Smith, James K. A. *How (Not) to Be Secular: Reading Charles Taylor*. Grand Rapids: Eerdmans, 2014.

Stats NZ, General Social Survey. "Loneliness." July 29, 2022. https://statisticsnz.shinyapps.io/wellbeingindicators/_w_bd18b946/?page=indicators&class=Social&type=Social%20connections&indicator=Loneliness.

Taylor, Charles. *A Secular Age*. Cambridge, MA: Harvard University Press, 2007.

Taylor, Lynne. "2023 Religious Affiliation: The Numbers." Oct. 23, 2024. https://lynnetaylor.nz/2023-religious-affiliation-the-numbers.

———. "Attendance of Baptist Churches in New Zealand: A Case Study." In *Strengthening the Church in Aotearoa*, edited by Mark Nichols, 39–44. New Vision New Zealand 5. Papaparaumu, New Zealand: New Zealand Christian Network, 2024.

———. "Redeeming Authenticity: An Empirical Study on the Conversion to Christianity of Previously Unchurched Australians." PhD diss., Flinders University of South Australia, 2017.

World Health Organization. "Social Isolation and Loneliness." https://www.who.int/teams/social-determinants-of-health/demographic-change-and-healthy-ageing/social-isolation-and-loneliness.

Zimmermann, Jens. "Being Human, Becoming Human: Christian Humanism as a Foundation of Western Culture." In *Humanism in Economics and Business: Perspectives of the Catholic Social Tradition*, edited by Domènec Melé and Martin Schlag, 49–67. Dordrecht: Springer, 2015.

Chapter 14

Beyond "Them" and "Us"

Bumping into God in the Marketplace

BRIAN HARRIS

INTRODUCTION

IT WAS 2021. AFTER completing seventeen years as principal of a theological college, I embarked on a new challenge and with a few friends helped found the Avenir Leadership Institute. We imagined that the bulk of our consultancy work would be with clients from the church and not-for-profit world, and this assumption has largely proved right. Largely—but not entirely because through a friend we were invited to put in a proposal to do some work with one of the world's largest mining companies. In inviting us to apply, our contact said, "I've just come from the most boring PD session imaginable. There is no way you could be worse. Why not put in a proposal to do some work with us? I'll make sure it gets a look in and that you have a fair chance."

A fair chance was all we were looking for, so we put together our CVs and a proposal and emailed them off. My friend got back to me quickly. "About your CV. Very impressive and all that, but this is a mining company. They really don't need to know that you have all these degrees in theology. Or that you have spent years training people to be pastors. Fortunately, your first degree was in social work—and I think that if they know you have a degree in the social sciences, well, that's all they need to know. And that you have spent years in the higher education sector—yes, that's good, we just won't elaborate and say that it was heading a theological college. And great that you have been a non-executive director on several boards, but let's not make it so obvious that they are related to Christian endeavors. Happy that I simply delete some of these details?" I agreed, and with the religious components of my life effectively removed, we were contracted to oversee a modest project—the first of five we have now undertaken for them, each one larger than the last.

As I signed us up for their most recent project, I reflected on some of the discussions I had with my friends when we started Avenir. We imagined we would largely be serving Christian groups, but when not, we had committed to making sure that our work would, at least in some form, be an exercise in public theology.[1] By that we meant that the training we offered and the recommendations we made would be consistent with the big ideas of the Christian faith. We fully understood that we wouldn't be able to insert Bible verses into the playbooks that accompany the professional learning days we offer or directly talk about Jesus, but we wondered if it was possible to guide in such a way that key principles of the Christian faith were being promoted.

A Bible verse that has always resonated with me is Jer 29:7—"Seek the peace and prosperity of the city to which I have carried you into exile. Pray to the LORD for it, because if it prospers, you too will prosper" (NIV). It implies that even when in exile, God's people do good in the world. They can pray for it in private, but daily work for the peace and prosperity of the city of their exile.

Perhaps at another level I was remembering the comment by Morgan Phillips: "The (British) Labour party owes more to Methodism than to Marxism."[2] The social impact of Christianity on society has been—and I would argue, continues to be—enormous. Be it in the support given to help form trade unions to protect workers rights, or the birthing of multiple charitable organizations, or the repeated insistence that because all people have been made in the image of God, all people have infinite dignity and worth—the Christian faith has been an active participant in the shaping of our world.[3] Even though it is common to talk about this being a post-Christian world, it is important to note that no one suggests that it is a

---

1. A helpful work that explores this more fully is Wright, "God in Public."

2. Phillips was the general secretary of the British Labour party between 1944 and 1961. Sellers, "Marxism."

3. For a more extensive development of this argument, see Harris, *Why Christianity*, 71–81; or Sheridan, *God Is Good*.

pre-Christian world.[4] In other words, though the Christian faith might no longer be setting the pace for societal change and development, its historic impact continues to be felt and is unlikely to be completely undone.

Christian churches who might be discouraged by their declining attendance could be heartened by looking at recommendations that flow from culture reviews we conduct at Avenir. When we have identified workplace bullying or harassment, management has always readily embraced recommendations we have made and has been determined to see its eradication. It's worth asking, "Why?" Why this concern for workers' well-being? Much of the answer lies in the impact of the Christian conviction that people matter and that you therefore should not treat them unfairly or poorly. Christianity has been successful in convincing people of all faiths and none that this is a principle that should find expression in practice, with many protections now being entrenched in law.

The impact of what we could call the *imago Dei* principle was underlined for me in a culture review we were asked to undertake by the mining company I mentioned. The study was a prelude to making some recommendations for a program to assist the well-being of "fly-in, fly out" workers. After accepting our proposal, we were instructed to closely consult the mining company's stated values and to make sure all our recommendations both upheld and were consistent with these values.

While it would be inappropriate to disclose our client's name, I can share the stated values of three of Australia's largest mining companies. For BHP they are "do what is right"; "seek better ways"; and "make a difference."[5] That sounds a little like Mic 6:8. For Rio Tinto they are "care, courage, and curiosity."[6] If you read more of their literature, care heads the list because they have a deep commitment to worker safety. Mining is a dangerous business and prioritizing worker safety is appropriate. Interestingly, while earlier versions of their values thought of care primarily in terms of physical safety, more recent discussions now include emotional safety and well-being. Fortesque has a list of ten values, namely, "family, empowerment, frugality, stretch targets, integrity, enthusiasm, safety, courage and determination,

---

4. A strong argument can also be made that the claim of a post-Christian world is premature, given that the percentage of the world's population identifying with the Christian faith has been reasonably stable for over one hundred years. The third edition of the *World Christian Encyclopedia* claims that in 1900 34.5 percent of the world's population claimed to be Christian and that in 2020 this was 32.3 percent—a drop of just 1.2 percent in a 120 year period. What has changed more dramatically is the location of where Christians live—the global spread being substantially wider in 2020 than in 1900. Zurlo and Johnson, "Is Christianity Shrinking?"

5. BHP, "Our Values."

6. Rio Tinto, "About."

generating ideas, humility."[7] While it is a little less obvious how these values link together, or how, for example, frugality might relate to enthusiasm, it is a start.

Examining the stated values of significant public companies helps us to understand what is more broadly valued in the public space. While we might dismiss them as a secular version of what would previously have been a set of faith propositions, that is to forget that Christian faith expresses itself in the world. It does not simply talk about God, but also about the way we are called to relate to each other in the light of the story of God. In their own way, the espoused values of a company tell us about their theological architecture. Sometimes they flow directly from the Christian faith, at other times they might be at odds with it—but they point to principles they expect their employees to abide by and in their own way are the statement of faith of the company.

UNDERSTANDING THEOLOGICAL ARCHITECTURE[8]

Let me unpack the idea of theological architecture, first as it applies to explicitly Christian organizations and then as it can be inferred from groups who make no obvious claim to holding a faith position.

Theological Architecture and Christian Organizations

Ever since the 1054 Great Schism between the church in the East and West we have lived with the idea of a divided church. This was accelerated by the 1517 Protestant Reformation that went on to birth a plethora of new denominations. Over five hundred years later, there is no sign of this abating. When a new denomination or church group is formed it is common for it to adopt its own "confession" or "statement of faith"—a creedal statement outlining what the group considers to be non-negotiable about their expression of the Christian faith.

In earlier years these focused on what was believed about God, Jesus, the Spirit, the cross, the church, the Trinity, and the Bible—with perhaps some additional clauses on baptism, communion, eschatology, and the final judgment. There is also often a clue about the group's position in the free-will–predestination juggle, and sometimes there are more exotic inclusions;

---

7. Fortescue, "About Fortescue."

8. Parts of this section initially appeared in a post on my blog: Harris, "From Statements of Faith."

for example, based on Mark 16:18, some see efficient snake handling as a test of genuine faith, while the same verse sees others stress the importance of drinking poison without serious mishap. While there is usually a great deal of overlap with what other churches say, tucked away in at least one of the clauses you will find a rationale for why this group's separate identity is justified. Sometimes it isn't so much a particular clause but the overall configuration of faith that is seen to be different. A statement of faith is often intended to define who is in and who is out. Agree with it, and you are part of the inner circle. Disagree, and the accusation of heresy might not be far away. Today that would probably see you excluded from the group, but in an earlier era sometimes meant you were burnt at the stake or beheaded.

In a post-denominational era, statements of faith have been slipping in prominence, and a decade ago many wondered if they would have any role in the future. However, with recent challenges to traditional understandings of gender, marriage, and sexuality, a fresh round of work has been taking place, and many statements of faith have now been updated with new clauses on these questions, some to affirm what is held to be a traditional position, others to embrace a more progressive one. Some even specify if a group holds a complementarian or egalitarian view of gender roles, so specific detail is sometimes added. These additions will inform historians of the future what the church in the 2020s prioritized or saw to be of great concern.

Although some of the clients I work with at Avenir Leadership Institute claim no Christian faith, most do, and noting how many theologians we have on our team, we are often engaged to undertake a theological consultation. If anyone had asked me if there is a living to be made in theological consultation I would have smiled and said, "Sadly no," but I have proved myself wrong—we have had no shortage of work in this sphere. Indeed, Avenir's first contract was to help a group review and refresh their statement of faith. In this review it became clear that there was a significant gap between what the statement of faith affirmed and what we knew to be the belief of many of the staff. It claimed, for example, to believe in the perpetual torment of the damned, but we knew that many, perhaps most, of the staff believed in annihilationism. They were, however, signing their affirmation of this statement, knowing that their continued employment depended on it. When I pointed this out, I was told not to worry about it—it had been there for a very long time, and no one bothered about it anymore. When I asked if it might be better to delete it, I was told that it wasn't worth the fuss it would cause. Personally, I would have thought that the potential eternal torment of the majority of the world's people is worth a bit of a fuss, but the client is always right—so it stayed in.

What became clear from this contract and other similar ones is that many Christian groups are struggling to articulate what being a Christian organization means for them, what they hold to, and how it shapes their practice. While statements of faith attempt to summarize the key beliefs of a group, we were being asked to provide language to describe how faith was lived out on a daily basis, and how it looked in action. In this context we started to advise groups to construct their theological architecture. Put differently, we suggested that they embark on the journey from statements of faith to theological architecture.

What's the difference? While a statement of faith summarizes what is believed and helps decide who is in and out, theological architecture focuses on the key beliefs that drive us and how they work out in daily practice. It's as much about how faith looks and what it does as it is about what faith says. There is a strong aesthetic element to theological architecture—a few evocative words helping to clarify what holds the group together. For example, after being consulted by a large Christian group who work in the hospitality arena we suggested they build their theological architecture around three words—Community, Place, and Pilgrimage—because they are essentially trying to live out their faith by giving people a rich experience of Christian community, doing this by creating "thin" places where it is easier for people to sense the presence of God, while being alert to those on a pilgrimage—a journey of seeking and finding. While I don't doubt those employed by that Christian group believe in the humanity and divinity of Jesus, and probably hold some convictions about baptism, the Bible and the like, on a day-by-day basis their Christian faith is expressed as they build community, shape thin places, and look out for the pilgrims in their midst. This is what unites them and keeps them focused on their mission. It is their theological architecture, shaping the contours of their interaction with the world.

A major Christian media group asked us for similar guidance. In their case we suggested that they adopt the three commonly embraced transcendental virtues of truth, goodness, and beauty, all understood in the light of the hope provided by the resurrection of Jesus. Imagine if the media everywhere filtered what they report in the light of truth, goodness, and beauty—and imagine if this was informed by the underlying hope birthed by the resurrection of Jesus. Many in Christian media now adopt this as their theological architecture, a lens that helps them to decide what to include in programming and what to exclude. They simply ask, "Is this true, is it good, does telling this story help to build something beautiful?" If the answer to any of these three is "no" you might decide against telling it. True, the group agreed that qualifiers were needed. Some stories are not beautiful, but they are true, and in telling difficult truths we might create the necessary conditions for beauty to be birthed. Some nuance is always important in birthing mature versions of the Christian faith.

I could go on, but this gives a feel for theological architecture. It is a more intuitive form of theology. Don't read me as being dismissive of the role of statements of faith, but I am noting the significant limitations when we simply hold onto a series of propositions woven together decades (or centuries) back. While statements of faith erect fences to hold some in and keep others out, theological architecture is essentially invitational. It clarifies the big things we focus on. It alerts us to some of the less obvious partners we might find for the journey.

Theological Architecture in the Marketplace

How does theological architecture work its way out in the marketplace? Can we assign a concept as lofty as theological architecture to an organization that makes no claim to hold to any faith? Is the assumption that there is a vast gap between "them" (secular organizations) and "us" (Christian organizations) valid?

The question came into focus in an assignment we had with an aged-care provider who wanted to honor the Christian faith of the organization's founders, while acknowledging that they no longer claim to be a Christian provider. It was a fascinating assignment—the organization wishing to be clear that it was not in the business of excluding people because of their faith (all are welcome—be they of any faith or none) or of proselytizing them. But they were anxious to respect the faith of their founders, and so were keen to discuss ways in which the founders' faith should continue to impact them.

One staff member suggested a way forward early in the exercise. She reminded the group that after a poor satisfaction rating from many of their clients, they discovered that the most common objection against staff was that they were always in such a hurry. A typical resident complaint was "I appreciate having my cottage tidied and being given assistance to bathe and dress. But the thing I really want is to have someone to talk to—and the staff are always in a hurry. I feel invisible, as though I'm just another body to be washed or another bed to be made."

She then asked the group, "Do you remember our response to these findings? We agreed that we needed to train our staff to be better listeners. And we had been debating whether we really needed chaplains—well that gave a clear answer to that question. And do you remember that we agreed to get our staff to adopt a slogan, 'I have time.' Instead of the usual, 'I am too busy', the mantra had to become, 'I have time.' The Board had to change the budget to make this possible. We improved staffing levels. But we did it because we realized you can't be in aged care and not give time to the people you are caring for." And then she said, "That's how we honor the founders' vision. That's the heart of being a Christian, isn't it? Being there for other people. Isn't that what the Jesus story is about? God living with us. Well, that's what I heard at a Christmas church service I went to—that Christmas is about God living with us. That sounds like 'I have time' to me."

Unpacked then, this organization hopes to show faithfulness to the Christian tradition that shaped it by continuing to fund chaplains, and by ensuring that staff are willing to stop and listen to residents, assuring them "I have time." They see the willingness to be respectfully present with another as an aspect of Christian faith they wish to hold onto, even though they now view their organization as non-religious.

MORE DETAILED THEOLOGICAL ARCHITECTURE

The examples of theological architecture I have given have been in broad brush strokes, where a few words evocatively capture an ethos that in some way reflects the implicit Christian faith of a group. Some organizations want more detail without having to go the full route of a statement of faith.

Carey Ministries, a Christian organization located in Perth, has opted for a framework that outlines in a horizontal column some expansive words that helped capture their faith, and then asks how that looks when viewed through four lenses listed in the vertical column. The faith words spring from a light rework of the Bebbington Quadrilateral of Evangelical priorities, with the addition of a fifth to reflect the group's commitment to creating community.[9] This is consistent with Carey's stated mission to "establish flourishing communities of hope."[10]

---

9. The Bebbington Quadrilateral of Evangelical Priorities are biblicism, crucicentrism, conversionism, and activism. Bebbington has written, "There are four qualities that have been the special marks of Evangelical religion: conversionism, the belief that lives need to be changed; activism, the expression of the gospel in effort; biblicism, a particular regard for the Bible; and what may be termed crucicentrism, a stress on the sacrifice of Christ on the cross. Together they form a quadrilateral of priorities that is the basis of Evangelicalism." Bebbington, *Evangelicalism in Modern Britain*, 2–3.

10. Avenir is closely associated with Carey Ministries and the example is used with permission.

What/How	Christologically	Incarnationally	Missionally	Invitationally
Community	Unity	Together	Love	Welcome
Cross	Forgiveness	Humility	Grace	Participation
Encounter	Rebirth	Transformation	Spacious	Winsome
Bible	WWJD	Spirit	Contextual	Compassionate
Action	Courage	Service	Faith	Freedom

A mapping exercise of the intersection of each vertical belief with its horizontal lens led to a word to describe how the group operates in each of these overlapping spaces.

Among several other ministries, Carey runs two schools with a combined enrolment of around twenty-six hundred students. In trying to establish schools that birth flourishing communities of hope, Carey interacts with families who sometimes operate with values and convictions that bear little resemblance to the Christian faith, and over 80 percent of the families linked to the school have no church allegiance. While attempting to hold to their core Christian convictions, Carey's theological architecture indicates how they hope to work their faith out in their context. Even when facing a difficult situation, for example, having to follow up the non-payment of fees, or when excluding a student because of antisocial behavior, they try to ask how it looks if they do this in a way that is consistent with the big blocks of their faith—community, cross, encounter, Bible, action. They then filter these blocks through each of the four lenses—Christologically, incarnationally, missiologically, invitationally. In reviewing the action taken, they ask if the key words in their grid are valid descriptors of the way they acted. Put differently, they will select words like together, humility, love, grace, or welcome and ask if any can be used to describe the process.

It's important to note that not only "soft" words are chosen. There are those that require rigor, as words like courage, service, and transformation are also part of the vocabulary. If the words they use to describe the process are consistent with their theological architecture, they know they are on target. If not, for example if the best description of the process is that it was, angry, accusatory, blaming, disrespectful, they will ask how they can be more faithful to their architecture next time around. Put slightly differently, the words they have chosen are their description of how Christian faith expresses itself in their ministries. They are their theological architecture.

THE THREE ORTHO TEST

Beneath this is a conviction that faith is not purely theoretical. It works its way out in practice. In testing faith in the marketplace, it helps to ask if it meets the "three ortho" test—the place where orthodoxy (right belief), orthopraxy (right practice), and orthopathy (right feeling) meet.[11] Traditional statements of faith usually focus their attention on orthodoxy—or on answering the question, "What constitutes right belief?" This is often seen as the most important question, and it is argued that if our beliefs are faulty, all else will also be flawed. However, it is possible to pass a test of orthodoxy, and yet fail the tests of orthopraxy and orthopathy. James 2:19 notes, "You believe that there is one God. Good! Even the demons believe that—and shudder." Verse 20 goes on to claim, "Faith without deeds is useless" (TNIV).

Many of the missiological challenges faced by the church have little to do with its doctrines. Realistically, while once the wider community was reasonably knowledgeable about basic Christian beliefs and had a rudimentary knowledge of the content of the Bible, this era has largely ended. Ask an average twenty-year-old to name the four Gospels and unless they are able to ask Google for the answer, you are likely to be met with silence. This is part of what it means to live in a post-Christian era. However, ask the same twenty-year-old to tell you about some of the failures of the church and a lengthy list is likely to follow. Expressed differently, people know more about the scandals that have faced the church than they do about the content of the church's teaching. This is part of the reason why relying on statements of faith to establish credibility has little impact. People don't so much want to be told what Christians believe, they want to *see* what they believe.

It is, however, possible to act in a way consistent with a set of beliefs and yet to fail the third test—the test of orthopathy. Though the most intuitive of the three orthos, in our current context it could be the most important. It is about genuine empathy—caring about the lived experience of those we encounter. The Bible gives a hint of its importance in Luke 15:11–32. Often called the Parable of the Lost or Prodigal Son, the passage ends by provocatively suggesting that the lost son was not necessarily the one who left home, but the older brother who had remained at home. While this son both believed and did the right things, his lack of compassion for his brother's plight marked him as being far from his father's heart. He refused to attend the party to celebrate his brother's return. There is something troublingly wrong with this. Orthodoxy backed with orthopraxy but failing the orthopathy test, is an inadequate expression of Christianity.

---

11. You can read more of this in Harris, *When Faith Turns Ugly*, 134–48.

What Does This Have to Do with the Local Church?

I have adopted a narrative approach in this paper, intentionally telling stories from my post-theological college days. I will now pull together what I am saying a little more tightly.

First, if the church is to be a place of transformation and healing, a little humility is in order. Much church language is about "them" and "us." But "them" is not always that different from "us." At times, "them" is even more compassionate than "us." Could it be that the church needs to learn from those it is trying to reach? We often assume that "the world" has nothing to teach us and should simply be the recipient of our wisdom. Yet Jesus often found expressions of genuine faith far away from the temples and synagogues of his day. Think about his daring portrayal of the Good Samaritan in Luke 10:25–37. He refused to escape into a religious ghetto and seemed untroubled by the accusation that he ate and drank with tax collectors and sinners (Luke 5:27–32). Perhaps there is less of a "them" and "us" than we have imagined, and perhaps we would receive a warmer reception if we entered the world of "them" with respect, empathy, and an embrace of our shared humanity. Reflect on the stated values of BHP: "Do what is right"; "Seek better ways"; "Make a difference." Instead of entering the marketplace by emphasizing our differences, perhaps we should enter by noting how much we have in common.

Second, while the church has made many mistakes for which it is rightly being called to account, it has done many things right. These continue to impact the world for good. We should not lose heart. We should again trust in the transforming power of God's Spirit as the world faces a new set of urgent questions. The increasing proliferation of Artificial Intelligence raises the question of what it means to be human with a fresh urgency. It is also possible that it will leave the wealthy and powerful wealthier and yet more powerful, while those on the margins are more exposed than ever before. There are many times in the history of the church that it has navigated these spaces well. The church has often been a courageous force for good. There is no reason why such examples should remain in the past. There are new stories to be written.

Third, the church is a sign of hope when it moves away from the ghetto and enters the marketplace. It should take seriously the task of equipping its people to do this well. During my years in theological colleges, I often taught homiletics. My time at Avenir has convinced me that I would teach it differently now. I would still encourage preachers to unpack the Bible systematically and clearly and I would continue to encourage them to tell stories their listeners can relate to, but I would warn them that the longer they are preachers, the more likely it is that their stories will become church-centric. It's natural enough. If you are a pastor, your world revolves around the church. Unwittingly, we make it sound as though God's concern for the world is limited to the well-being of the church. We subtly persuade people that their faith is best expressed through programs hosted by the local church. These programs often have very little contact with people who don't know Jesus. Our congregants most often meet unchurched people in their workplaces—but very few sermons focus on faith in the workplace, and even fewer tell the stories of how people are living out their faith in their workplace.

I was once advised to remember the TTT question when preaching. Simply stated, TTT stands for any of "this time tomorrow," "this time Tuesday," or "this time Thursday." When preaching we should ask where our listeners will be living out their faith TTT—this time tomorrow? Most often it is in their workplace. We should then ask in what way our preaching assists them to do it well.[12] At the local church I attend we are often reminded that "the reason for the gathering is the scattering." We come together for worship, prayer, teaching, and encouragement. But we are then scattered to live out our faith during the other six days of the week. Much of this will be spent in our workplaces, and if we do this well, the church will be a sign of hope to those who experience the difference faith makes in our life.

Fourth, think about the theological architecture we are constantly bumping into. Much of it has been birthed from the Christian faith. When the "them"-"us" divide is lessened, it is possible for us to enter discussions about the values of our workplaces and where they come from and why they matter and how we can uphold them better. In joining such conversations, we plant seeds that might produce fruit for decades to come. Perhaps in deciding a core value is "I have time," I might have enough time to listen to the story of the other in such a way that they lean in when I tell the story of Jesus.

BIBLIOGRAPHY

Bebbington, David. *Evangelicalism in Modern Britain: A History from the 1730s to the 1980s*. Grand Rapids: Baker, 1989.
BHP. "Our Values." https://www.bhp.com/about/our-values.
Fortescue. "About Fortescue." https://www.fortescue.com/en/about-fortescue.
Harris, Brian. "From Statements of Faith to Theological Architecture." Mar. 26, 2023. https://brianharrisauthor.com/from-statements-of-faith-to-theological-

---

12. A helpful resource in this connection is Stevens. *Other Six Days*.

architecture/#:~:text=While%20statements%20of%20faith%20erect,little%20too%20in%20your%20face.

———. *When Faith Turns Ugly: Understanding Toxic Faith and How to Avoid It*. Milton Keynes: Paternoster, 2016.

———. *Why Christianity Is Probably True*. Milton Keynes: Paternoster, 2020.

Rio Tinto. "About." https://www.riotinto.com/can/about#:~:text=Our%20values%20%E2%80%93%20care%2C%20courage%20and,how%20we%20treat%20each%20other.

Sellers, Ben. "Marxism and the Labour Party." Aug. 4, 2021. https://labouroutlook.org/2021/08/04/marxism-the-labour-party-ben-sellers/.

Sheridan, Gregg. *God Is Good for You: A Defence of Christianity in Troubled Times*. Sydney: Allen and Unwin, 2018.

Stevens, R. Paul. *The Other Six Days: Vocation, Work, and Ministry in Biblical Perspective*. Grand Rapids: Eerdmans, 2000.

Wright, N. T. *God in Public*. London: SPCK, 2016.

Zurlo, Gina A., and Todd M. Johnson. "Is Christianity Shrinking or Shifting?" Lausanne Global Analysis, Mar. 2021. https://lausanne.org/global-analysis/is-christianity-shrinking-or-shifting#:~:text=The%20percentage%20of%20the%20world,dramatic%20changes%20in%20Christianity's%20demographics.

Chapter 15

Carrying Hope

SARAH PENWARDEN AND GREGORY J. LISTON

IN REFLECTING ON THE contributions and message of this book, three aspects of value have emerged: the value of listening for notes of hope, the value of a chorus of scholar-practitioner voices, and the value of carrying hope for the church's future.

CHOOSING TO LISTEN FOR HOPE

The vision of this book called for its authors to recognize the tensions currently underlying the church in Aotearoa New Zealand. It asked them to acknowledge the way parts of the church have contributed to societal distress through enabling past abuses[1] *and also* to continue to believe in the calling, purpose, mission, and ministry of the church. The authors responded to this call, and across all the chapters, one can hear the intertwining of two particular melodies—the reality of the challenges in the church and the overwhelming sureness of the gift of God to us that the church can be.

Many authors showed that it is possible to hold the tension and play both these melodies simultaneously. Some authors looked toxic church elements squarely in the eye and also offered hope (such as Maja Whitaker's chapter on Christian attitudes to diet culture and the body). Others acknowledged the relevance of groaning, but noted that this grief in itself can

---

1. Royal Commission of Inquiry, "Executive Summary," 1–2.

be how the Spirit communicates to and through us (Geoff New). Others, such as Karen Kemp's chapter on compassionate realism, exemplified the ability to play both sequences of notes, and ultimately sound hope.

As well as those sounding both melodies, many authors deliberately chose to pay attention to hopeful elements. Lyndon Drake highlighted examples of implausible hope but then went on to lay out a clear picture of where hope for the Aotearoa New Zealand church might be found (such as through restoring missionary activity by Māori, and taking seriously the stories of the land underneath the churches we worship in). Sarah Penwarden focused on where flourishing is already happening in her church through an Appreciative Inquiry of what brings life. This is a seeking to find "bright spots";[2] to look for "what gives 'life' to a living system when it is most effective, alive, and constructively capable,"[3] and then to focus on growing this aliveness. In this sense, many chapters illuminated these "bright spots," or green shoots, of where transformation is already occurring.

Jonathan Dove's chapter highlighted how within experiences of church conflict and individual disappointment, personal growth can occur as people grow in their formation beyond who they thought they could be. Watiri Maina described practices from her own church life in which healing can occur, such as restorative conversations and peace-making initiatives. Writing from the spaces between the church and the surrounding communities, Lynne Taylor told stories of what it is about God and Christian faith that draws the unchurched to church today. Greg Liston described two examples of churches that retain a core commitment to being different from the surrounding culture (rather than seeking to match it) and are being fruitful in this. In these authors' chapters, one can see an ability to listen for the subtle notes of hope in/about the church and allow these to be heard. In this sense, the old idea that "what you pay attention to grows," is very relevant for the church of Aotearoa New Zealand today. It might be of use to remember that what we are paying attention to (in regard to subtle notes of hope) can actually grow hope.

A CHORUS OF SCHOLAR-PRACTITIONER VOICES

A distinctive feature of this book has been the bringing together of a chorus of voices from scholars (systematic theologians, biblical theologians, practical/interdisciplinary theologians) and practitioners (priests, pastors, leaders). The vision was to bring together those thinking/reading/teaching

2. Heath and Heath, *Switch*.
3. Cooperrider et al., *Appreciative Inquiry Handbook*, 3.

about the church and those serving at the coal face. Yet even that description is a dichotomy. Pastors think and teach about the church, and theologians serve. This book challenges some of the easy stereotypes—that pastors do not think theologically and that systematic theologians are not practical. In these chapters, authors believe, ponder, think, speak, and live. It shows us who we are—whole people; and the whole body of Christ.

The result is a multifaceted picture where scholars build on each other's work or offer counterpoints to it. Systematic theologian Christa McKirland's picture of a church power structure where each member of the flock has a role in listening to the Shepherd's voice echoes with counsellor-priest Sarah Penwarden's chapter on how the church members can hear their own vision, and also in priest Watiri Maina's description of restorative practices that a whole church community engages in together.

While there are other threads connecting various chapters, some authors provide a counterpoint to another author. In the first section, while biblical scholar Mark Keown focuses on three understandings of the body of Christ (Jesus' body, the local church, and the global church), practical theologian Maja Whitaker focuses on the actual human body and how Christian ideas of the healthy/unhealthy body can impact people's lives. Emerit leadership professor MaryKate Morse focuses on how as leaders we lead *from* our bodies, in the place where the presence of the Spirit dwells. This section exemplifies a complex and rich picture offered in considering what hope looks like for individual bodies and the church.

In another example of counterpoints, Brian Harris suggests that the church-world divide is not as great as one might think. He goes on to give examples of "theological architecture" embedded in the values of three corporate businesses. He has adapted his focus to working with companies to grow their values that are implicitly (though not explicitly) Christian. In contrast, Greg Liston's message is that as the church we should lean towards our distinct difference with communities around us. In a sense, Liston's chapter is calling us back to core beliefs and to a position that is intentionally away from the central narratives of the society which we indwell. Lyndon Drake's chapter similarly advocates for a new way of being that seriously acknowledges the history of colonization in New Zealand and so calls for change beyond the status quo. This book can hold such complexity. It offers an invitation to be open; to be open to reciprocity with others both alike and different from us in their faith. In these often polarized times, there is significant value to being open to hear where another Christian believer finds hope in the church.

CARRYING HOPE FOR THE FUTURE

This book has acknowledged something of the past elements of the church in Aotearoa New Zealand, shared stories of where we are in the present, and has highlighted the journey we are on—the bumpy journey of sanctification. It has brought a focus both on realism and hope. It is worth saying again that there is something particular about Christian hope. It is stubborn. As Migliore says, "Christian hope resists every repression or distortion of our yearnings for healing and wholeness in our personal life, and for justice and freedom in our social order. Christian hope fuels the passion for new life and for human flourishing. It strengthens the longing for a new, transformed humanity in a redeemed world."[4] In this way, "Christians boldly hope."[5] In considering how to think about the future, we commend a view that, while realistic, resists repressing the Spirit's yearning in us for communal flourishing. The church is being called into being by the one "who is, and who was, and who is to come" (Rev 1:8 NIV). It remains God's chosen vehicle to show the world what a relational, reciprocal, wounded-but-healing community is. And in this way, we continue to carry a candle of hope for the world.

BIBLIOGRAPHY

Cooperrider, David, et al. *Appreciative Inquiry Handbook: The First in a Series of AI Workbooks for Leaders of Change*. Bedford Heights, OH: Lakeshore, 2003.

Heath, Chip, and Dan Heath. *Switch: How to Change Things When Change Is Hard*. New York: Random House, 2011.

Migliore, Daniel. *The Power of God and the Gods of Power*. Louisville: Westminster John Knox, 2008.

Royal Commission of Inquiry. "Executive Summary: He Whakarāpopototanga rīpoata." Abuse in Care. https://www.abuseincare.org.nz/reports/whanaketia/preliminaries/executive-summary.

---

4. Migliore, *Power of God*, 109.
5. Migliore, *Power of God*, 109.

Author Index

Adeney, Frances S., 238, 244
Aikman, Ian, 103, 120
Aked, Jody, 240, 244
Anderson, David A., 64, 68
Anderson, Neil T., 128–29, 140
Aquinas, Thomas, 140
Arnold, Clinton E., 19, 26
Augustine, 123–24, 190

Baab, Lynne, 168–69, 181
Bacon, Hannah, 45, 46
Bacon, Linda, 33, 46
Barash, David, 75, 85
Barringer, Laura, 61, 69, 117, 121, 135, 165–66, 181
Barth, Karl, 163, 190, 199
Basil the Great, 191, 199
Bass, Dorothy C., 102–3, 119–20
Bauckham, Richard, 92, 101
Bebbington, David, 254, 258
Beck, Amanda Martinez, 4
Beeb, Gayle D., 37, 47
Belich, James, 193, 199
Best, Ernest, 21
Blair, David, 187, 199
Blanchard, Joshua, 110, 113, 120
Blum, Deborah, 75, 85
Boero, Natalie, 33, 47
Bogen, Katherine W., 229, 244
Bonhoeffer, Dietrich, 61, 68, 105–6, 116, 120, 190, 199
Bowden, Jennifer, 214, 216, 225
Braganza, Morgan E., 119, 122
Branson, Mark Lau, 171, 181
Brierley, Justin, 239, 244

Brock, Brian, 42, 47
Broughton, Geoff, 106, 108–9, 120
Brown Taylor, Barbara, 107, 120
Brown, Robert McAfee, 140
Brown, Warren, 166–68, 181
Brueggemann, Walter, 117, 120, 132, 140
Buckley, Michael, S.J., 150, 152, 163
Buechner, Frederick, 237, 244
Busetta, Giovanni, 34, 47
Butler-Kisber, Lynn, 176, 181
Bynum, Caroline Walker, 31, 47

Calvin, John, 14, 26, 190, 199
Campbell, Andrew, 80, 85
Carli, Linda L., 75, 85
Carlson, Kent, 106, 120
Carpenter, Sam, 187, 197, 199
Carr-Ruffino, Norma, 77, 85
Chae, Young S., 90, 92, 94, 101
Chambers, Douglas A., 187, 199
Chan, Simon, 63, 69, 191, 199
Chryssides, George D., 54, 68
Coakley, Sarah, 32, 47–49
Comer, John Mark, 37, 47
Congar, Yves, 190, 199
Cooper, Mick J., 133, 140
Cooperrider, David, 171, 181, 261, 263
Copeland, Gloria, 31, 47
Croasmun, Matthew, 114–15, 122
Cummings, Charlotte, 104, 228, 244
Cunningham, Loren, 75, 85

Davidson, Allan K., 187, 192–93, 199–201

Deary, Vincent, 109, 120
Deci, Edward L., 241, 244
Demuth, Mary, 9, 47
Descartes, René, 31, 47
DeSilva, Dawna, 125, 140
DeYoung, Rebecca Konyndyk, 43, 47
Dine, Jonty, 118, 120
Dixon, Nigel, 211, 22
Douglas, Brian, 175, 181
Douglas, Mary, 40, 47
Drake, Lyndon, 4, 183, 185, 187, 189, 191–95, 197, 199–201, 261–62
Durie, M. H., 230, 244
Dykstra, Craig, 102–3, 119–20

Eagly, Alice H, ., 75, 85
Eiesland, Nancy, 36, 47
Eriksson, Paivi, 169, 181

Fahs, Breanne, 42, 47
Falloon, Malcolm, 187, 193, 200
Farley, Harry, 103, 120
Fee, Gordon, 13–14, 26, 43, 47, 159, 163, 255
Fels, Anna, 75, 85
Fernandes, Kimberlee, 198, 200
Fischer, David Hackett, 195, 197, 200
Foster, Richard J., 37, 47
Frankel, Lois, 75, 85
Freeman, Sue, 75, 85
Friedman, Edwin H., 106, 120
Furborough, Luke Paul, 229, 244
Furman, Rich, 176, 181

Galvin, Kathleen, 176, 181
Ganesan, Asha, 234, 245
Garland, David E., 14, 26, 97, 101
Goheen, M. W., 207–10, 213, 225
Goldsmith, Marshall, 72, 85
Gonzales, Laurence, 74, 76, 85, 104, 120
Gorman, Michael J., 149, 154, 159, 163
Green, Joel B., 243, 245
Greggs, Tom, 167, 181
Grenz, Stanley, 14, 167, 181, 238–39, 245
Griffith, R. Marie, 38–39, 47
Gunton, Colin E., 186, 200

Gurien, Michael, 75, 85
Gushee, David P., 119, 122

Habets, Myk, 214, 216, 225
Haley Barton, Ruth, 165, 168, 180–81
Hall, Edward T., 78–79, 81, 85
Hamilton, David Joel, 75, 85
Han, Byung-Chul, 156, 163
Hardy, Daniel W., 186, 200
Harris, Brian, 248–49, 256, 258
Hauerwas, Stanley, 5–6, 113, 120, 207, 225
Haymes, Brian, 100–101
Heath, Chip, 171, 181, 261, 263
Heath, Dan, 171, 181, 261, 263
Hedahl, Susan, 168–69, 180–81
Heifetz, Ronald A., 80, 85
Heiss, Sarah, 36, 47
Helgesen, Sally, 75, 81–82, 85
Hendricks, Bill, 73, 86
Heschel, Abraham Joshua, 153–55, 158, 163
Hilliard, David, 187, 200
Hurtado, Larry W., 223, 225

Ibarra, H., 77, 85
Ingham, Harry, 113, 121
Innes, Jeanine, 138, 141

Jaschik, Scott, 75, 86
Jessel, David, 75, 86
Jinkins, Michael, 1, 6
Johnson, Julie, 75, 85
Johnston, David W., 34, 48
Jones, Zachary, 136, 140

Kaa, Hirini, 192, 200
Kärkkäinen, Veli-Matti, 165–66, 181
Katongole, Emmanuel, 117, 120
Kayser, Udine, 113, 121
Kearsley, Roy, 95, 97–98, 101
Keenan, Danny, 186, 200
Keener, Craig S., 156, 159, 163
Keller, Tim, 221–23, 225, 241
Kemp, Karen M., 3, 102–3, 105, 107, 109, 111, 113, 115, 117, 119, 121, 261
Kent, Elizabeth, 45, 48

Keown, Mark J., 2, 9, 11, 13, 15–17, 19, 21–23, 25–27, 262
Kierkegaard, Søren, 209, 225
Kinnison, Quentin, 90–99, 101
Kornfield, David, 186, 200
Kovalainen, Anne, 169, 181

L'Engle, Madeleine, 159, 163
LaCelle-Peterson, Kristina, 75, 86
Lange, Raeburn, 187, 193–94, 200
Laniak, Timothy S., 90–93, 95–96, 101
Lederach, John Paul, 114, 121
LeDoux, Joseph, 76, 86
Lee, Yongbom, 10, 26
Leech, Kenneth, 132, 140
Lelwica, Michelle, 37–38, 48
Leuken, Mike, 106, 120
Lewis, Thomas, 86
Liebscher, Teresa, 125, 140
Lincoln, Andrew, 20, 27
Lineham, Peter, 187, 200
Linsky, Marty, 80, 85
Liston, Gregory J., 1, 3–5, 205, 207, 209, 211, 213, 215, 217, 219, 221, 223, 225, 241, 260–63
Loebs, Pat, 229, 245
Louth, Andrew, 31, 48
Luft, Joseph, 113, 121
Lupton, Robert D, 65, 69
Luther, Martin, 14, 167, 190, 200
Lutz, Matthew, 110, 121

MacCulloch, Diarmaid, 163
Macy, Gary, 165, 181
Maier, Francis X., 140,
Mangum, Douglas, 24, 27
Mann, T. W., 91, 101
Manne, Kate, 36, 44, 48
Mannen, Sarah, 160, 163
Markus, R. A., 190, 200
Marshall, Christopher, 105, 110–12, 121, 214, 225
Marshall, Colin, 110, 114, 116, 121
Marshall, Ellen Ott, 140
McCrindle, 230, 245
McKay, Heather A., 75, 86
McKirland, Christa L., 3, 89, 91, 93–95, 97, 99, 101, 262

McKnight, Scot, 61, 69, 106, 117, 121, 135, 165–66, 181
Mearns, Stephen, 133, 140
Melton, J. Gordon, 54, 69
Mickulas, Peter, 33, 47
Middleton, Richard J., 93, 98, 101
Migliore, Daniel, 263
Miller, Arthur, Jr., 73, 86
Miller, Sharon Hodde, 39, 48
Moir, Anne, 75, 86
Moltmann, Jürgen, 191, 200
Moo, Douglas J., 11, 27, 153, 163
Morgan, J. Nicole, 33, 43
Morley, William, 187, 201
Morse, MaryKate, 2, 70–71, 73–75, 77, 79, 81, 83, 85–86, 262
Moschella, Mary Clark, 169–70, 180–81
Mulholland, Robert, 124, 132–34, 140
Muller, Wayne, 74, 80, 86
Mwiti Gladys, 137, 140
Mylander, Charles, 129, 140

Newbigin, Lesslie, 205–13, 216, 218–25
Newman, Keith, 192, 201
Nicol, Charissa, 148, 163
Nieuwhof, Carey, 67, 69
Norfolk, Donald, 74, 86
Nouwen, Henri J. M., 66, 69, 125, 140
Nussbaum, Martha C., 112, 121

O'Malley, Vincent, 192, 201
Obodaru, O., 77, 85
Origen, 30, 48
Owens, J. M. R., 193, 201

Palacio, R. J., 36, 48
Pannenberg, Wolfhart, 191, 201
Parsons, Mikeal C., 36, 48
Pearcey, Nancy R., 40–41, 48
Pelikan, Jaroslov, 6
Peterson, Eugene H., 157, 163
Phillips, Susan, 130, 140
Piff, Paul K., 241, 245
Pikaahu, Te Kitohi, 192, 197, 201
Pimlott, Nicholas, 235, 245
Plantinga, Cornelius, 107–9, 121

Pohl, Christine D., 64–65, 67, 69, 117–18, 121
Porter, Thomas W, 118, 121
Powell, Kara, 245
Poyner-Smith, Karly, 229, 245
Prendergast, Monica, 176, 181
Price, Terry, 80, 86
Pritchard, G. A., 210, 225
Purves, Andrew, 205, 225

Rah, Soong-Chan, 63, 69
Ratzinger, Joseph, 190, 201
Rice, Chris, 117, 120
Richardson, Laurel, 176, 182
Riley, Cole Arthur, 240, 245
Rochford, Tim, 41, 48
Root, Andrew, 161, 163
Rosener, Judy B., 75, 86
Routledge, Robin, 47–48, 101, 111–12, 120–21, 245
Rusbult, Caryl E., 241, 245
Ryan, Richard M., 241, 244

Salter, Leah Karen, 132, 140
Sanchez, Michelle T., 63, 69
Sanfey, Alan G., 35, 48
Scazzero, Peter, 67, 69
Schreiter, Robert, 108, 114, 116, 121
Schroeder, Jessica J., 41, 48
Scott, Dick, 186, 201
Scott, Kim, 116, 122
Sebba, Rachel, 77, 86
Sellers, Ben, 248, 259
Serratt, Olivier, 84, 86
Shamblin, Gwen, 38, 48
Shedd, Charlie, 38–39, 48
Sheridan, Gregg, 248, 259
Simmons, David R., 187, 193, 201
Sittser, Gerald L., 103, 122
Slocum, Robert Boak, 141
Smale, Aaron, 115–16, 122
Smith, Bradford, 137, 140
Smith, Gordan T., 72, 86
Smith, James K. A., 205, 225, 240, 245
Snyder, C. Richard, 141
Stafford, Tim, 206, 225
Stassen, Glen H., 119, 12
Steger, Michael F., 73, 86
Stetzer, Ed, 136, 141

Stevens, R. Paul, 258, 259
Strawn, Brad, 166–68, 181
Strings, Sabrina, 38, 48
Studebaker, John A., Jr., 94, 101
Swinton, John, 127, 137–38, 141
Sykes, Bryan, 75, 86
Synnott, Anthony, 33–34, 48

Taylor, Charles, 230, 238, 245
Taylor, Lynne, 230, 237, 245
TerKeurst, Lysa, 38, 48
Theilman, Frank, 12, 27
Thiselton, Anthony C., 43, 48
Tillich, Paul, 141
Torrance, Thomas F., 180, 201
Troughton, Geoffrey, 187, 201
Turner, Bryan S., 30, 48
Tybur, Joshua M., 35, 48

Van Ingen-Kal, Tyran, 214–15, 225
Van Leeuwen, Mary Stewart, 75, 86
Van Norstrand, Catherine Herr, 77, 86
Vennen, Mark Vander, 119, 122
Volf, Miroslav, 64, 69, 114–15, 122, 131–32, 141, 191, 201

Wall, Terry, 187, 201
Wallace, William E., 68–69
Ward, Alan, 193, 201
Ward, Kevin, 212–13, 225
Ware, Kallistos, 30, 49
Warren, Rick, 38, 49, 210, 226
Webb, Howard, 218–20, 226
Weld, Nicki, 109, 122
Wells, Samuel, 65, 69, 115, 118, 119, 122
Whitaker, Maja I., 2, 28–29, 31–33, 35, 37–39, 41, 43, 45–49, 225, 260, 262
Widdows, Heather, 34, 36, 37, 45, 49
Wiesel, Elie, 162–63
Wilkinson, John, 41, 49
Williams, C. Peter, 187, 194, 202
Williams, David V., 193, 202
Williams, Michael, 130, 141
Williams, Rowan, 188, 190, 202
Windsor, Paul, 211, 226
Winslade, John M., 130, 141
Witherington, Ben, III, 15, 27

Wolf, Naomi, 39, 49
Wood, Kevin, 217, 226
Woodfield, Elaine, 187, 202
Workman, Clifford I., 35, 42, 49
Wright, N. T., 153, 159, 161, 163, 248, 24
Wright, Walter, 82, 86

Yong, Amos, 139, 141

Zahl, David, 37, 49
Zimmermann, Jens, 242, 246
Zizioulas, John D., 191, 202
Zurlo, Gina A., 254, 259

Subject Index

Aaron, 67, 115–16, 122
abide, abiding, 79, 128, 133, 229, 250
abortion, 41, 223
Abraham, 62, 90, 93, 98, 139, 153, 155, 158, 163, 238, 245
absence, 106–7, 118, 222
abundance, abundant, 58, 108, 119–20, 213
abuse, 3, 13, 32, 57, 66, 69, 93, 100, 103–5, 112, 115, 118, 120–21, 137, 165, 181, 227, 229, 245, 260, 263
accountable, accountability, 51, 100, 104, 130, 189, 100, 217, 220
adoption, adopted, 2, 34, 38, 51–52, 62, 68, 137, 145, 152, 210, 212, 214–18, 221, 224, 257
advocacy, advocate, 11, 39, 127, 165, 170, 262
aesthetic, 29, 34, 36, 39, 252
agency, 94, 100–101, 116, 149, 157, 192–93, 207, 227, 229
alive, 11–12, 17, 32, 171, 177, 261
anger, 34, 71, 77, 79, 117, 126, 234
Anglican, 4, 103, 106, 120, 140, 167, 170, 175–76, 179, 181–82, 185–87, 194, 196–97, 199–201, 228
animals, 78, 93, 95
anointing, 95, 127
anthropology, 29–30, 37, 40–41, 49, 216
anxiety, anxious, 30, 106, 109, 131, 133, 138, 156–57, 253

apostle, apostolic, 2, 21, 60, 66, 96, 107–8, 214
atheism, atheist, 231–32, 239, 244
attitude, 2, 5, 14, 18, 43, 104, 127, 168, 195, 206, 229–30, 260
attract, attractive, 33–34, 40–42, 51, 55, 83, 158, 188, 210, 220, 223–24
attribute, 21, 42–43, 228, 231, 233–34, 241–44
authentic, authenticity, 55, 62, 78–79, 83, 86, 120, 133, 161, 179, 217, 230, 237, 243

baptism, baptized, 15, 18, 21, 29, 45, 52–54, 58, 124–25, 127, 139–40, 167, 190, 212, 228, 232, 234, 241, 250, 252
Baptist, 100–101, 146, 163, 184, 187, 199, 202, 205, 230, 234, 241–42, 245
Barth, 163, 190, 199
battle, 91, 146, 198, 200
beliefs, 54, 66, 68, 208, 237, 252, 256, 262
believer, 10–11, 15, 18, 20, 23–25, 60, 84, 124–25, 133, 136, 154–55, 165–67, 169, 180, 192, 210, 262
beloved, 66–67, 74, 83, 229
bias, biases, 29, 36, 61, 86, 112
biology, biological, 30–31, 35, 41, 85, 137, 239
bless, blessed, blessing, 53, 90, 93, 126, 177, 183, 186–87, 194, 196
bodily, 26, 30–32, 39, 44, 74, 127

Subject Index

bondage, 18, 128–29, 145, 147, 150, 152, 158
boundaries, 31, 65–68
brain, 29, 31, 73–76, 80, 85–86
breath, breathe, breathed, 152, 161, 165–66, 180–81

canon, canonical, 96, 196
care, cared, caring, 75, 84, 91, 93, 94, 97–98, 104, 111, 127, 129, 137, 172, 174–75, 178, 254, 256, 259
catalyst, 50–51, 53, 55, 57, 59, 61–65, 67, 69, 231
Catholic, 14, 31, 48, 114, 140, 165, 175, 186, 194, 201, 246
catholic, 21
characteristic, 14, 35, 40, 71, 154, 166, 231, 242
charity, 57, 65, 69, 104
children, 22, 26, 31, 98, 103, 138, 145–46, 152, 154, 159, 186, 212, 239
chose, chosen, 51, 56, 60, 77, 92, 115, 123, 125, 130, 173, 190, 192, 215, 220–21, 233, 255, 261, 263
Christlike, Christlikeness, Christoformity, 17, 79, 138, 241–42
Christology, Christological, 108–9, 120, 189–90, 255
colonial, colonialism, colonization, 38, 194, 195, 262
command, commandment, 24, 78, 80, 92, 95, 126, 131, 196
commission, 102–5, 108, 119, 121, 227–28, 245, 260, 263
commune, communal, 3, 5, 44, 54, 63, 73, 82, 115, 124, 130–33, 135, 180, 183, 198, 211, 215, 219–20, 241, 263
communion, 14, 18, 80, 118, 130, 133, 174–78, 190–91, 200, 250
confess, confession, 5–6, 17, 124, 128, 133, 140, 149, 191, 250
conflict, 15, 27, 53, 57, 61, 106–7, 109, 121–22, 128–30, 141, 173, 199, 261
conform, conforming, 24, 30, 39, 46, 72, 136, 138

conscious, consciously, consciousness, 33–34, 36, 44, 63, 69, 73–74, 104, 111–13, 180
consumer, consumerism, 118, 213–15, 217, 219, 222
conversion, 58, 185, 187, 192–93, 197, 200, 211, 213, 232, 245
converts, converted, 10, 26, 54, 174, 192, 200, 221
conviction, 56, 59, 66, 84–85, 164–65, 168, 249, 252, 255–56
cosmic, cosmos, 10, 16, 19, 25–26, 165
council, 11, 170–71, 190,
countercultural, 128, 136
courage, 72, 86, 126, 130, 249, 255, 259
covenant, covenantal, 93–94, 98, 111–12, 118–19, 163, 184
creation, 11, 19, 23, 39–40, 42, 80, 89, 93, 102, 107, 109, 119, 124, 145–48, 152–54, 158, 161–62, 171, 233, 239
Creed, 5–6, 191
crisis, 83, 90, 104, 134–35, 156, 161, 163
crown, 48, 151, 201
crucified, crucifixion, 10–11, 40, 124, 205, 225

darkness, 5, 125, 154, 184, 245
daughters, 34, 66, 85, 126, 140
David, Davidic, 26, 37, 48–50, 64, 68, 85–86, 92–93, 95, 101, 119, 122, 181, 184, 197, 199–202, 258, 263
decline, 1, 50, 161, 163, 186, 213, 225, 229–30
deity, 13, 23, 90
demographic, 173, 245, 259
denomination, denominational, 21, 102, 105, 175, 186–87, 194, 196, 213, 250–51
depression, 137, 214–15, 218, 225
destroyer, 61, 105, 223, 225
devil, 37, 42
diet, 38, 48, 214, 216, 218, 225, 260
dimension, 65, 78–79, 85, 103, 111–13, 118, 141, 179, 230

Subject Index

disability, 29, 33, 36–37, 42, 44, 47, 104, 137, 141
disciple, discipleship, 13, 17, 44, 63, 69, 79, 105–6, 108, 131, 135, 147–48, 151, 158, 217, 220, 229, 242
disruption, 51, 53, 58–60, 62–63, 66, 68, 103, 107, 245
distinct, distinction, distinctive, 4, 158–59, 171, 205–7, 209–11, 213, 215, 217–21, 223–25, 261–62
diversity, 2, 16, 21, 25, 28–29, 37, 47, 50–51, 53, 55–59, 61, 63–69, 83, 104, 243
divine, divinity, 2, 13, 24, 32, 50, 52–54, 56, 62, 91, 96, 98, 101, 107–8, 124, 128, 130–31, 133, 139, 141, 148–49, 153–54, 156–57, 159–60, 167, 170, 191, 243, 252
doctrine, doctrinal, 31, 190, 195, 199, 208, 225, 200
dream, 59, 61, 65, 69, 105, 118–19, 122, 171, 179
dualism, dualist, 31, 41, 105–6
dysfunction, 50, 52, 56, 60–61, 66–67, 126

earthly, 4, 24, 40, 43, 190
eating, 33, 43–45, 48, 82–83, 132
ecclesial, 166, 210, 225
ecclesiology, ecclesiological, 6, 163, 165–67, 181, 191, 199–200, 207, 214–15, 225
echo, 46, 176, 191
echoes, 62, 207, 262
economic, 18, 35, 48, 60, 65, 77, 219, 244, 246
education, 86, 120, 199, 248
egalitarian, egalitarianism, 167, 188, 194, 251
elders, 71, 74, 78, 96, 100, 134
embody, embodied, 2–3, 24, 30–31, 40, 45–46, 59, 72, 80, 82, 84, 92, 100, 103, 105, 112, 117–18, 126–27, 132–33, 138, 161, 164, 184–85, 194, 215–16, 223
Emmanuel, 120, 159

emotion, emotional, 30, 41, 71, 76, 80–81, 86, 103, 110–11, 121, 124–25, 128, 130–31, 228, 232, 249
empathy, 52–53, 55–58, 63, 133, 256–57
enemy, 16, 37, 47, 49, 59, 98, 107, 160, 184
environments, environmental, 52, 61, 63–64, 68, 71, 74, 76–77, 81, 215
epistemic, epistemological, 97, 110, 112
eschatological, 90, 92, 94, 101, 114, 136, 153, 160, 191
eschaton, eschatology, 24–25, 42, 101, 119, 250
eternal, eternity, 12, 18, 20, 40, 152, 192, 251
ethic, ethical, 20, 32, 42, 49, 51, 66, 80, 86, 100–101, 106, 110, 116, 119–20, 122, 170–71, 207, 223
ethnic, ethnicity, 15, 20, 23, 25, 55–56, 58–59, 74–76, 223
ethnography, ethnographic, 164–65, 169–71, 180–81
Eucharist, Eucharistic, 21, 45, 118, 124–25, 127, 131–33, 139–40, 165, 175, 181, 215
Evangelical, Evangelicalism, 12, 39, 187, 199, 201, 213, 225, 231, 239, 245, 254, 258
evangelism, evangelists, 4, 96, 185, 193–94, 211, 220, 237–38, 242–44
evil, 17, 30, 35, 90, 141
exile, exilic, 62, 90, 120, 248

failure, 1, 5, 18, 83, 103–4, 106–8, 110, 120, 134, 150, 213, 256
faith, 4–6, 11–12, 16–19, 21–23, 39–40, 46, 48–50, 52, 54–56, 58–60, 62, 64, 66, 69, 78, 84–85, 98, 103–5, 108, 119, 121–22, 124–25, 131–32, 134–35, 137, 139–40, 149, 153, 158, 163, 169–70, 172–73, 177–81, 192, 197, 211–12, 216, 225–45, 248–59, 261–62

faithful, faithfulness, 4–5, 23, 26, 33, 43, 48, 66, 93–94, 104, 111, 118, 126, 147, 153, 161, 234–35, 242, 254–55
fallen, fallenness, 5, 24–25, 29, 94, 113
fat, fatness, 33–34, 36, 38–39, 42–48, 94, 214, 216, 225
fathers, 5, 30, 191
feast, feasting, 13, 31, 43, 47, 129
fellowship, 20, 25, 51, 106, 134, 216, 234
female, 31, 46, 48–49, 71, 75, 77, 85, 225
flesh, 15, 18, 23, 25, 31, 37, 42, 47, 72, 85, 192, 240, 245
flock, 3, 89–91, 93–101, 112, 197, 262
flourish, 9, 11, 16, 20–23, 26, 100, 126, 163–64, 170, 172, 176, 179, 216, 237
forgiveness, 53, 77, 106, 108, 111, 114, 121, 125, 127–28, 130, 133, 184, 223, 255
formation, 3, 42, 63, 76, 120, 131, 134, 192, 216, 225, 228, 230, 237, 242–43, 261
freedom, 9, 20, 23, 29, 46, 77, 129, 140, 145, 147, 151, 158, 195, 197, 200, 222, 255, 263
friends, 56, 79, 146, 219, 228, 231–33, 236–38, 243, 247–48
fruit, fruitful, fruitfulness, 97, 104, 107, 117–18, 152–53, 161, 172, 185–86, 193, 197, 212, 216, 243, 258, 261
functional, functioned, 35, 42, 137, 219–20, 231
fundamental, fundamentally, 30–31, 37, 42, 53, 63–64, 77–78, 93, 132, 151, 205, 209, 214

gender, 20, 41, 47, 74–77, 85–86, 97, 251
Gentile(s), 10–11, 16, 20, 25, 60
gift, 12–13, 15–16, 18, 21–22, 72, 82–83, 102, 119, 126, 135, 137, 140, 147, 155–56, 164, 166–67, 171–72, 175, 178–79, 260
girls, 75, 77, 85–86

global, 52, 73, 136–37, 140, 146, 181, 249, 259, 262
glorious, 17–18, 26, 28, 151
glory, 17, 72, 124, 128, 130, 136, 145, 147, 151, 155, 160, 192, 238
gospel, 2, 4, 6, 11, 16–17, 19–21, 23–25, 38, 43, 46, 60–62, 101, 103, 106, 108–9, 120–21, 133, 136, 141, 179, 185, 193–94, 196–97, 199, 207–12, 214–15, 217–18, 221–26, 228–29, 231, 235, 239, 243, 254
grace, 12, 15, 18–21, 26, 50–51, 55–56, 58, 60–62, 64–68, 72, 75, 86, 109, 116–17, 124, 127–28, 130–31, 133, 135–36, 139–40, 150, 160, 163–69, 171, 173, 175–77, 179, 181, 190, 232, 255
Greek(s), 22, 30, 38, 40, 49, 125–26, 139, 153, 157, 188, 207, 221–22, 225
growing, 1, 3, 20, 22, 54, 56, 64, 87, 99, 137, 149, 163, 167, 171, 179, 210, 212–13, 229, 238, 245, 261

hands, 5–6, 16, 18, 127, 156, 184
harm, harmful, 29, 34, 37, 40, 43–46, 62, 103–6, 111, 115–17, 119, 130, 136, 138, 195, 228–29, 241
harmony, 53, 86, 108, 126, 156
heal, healed, 5, 11, 15, 17–18, 21, 26, 52, 72, 90, 94, 107, 124–25, 127, 131, 140, 177
healer, 124–25, 140
hearts, 17, 19, 25, 59, 146, 155
heaven, heavenly, 16, 19, 40, 93, 98, 101, 150, 152, 155–56, 165, 190, 192
hesed, 111–12, 118, 121
historic, 91, 196–97, 249
holistic, holistically, 2, 30, 41, 44, 125–28, 137, 215
holy, holiness, 5, 23, 28–29, 31, 33, 35, 37, 39–41, 43, 45, 47, 49, 84, 93, 95–96, 101, 124–25, 129, 140, 147, 155–56, 163, 165, 168, 171, 177, 180, 184, 190–91, 199, 216, 220, 224, 242

Subject Index

honor, 17, 25, 105, 121, 135, 176, 216, 253–54
hopes, hopeful, 2, 4–5, 11, 26, 36, 99, 116–17, 119–20, 130, 145, 147, 152, 160, 163, 171–72, 177, 181, 184–85, 192, 234, 254, 261
hospitality, 58, 65, 67–69, 108, 134–35, 138–41, 172, 211, 216–17, 228, 232, 252
humanity, 29, 54, 64, 68, 98, 103, 113–14, 122, 132, 138, 156, 167, 189, 205, 208, 252, 257, 263
humankind, 16, 23
humility, 21, 61, 92, 97–98, 101, 105, 117, 119, 168, 239, 242, 250, 255, 257
hurt, 24, 69, 80, 83, 108, 228

identity, 12, 15, 45, 51, 59, 67, 69, 76, 78, 81, 86, 98, 102–4, 108, 115, 126, 128, 130–32, 138, 160, 190, 207–8, 222, 244, 251
ideology, ideological, 36–37, 86, 134, 208, 217
idol, idolatry, 11, 13–14, 53, 136, 209, 213, 218, 222
illness, 13, 18, 127, 136–38, 141
image, imaging, imagery, 2–3, 11, 41, 49, 52, 72, 75, 80, 82, 90–91, 98, 111–12, 114–15, 140, 161, 178, 184, 201, 214, 227, 229, 231, 233–36, 239, 241–45, 248
imagination, imagined, imagining, 42, 44, 47, 75, 77, 108–9, 117, 120, 132, 140, 171, 185, 194, 215, 247–48, 257
immigrant, 55–56, 64–65
immortal, 17–18, 30
imperfection, 60–61, 68
incarnation, incarnational, incarnationally, 5, 40, 115, 122, 154, 158, 255
inclusion, inclusive, 29, 36–37, 46, 57, 60, 64–65, 81–82, 85, 134, 137–39, 141, 177, 250
Indigenous, 41, 192–94, 199–201, 230
individualism, individualistic, 12, 135, 209, 213–15, 217, 220, 222

indwell, indwelled, indwelling, 12, 72, 84, 114, 208, 210, 262
infinite, 243, 248
inherently, 132, 234, 236, 238, 241, 000
inheritance, 5, 19, 36, 153
injustice, 4, 34, 49, 135, 186, 194, 196–98
inspire, inspired, 1–2, 52, 58, 85, 129, 171, 191–92, 207, 228, 240
institution, institutional, 50–51, 60, 73–74, 77–78, 82, 84–85, 103–4, 124, 206, 214–15, 227
intercede, intercession, 146–48, 154–59, 161–62, 167
interdisciplinary, 2–3, 121, 166, 261
intimacy, intimate, 13–14, 78–80, 92–94, 97, 217
invisible, 3, 124, 128, 165, 219, 200
isolation, 20, 36, 62–63, 65, 67, 89, 106, 134, 139, 235, 245
Israel, 3, 89–96, 183, 191
iwi, 183–84, 196, 199

Jew(s), Jewish, 10–11, 16, 20, 24–25, 131, 222
joy, joyful, 53–54, 138, 183, 195, 201, 215
judgment, 13–14, 78, 112–13, 116, 130, 135, 138, 192, 250
justice, 5, 71, 94, 98, 106–7, 110–12, 120–21, 126–28, 132, 135, 179, 187, 196, 201, 222, 263
justify, justified, 11, 33, 36, 114, 185, 251

kindness, 36, 55–56, 65, 111, 126, 135, 178
kingdom, 5–6, 19, 25, 91–92, 103, 105, 109, 114–15, 119–20, 122, 135–36, 139, 141, 162, 185, 192, 207–8, 215, 219, 225

lament, 106, 117, 128–29, 146
Last Supper, 13–14, 18, 60
liberating, liberation, 75, 86, 129, 140, 206, 222, 245
lies, 6, 11, 35, 37, 42, 47, 61, 103, 114, 116–17, 131, 150, 192, 224, 249

life, 11, 21, 55, 60, 62, 67, 72–73, 82, 85–86, 96–97, 99, 104, 116, 119–20, 128, 130, 135, 137–38, 141, 150, 153, 164, 169–70, 191, 195, 207–10, 214, 231–33, 237, 241, 243–44, 254, 262
liturgy, liturgical, 132–33, 191–92, 197, 214–15
location, 30, 51, 74, 76, 83, 102, 223, 249
loneliness, 20, 219, 235–36, 240, 245

Māori, 193, 200–201, 230, 244
marriage, 11, 18, 53, 213, 251
mediation, 190, 201
medical, 35, 41, 49, 129, 134
medieval, 6, 31, 47
memories, 63, 71, 116, 132, 141, 171, 181
mercy, 5, 11–12, 110–13, 135, 184, 196
messiah, messianic, 94, 98, 106, 112, 151, 200
metaphor, 3, 10, 19, 43, 68, 89–91, 99, 101, 124–25, 166
methodology, methods, 65, 169, 181, 199, 201
ministers, 5, 22, 125, 128–29, 149, 188–89, 194–95
miracles, 16, 18, 24
missiology, missiological, 206–7, 209–12, 221, 223, 256
missionary, 122, 185–87, 192–94, 199–202, 206–7, 220–21, 225, 261
modern, modernity, 6, 32, 35, 38, 40, 46–47, 122, 160, 188, 218, 220, 254, 258
moral, 33–36, 44, 47, 80, 83, 103, 110, 116, 120–21, 126, 131, 195
mystery, mysterious, 4, 15, 20, 86, 115, 148, 151, 158–60, 162, 190, 199, 227–28, 235, 238–40, 243–44

neighbor, 30, 43, 46, 48, 91, 113, 141, 167
nourishing, 4, 203, 227, 229, 231, 230,

nurture, nurtured, nurturing, 12, 66, 75, 78, 125, 127–29, 131, 133, 135

offering, 4, 17, 34, 41, 124, 134–36, 138–40, 197, 225, 237
oppressed, oppression, 14, 18, 93–94, 129
ordination, ordained, 3, 150, 97, 150, 163, 189–90, 194, 198, 200
orthodox, orthodoxy, 4, 54, 61, 66, 221, 256

pain, painful, 9, 18, 20, 24, 32, 34, 51–52, 57, 59–60, 62–63, 68, 110–11, 118, 128–31, 145, 147, 152, 156, 159, 161, 208–10, 245
parable, 110, 112, 121, 131, 256
participation, participatory, 3, 6, 13, 111–13, 132, 154, 166, 179–80, 190–92, 255
pastor, 2, 50–51, 59, 71, 74, 83–84, 99, 146, 149, 156–57, 164, 168–70, 194, 205–6, 247, 258, 261–62
patience, 3, 21, 53, 58, 101, 117, 139, 157, 160, 168, 234
Paul, 2, 9–27, 37, 41, 43, 60, 96, 98, 107, 109, 114, 121, 125, 141, 148–49, 154, 159, 161, 163, 166, 206, 214, 222, 226, 244–45, 259
perfection, 38, 46, 48–49, 126, 225
philosophy, philosophical, 24, 29–30, 38, 47, 49, 80, 110, 120–21, 171, 175, 181
plausibility, 185–86, 189, 197, 209–11, 224
pluralist, 208–9, 221, 225
poetry, poetic, 176, 181–82, 239
postmodern, postmodernism, 111, 211, 225, 238–39, 245
powers, powerful, 29, 32, 34, 38, 45, 47, 53, 59, 62–65, 82, 92, 94, 97, 121, 130, 135, 222, 231, 233, 241–42, 257
praise, praised, 14, 125, 134
pray, prayer, 18–20, 24, 38–39, 48, 54, 73, 79–81, 100, 111, 121, 124, 127–30, 134, 136, 139, 145–50, 152–62, 167, 169, 172–73, 180,

182–83, 185, 191–92, 197, 199, 201, 213, 217, 234, 237, 248, 258
preach, preacher, 10–11, 21, 24, 58, 146, 257–58
prejudice, 20, 33, 37, 43, 112
presence, 5, 25, 51, 69, 72, 74, 79–81, 83–84, 91, 93, 95, 101, 103, 106, 108, 112, 115, 117, 124–29, 132–33, 139, 147, 154–57, 159, 163, 168, 172, 174–75, 177, 187, 215, 252, 262
priest, priesthood, 2–3, 91, 93, 98, 125, 150, 163, 167, 170, 173–74, 261–62
proclaim, proclamation, 14, 23, 25, 78, 160, 163, 193, 197, 207, 223
promise, promised, 20–21, 25–26, 53, 62, 94, 102, 118–19, 136, 146–47, 151–53, 156, 184–85, 189, 193, 197–98
prophet, prophetic, 66, 94, 96, 116, 120–21, 132, 140, 155, 158, 163, 184, 196, 213
psychology, psychological, 25, 35, 48, 181, 228, 234, 244–45
purposes, purposeful, 16, 40, 61–62, 72, 79, 84, 97, 136, 154, 176, 196, 206, 215
Pākehā, 51, 188, 194–95, 199, 229, 244

qualitative, 4, 164, 169–70, 172–74, 181, 242
quantitative, 164, 172–73, 179, 242

racial, 18, 48, 82, 199
realism, 3, 102–5, 107, 109–21, 261, 263
reality, 3, 5, 34, 50, 60–61, 63, 67, 74, 77, 80–81, 96, 103, 105, 109–10, 113–17, 119, 124, 128, 131–32, 148, 157, 165, 206, 220, 238, 260
redeem, redeemed, redemptive, 11, 18, 23, 25–26, 41–42, 46, 79, 97, 114, 127, 135, 139, 156, 218–20, 226, 263
renew, renewal, 3, 18, 22, 24, 26, 42, 50, 52, 60, 67–68, 80, 86, 125, 129, 131, 135, 183, 185–86, 189–91, 193, 198, 200, 218
restore, restoration, 3, 87, 90, 102–9, 116, 119, 123–24, 126–32, 135, 137, 139, 172, 193, 195–98, 220
resurrection, resurrecting, 5, 11, 26, 30–32, 40, 42, 72, 98, 108, 138, 141, 157, 163, 252
revealed, revealing, 5, 20, 38, 68, 74, 139, 145, 152, 160, 230
revelation, 19, 53, 148, 153,
righteous, righteousness, 11–12, 41, 90, 98, 113, 126, 184
royal, 94, 98, 102–5, 119, 121, 125, 193, 201, 227–28, 245, 260, 263

sabbath, 80, 86
sacrament, sacramental, 3, 13, 18, 123–29, 131–33, 135–41, 165, 177, 190, 197–98, 200
sacred, 31, 80–81, 86, 106, 124, 129, 131, 139–40, 159
sacrifice, sacrificial, 17–18, 48, 54–55, 61, 89, 94, 96, 106, 111, 121, 175, 196, 198, 242, 254
salvation, 20, 24, 52, 62, 120, 125–26, 128, 166, 175–76, 184, 190, 243, 245
sanctifying, sanctification, 124, 126, 128–29, 132, 169, 191, 263
saves, saved, 21, 61, 84, 125, 136, 140, 145, 152, 100, 000
savior, 16, 22, 184
Scripture, 3, 29, 39–40, 43, 46, 54, 89–90, 106, 121, 128, 130, 133–34, 138, 172, 190–91, 195–96, 214, 229
secular, secularism, 4, 38, 86, 105, 163, 188, 205–6, 208, 213–14, 230, 238, 244–45, 250, 253
sexual, sexuality, 18, 20, 32, 35, 40–41, 48, 53, 60, 103–4, 223, 244, 251
shalom, 11, 17–18, 22, 25, 41, 94, 107–9, 120, 124, 126, 132, 139
sin, sinful, 9, 11–12, 15–16, 18, 36–37, 39, 42–44, 47, 61, 81, 106–9, 114–15, 120–21, 150, 184
sociological, sociologically, 187, 195, 212–13, 226

Son, 22, 110, 112, 192
sonship, 145, 152
soul, 13, 30–31, 39, 47, 71, 90, 96, 127, 151, 165, 195
spirituality, 31, 47, 121–22, 127, 132, 137, 140–41, 146–48, 150, 152–53, 159–60, 230, 239, 245
status, 8, 20, 35, 81, 97, 99, 135, 194, 218, 234, 262
suffer, suffered, suffering, 3, 10, 12, 15, 17–18, 23–24, 42, 98, 105, 110–11, 115–16, 125, 127, 131, 138, 145, 147–56, 159–60, 222, 236
survive, survival, 31, 74, 76–77, 80, 85, 104, 120, 160–61
syncretism, syncretistic, 24, 209, 215, 218, 224

telos, 30, 46, 106, 148
temple, 13, 40, 101, 129, 257
testimony, 58, 133, 146, 157
toxic, 60–61, 65, 67, 69, 103–4, 117, 165, 259–60
tradition, traditional, 2, 6, 24, 29–31, 34, 36, 40, 46, 65, 69, 75, 78, 86, 101, 131, 135, 147, 149, 153, 156, 175–76, 212, 217, 246, 251, 254, 256
transcendence, transcendent, 31, 240
trauma, 35, 116, 131, 154, 245
Treaty, 105, 192, 201
trinitarian, 139, 156, 208, 225
triune, 72, 217, 236, 243
truth, 1, 41, 46, 64, 95, 109, 114, 116–19, 128–31, 133, 138, 158, 205–10, 212, 218, 223, 239, 252

unity, 15–17, 21–22, 25, 53, 59, 61, 66, 99, 106, 124, 128–30, 133–35, 140, 191, 194, 255

universal, 57, 66, 72, 107, 125
vicarious, 205
victim, 106, 112, 114–17, 245
violence, violent, 44, 121–22, 137, 141, 244
virtue, 4, 17, 21, 24–25, 38, 120, 148, 151–52, 157, 252
voice, 2, 28, 31, 89, 94, 96, 101, 119–20, 130, 170, 200, 213, 260–62
vulnerable, vulnerability, 13, 18, 44, 94, 98, 100, 104, 116, 119, 127–28, 133, 149, 168, 243

Waitangi, 105, 186, 201
weak, weakness, 15, 18, 20, 39, 94, 98, 145, 147–55, 157–59, 161–63, 234, 242
wisdom, 19, 24, 26, 66, 69, 128, 134, 138, 222, 257
witness, witnessed, 15, 55, 59, 62, 99, 106, 113, 115, 124–25, 128, 140, 151, 159–60, 167, 192–93, 209, 233, 235, 244
worldview, 29–32, 34, 40–41, 64, 113, 225
worship, worshiping, 18, 24, 40, 45, 60, 71, 79, 81, 128, 134–36, 172, 174–79, 183–85, 192–93, 197, 199, 201, 206, 214, 218, 225, 229, 243, 258, 261
wounds, wounded, 103, 105, 108, 116, 125, 129–31, 140

youth, 44, 138, 146, 236

www.ingramcontent.com/pod-product-compliance
Lightning Source LLC
Chambersburg PA
CBHW070236230426
43664CB00014B/2317